Contents

A Village Named Dowgalishok

The Library of Holocaust Testimonies

Editors: Antony Polonsky, Sir Martin Gilbert CBE, Aubrey Newman,
Raphael F. Scharf, Ben Helfgott MBE

Under the auspices of the Yad Vashem Committee of the Board of Deputies of
British Jews and the Centre for Holocaust Studies, University of Leicester

SPECIAL OFFER
Books in the Library of Holocaust Testimonies series may be bought in groups at a
discount of 25%. For furthur details contact Toby Harris toby.harris@vmbooks.com
Tel.: 020 8952 9526 Fax.: 020 8952 9242

A Village Named Dowgalishok

The Massacre at Radun and Eishishok

AVRAHAM AVIEL
Translated from the Hebrew by Atalya Broide

VALLENTINE MITCHELL
LONDON • PORTLAND, OR

First published in 2006 in Great Britain by
VALLENTINE MITCHELL
Suite 314, Premier House
Edgware, Middlesex HA8 7BJ

and in the United States of America by
VALLENTINE MITCHELL
c/o ISBS, 920 NE 58th Avenue, Suite 300
Portland, Oregon 97213-3786

Website: www.vmbooks.com

British Library Cataloguing in Publication Data

ISBN 0-85303-583-0 (paper)
ISBN 978-0-85303-583-1 (paper)
ISSN 1363-3759

Library of Congress Cataloging-in-Publication Data

A catalog record for this book is available
from the Library of Congress

Originally published in Hebrew by the
Israeli Ministry of Defence Publications

Printed and bound in Great Britain by MPG Books Ltd, Bodmin, Cornwall

Acknowledgements

I bless and thank my dear wife, Ayala, who encouraged me by reading the text, which often moved her to tears.

I would like to offer warm thanks to all the friends and acquaintances who helped and encouraged me to write up these long-closeted memories.

Finally, special appreciation to my publisher, Mr Frank Cass, for deciding to publish an English translation of this book.

*This book is dedicated to the following people:
My late mother, Sara Mina, who imbued me
with love of Jewish values;
My late father, Moshe David, who was to me a
symbol of valor and struggle;
My late brothers, Pinchas and Yekutiel, for
whom my love remains eternal;
The Jews of the Radun ghetto, whom I saw on
the edge of the pit, and who died with the
prayer 'Hear O Israel' on their lips*

Glossary

AK	Armia Krajowa: the 'White Poles'. Polish underground movement hostile to Jews and Russians.
babka	Domed cake, sometimes made with raisins.
Betar	Zionist movement.
challah	White bread made with eggs and eaten on the Sabbath.
cheder	School for teaching boys the fundamentals of Judaism.
cholent	Stew kept warm from Friday and eaten on the Sabbath.
Flowers of Agudath Israel	Youth wing of the Agudath organization. Orthodox and anti-Zionist.
gefilte fish	Stuffed fish, traditionally served at the Passover and often flavoured with horse-radish.
Hafetz Haim	Israel Meir Ha-Kohen (1838–1933): world Jewish leader, still influential today.
Judenrat	Governing Jewish council of each ghetto.
kishke	Stuffed cow gut.
kugel	Potato and onion balls, eaten with *cholent*.
kashrut	Jewish dietary laws.
Lag Ba'omer	Holiday on 18 Iyar (May).
maggid/im	Travelling preacher/s.
maskilim	Followers of the Haskalah (Enlightenment), who embraced secular learning.
matza/oth	Flat bread eaten by the Jews during the eight days of Passover.

mezuzah	Little container with scrolls of parchment inscribed with Torah verses affixed to doorpost.
mussaf	Additional prayers used on the Sabbath and holy days.
NKVD	Soviet Security Police.
Otriad	(Russian): military unit comprising Russian, Jews and other Partisans.
Rashi	Rabbi Shlome Yitzhaki: Biblical and Talmudic commentator of the eleventh century.
piyutim	Prayers in the form of poems used on the holy days (e.g. Yom Kippur, Passover, etc.).
puszcza	Ancient forests of Lithuania, Poland, and Russia.
Seder	Ceremony of the first night of Passover.
Shavuoth	(Hebrew: 'weeks'). Feast taking place seven weeks after the beginning of harvest to celebrate the giving of the Torah.
shofar	Ram's horn to trumpet Rosh Hashanah (New Year).
Simchat Torah	Holy day celebrating the Torah.
Sukkah	Booth erected for the feast of Tabernacles.
Tefillin	Two black leather boxes, containing biblical verses, worn strapped to the left arm and forehead.
White Poles	See the AK.
yeshiva	Academy for the study of the Torah and rabbinic literature.
zimmes	Dish of sweet potatoes, carrots and prunes.

The Library of Holocaust Testimonies

Ten years have passed since Frank Cass launched his Library of Holocaust Testimonies. It was greatly to his credit that this was done, and even more remarkable that it has continued and flourished. The memoirs of each survivor throw new light and cast new perspectives on the fate of the Jews of Europe during the Holocaust. No voice is too small or humble to be heard, no story so familiar that it fails to tell the reader something new, something hitherto unnoticed, something previously unknown.

Each new memoir adds to our knowledge not only of the Holocaust, but also of many aspects of the human condition that are universal and timeless: the power of evil and the courage of the oppressed; the cruelty of the bystanders and the heroism of those who sought to help, despite the risks; the part played by family and community; the question of who knew what and when; the responsibility of the wider world for the destructive behaviour of tyrants and their henchmen.

Fifty memoirs are already in print in the Library of Holocaust Testimonies, and several more are being published each year. In this way anyone interested in the Holocaust will be able to draw upon a rich seam of eyewitness accounts. They can also use another Vallentine Mitchell publication, the multi-volume *Holocaust Memoir Digest*, edited by Esther Goldberg, to explore the contents of survivor memoirs in a way that makes them particularly accessible to teachers and students alike.

Sir Martin Gilbert
London, April 2005

Foreword

Avraham Aviel records through the eyes of a young boy the upheaval of a traditional pastoral way of life in a number of small rural villages in Poland (formerly Byelorussia). He charts the deterioration and annihilation of Jewish Life under the Nazi regime and the eventual state of chaos and inferno created by the Germans.

The book begins with an affectionate and detailed account of the occupations, customs, culture and spiritual background of a small, predominantly Jewish village.

When war came the innocent people of this area were subjected to humiliation and death. Those who survived escaped to the forest, or were sheltered by the few friendly Polish farmers, who hid them in exchange for all their worldly goods.

Eventually, Avraham Aviel joined the partisans in the forest, and later on part of the Red Army. He and his comrades faced not only the Nazis but also the intensely, anti-Semitic White Poles, the AK, who were determined to drive both Russians and Jews out of Poland.

After the events described in this book, came to an end, Avraham Aviel escaped to the liberated part of Poland in order to make his way to Israel.

He embarked on a journey, which lasted over two years, travelling through Romania, Hungary, Austria, Yugoslavia, and Italy. Eventually he arrived in Israel only to be deported to Cyprus by the British. However, he returned to Israel in time to take part in the War of Independence.

In 1949 he joined a kibbutz in the Negev. After leaving the kibbutz, he worked at a variety of jobs in industry as a metal worker. He also studied economics and other subjects, and served as the director of a cultural institution, until he settled down to establish his own firm, a wholesale book company.

In 1952 he married a Jewish girl who had survived the Second World War in Germany by taking on the guise of a Ukrainian Pole. They are the proud parents of three children and the grandparents of nine.

Introduction

Dear Reader,

Since 10 May 1942 the memory has been hidden deep inside me.

It has been trapped in my soul, soaked into the capillaries of my heart and brain, a safely kept deposit, from which I am unable to sever myself for even a moment. Sometimes it emerges as a smothered cry, at other times it stabs with all its stooped force, and events that were engraved on my inner soul have surface in all their power. Sixty-four years later, after two generations have grown up, the storm has blown over and the emotions have subdued – the memories have quieted, become clear and precisely phrased, and are coming out of me now, without the turmoil of an emotional storm. The safely kept deposit that has been preserved as part of my memory is now released from its prison and set free. It has exchanged its temporary home for one that is permanent, one that takes the form of words and pages.

I have tried, with the inadequate language at my disposal, to revive those sights that were preserved and absorbed into my memory and my heart, as they were reflected through the eyes of a child – the small town, those wonderful, simple Jewish people who lived there and who are no more, the lives of the Jews who worked the land in an exile that no longer exists.

My book is written in the first person, in order to show that these stories do not come from the wild imaginings of a young boy, but are things that happened in a reality in which many Jewish children lived, whose experiences were as bad and even worse than mine. These children have no voice to tell their story – theirs was silenced, their souls rose up in a pure and holy cloud of smoke. And I am no longer free forever to choke and imprison my trapped memories, if only because they include a tiny remnant of the memories and the stories of those who were destroyed and lost.

Avraham Aviel
Spring 2006

1 The Story of a Village

Memories of my childhood are associated with tears and farewells. Looming out of the mist, as it were, I seem to be aware of crowds of people dressed in woolen overcoats and sheepskins, donning hats with fur-lined earflaps. My father, the late Moshe David, of blessed memory, is holding me tightly in his powerful, bony hands. Suddenly, I am torn away from him and handed over to his cousin Berl, the tailor of Dowgalishok. I was then 2½ years old. It still astonishes and amazes me that this scene has remained in my memory until today. Even though 55 years have gone by, my mind's eye brings that scene to life, recalling that setting from the recesses of my memory from time to time, and with it, the pain endured by the little child – a pain which has not left me to this very day. I still hear echoes of my crying and weeping that rose from amidst the groups of people who had come to part from my father Moshe David and his brother Jacob Leb Lipkunsky. They were setting off to seek a new life across the ocean in Argentina.

My father was born in a village, the third of four valiant sons born to Grandfather Rabbi Pinchas Lipkunsky and Grandmother Esther Gordon from Grodno. The two elder brothers, Yekutiel and Nachum Jossel, felt they had to leave home for it was becoming too cramped for them, both physically and spiritually. The piece of land which the family owned was also too meager to provide the four sons with a living. So they were forced to leave their beloved hamlet of Dowgalishok, and went to live in Dziewienishok, a village some 50–60 kilometers away. They married daughters of the village, raised families, and settled down in the place. Some dozen years later, the two younger brothers, Moshe David (my father) and Jacob Leb, also had to follow in their older brothers' footsteps and leave their village behind.

The family's stretch of land covered 25 hectares and included pasture-land, areas of pine forest, stretches of natural grass, and also a plot consisting of poor soil and sand, intended for growing produce, which could not provide the two families with anything like a decent living.

In order to pay for their journey, and also to leave some money to provide for their families, who were moving to the nearby village of Radun, they sold their farm equipment, together with all the livestock, including the horses and the cattle and the herds of geese. They refused to sell their house and lands, however, deciding instead to lease them for a period of six years, in order not to lose their ownership rights over the land. The house and the farm buildings and the land were let to a Jewish family who had been farmers for generations, though they did not hail from Dowgalishok. But the brothers secretly hoped that after they had earned enough money overseas, they would return to their land and their beloved village.

The village of Dowgalishok did not resemble any of the other villages in the neighborhood and not only because of its Jewish character, for only three gentile families had succeeded in getting a foothold there. It is difficult to figure out how these families managed to get accepted by Jewish Dowgalishok, to strike roots and live among the Jews of the place: perhaps it was because they needed 'goys', for the Sabbath.

Dowgalishok was a many-faceted village – its winter aspect was not that of its summer manifestation, nor was the mundane Dowgalishok the same as the spiritual Dowgalishok. It had one long street paved with stone, which ran along the length of the entire village from west to east, and one dirt road which crossed it at its center, from north to south. This made up the entire layout of the village. The road was lined on both sides with homes and behind these were

2

the farm buildings: the outhouses, the stable, the chicken-coops and the barn. The gardens and yards surrounding the houses served as the dividing lines between the houses.

Both the homes and the farm buildings and outhouses were built of clapboard. The dried straw stuffed between the planks served as binding material and also to fill in cracks between the boards. The homes and the other farm buildings were differently roofed; some had sloping roofs covered with shingles while others were thatched with straw. The windows were double, and towards the winter season, the spaces and chinks between the window-frames were stuffed up to ward off any possible entry of the terrible cold that prevailed during the freezing winter months. Apart from the wood-burning oven that stood at the very heart of every house, there was also a large oven that was used for baking bread and *challah*, and on Friday afternoons, where the *cholent* was placed before the start of the Sabbath. The floors were partly wooden planks and partly flattened and smoothed-down plaster. On the eve of the Sabbath, when the household was being cleaned in preparation, clean and fresh golden sand was strewn on the plaster floors, as if a new carpet was being laid for the event. The earthy fragrance of the fresh sand inter-mingled with the odors of the dishes being prepared and the Sabbath atmosphere all combined to summon up an aura of sanctity and renewal.

There were only a dozen family houses in the village, nine of which were occupied by Jews, while gentiles of Polish origin lived in the remaining three. In the distant past, the Jewish families of the village consisted of the eight homes of the Lipkunsky family and four of the Paikovsky family. In delving into the roots of the past, some five generations back, it appears that the first to lay the foundations of the village was one of the offspring of the Lipkunsky family, and by the marriage of one of the daughters of this family to a son of the Paikovsky family, the village was developed by the two families. The story that has been handed down from genera-tion to generation is the following. At the beginning of the eighteenth century, a battle was being waged between the Polish and Russian armies. When the Polish army seemed to be gaining the upper hand, a well-known and important Russian general fled from the battlefield and found refuge in the home of a Jew. Indeed, the Poles won the battle, but the entire campaign ended with the Russian army as the victors. In recognition and gratitude to the Jew who saved his life, the Russian general, who was close to the Tsar, granted him the choice of a stretch of land in this region, on which he could settle and farm the land – a circumstance that was denied the Jews in those days.

Since then, for some generations, the descendants of the Lipkunskys stayed on their land and did not leave it. The single family became an entire village, a rural village whose livelihood was derived solely from farming the land. Only in the course of time, with the increase and growth of its families and when the soil was no longer rich enough to support its inhabitants, did some of them add other ways of earning a living, such as building, carpentry, smithing, and petty trading.

The Jewish village of Dowgalishok was set in a rural neighborhood, surrounded by similar pastoral villages inhabited mainly by farmers of Polish descent. The nearest village to the west was Pitzeluntze and there was a brook flowing from the north to the south dividing the two villages and on either bank of the brook was a rich variety of lush shrubbery, which was a rewarding and abundant source of wild berry picking for the children of the villages. To the east was a high wall of huge trees forming the pine forest, surrounded on the north and the south by a chain of family farmsteads, all within sight of one another.

The daily life of the Jewish farmer of Dowgalishok was essentially no different from that of the other farmers of the neighborhood. The life of a farmer who lives off the land is shaped by the livestock he breeds and determined by the seasons of the year. In the early spring, with the melting of the snows, they would lead the cattle and the sheep to the pasture, at first on the edge of the forest or its clearings, where the rays of the sun had managed to dissolve the mounds of snow which had accumulated during the winter. Later on, they would go into the depths of the forest where the pasture for grazing was rich and abundant. The shepherding of the herds was generally carried out communally; each of the shepherds would take his turn, in accordance with the number of head of cattle or sheep he possessed, and those families who could not supply a shepherd would pay for this service. It was also customary to trade certain services, reckoned according to the working day of a beast of burden or of a farmhand. Mutual help was a way of life and taken for granted in village mores.

With the melting of the snow and the loosening of the topmost layers of the soil from its frozen state, the ploughing and the sowing began. The iron ploughs were harnessed to a horse or an ox while the sowing and planting was done by hand. Towards the end of the summer, when the corn stood golden in the fields, the whole family would be recruited for the harvesting. The neighbors, whose fields were not yet ripe enough to harvest, also volunteered to help with the harvest, for corn which is dry and ripe enough to harvest is very sensitive to rain or hail, which could occur at any time and which frequently did in this area. A few minutes of heavy rainfall could flatten the harvest and prevent it from drying out again and spoiling, while a hailstorm would break the stalks and empty the ears of its grain, as if it had been threshed in the field.

One could see rows of reapers of all ages, male and female, bent down on their knees, with kerchiefs on their heads to protect them from the heat of the sun. Their right hands held the scythes which passed through the stalks an inch or two from the ground, while at the same time, their left hands were gathering and grasping the bunch of stalks that the scythe has just cut, and set them on the ground to their left. And so they advanced, step by step, harvesting the corn handful by handful, like well-oiled machines. The reapers were followed by the sheaf-binders, who deftly tied the sheaves together, sheaf by sheaf, with one encircling movement, and then they were mounted one layer upon the other in a sloping, cone-shaped mound to protect them from any rain that might penetrate to the grain. At the end of the harvest, when the corn was dry, it was stored in the barn.

After the harvest, it was time to collect the potato crop. The shovel was dug deep under the root of the plant, in order to loosen the clods of earth around it, the the whole plant was shaken and the potatoes gathered up and then sorted out into various pails and baskets. A part of the potato crop was stored in the cellar of the house and the remainder in pits in the field not too far from the house. The pits were dug in sandy, dry ground, and to prevent the icy cold of the winter from penetrating them they were covered with straw and sand. Potatoes, like bread, were an important element in the daily diet, and they were also used as cattle fodder.

As soon as the potato crop was collected, it was time to pick the fruit. There were no large orchards in Dowgalishok, but almost every farmer had a few fruit trees in his fields – usually apple or pear trees. The fruit was picked by shaking the trees and gathering the ripe fruit that fell to the ground. The fruit that was found to be in good condition was eaten in its natural state for many weeks of the year. Some of it was made into tasty preserves and jams, after slowly stewing with sugar for hours on end. In this way it was kept throughout the long winter. Some of the fruit was laid out in the sunshine to dry, but most of it was covered with straw and so kept for some time from going bad. Whatever was still standing when the frost and icy winds arrived was left to freeze and thus preserved from spoiling throughout the winter.

Preparations for the winter were an elementary part of the way of life. The food was generally produced on the farm and whatever could be preserved at home was. The carrots and the beets went down to the cellar and joined the potatoes. The cabbage and the cucumbers were pickled in brine in huge wooden barrels and supplied family needs until the spring-time when the new crops were harvested. With the approach of autumn and the darkly clouded skies, the scene of action moved to the woods, where logs were being prepared as fuel for the winter. Equipped with saws and axes, the men would go out to the forest to gather dry wood for burning and heating. Alongside every homestead stood a pile of logs, sawn to size, to fit the wood-burning stoves.

Now that the harvested wheat was in the barn, the potatoes, beet and carrots in the cellar, or in the pits, the wood for heating standing in piles alongside the house, one could face the winter. When the winter days had sheathed the ground in a blanket of snow from horizon to horizon, the farming labors out of doors ceased altogether. Apart from the daily round of tending the livestock, threshing was the only agricultural work that remained to be done. The threshing was done with a thin, long, stick, strong and smooth, two meters in length. At one end of this a forceful flailing stick some ten cubits in length was fastened by means of sturdy leather strips. The thresher would raise the stick on high and with one practiced swoop, come down with a tremendous blow on the spread-out stalks which were laid out sheaf by sheaf on the floor of the barn. The threshing was done in pairs, with each of the threshers facing one another, flailing the ears of corn in a synchronized rhythm, one after the other; the grains rapidly escaping and emerging from their husks. An enormous amount of strength and endurance was required to stand and flail in one measured beat for hours on end, and great skill to avoid hurting one another. It was necessary to be in full command of the flailing stick while bearing down on the ears of corn to propel them toward a central point, to be threshed once again. The threshers were not aware of the bitter cold that was raging outside, for the work kept them warm from head to toe.

During the weekdays, the daily routine of the Jewish farmer of Dowgalishok about the farm resembled that of the Polish farmer, in the main. The notable difference was in the education of the children, for there was not a single Jewish child who did not know how to read and write, and every Jewish child attended school or *cheder*, more or less. This was not the case with the Polish neighbors. I recall my mother saying to us: 'Children, if you don't study, you'll be swine-herds.' And indeed this was the fate of most of the children of the Polish farmers.

On holidays and feasts, and on the Sabbath, the Jewish farmer and his Polish neighbor were very dissimilar in their ways of enjoying the day of rest. The former spent his day in rest and prayer, studiously poring over the weekly Portion (from the Pentateuch) read on the Sabbath, listening to a lesson in *Mishna*, or mulling over the 'Sayings of the Fathers', and whoever was none the wiser as a result of these efforts, pored out his heart to the Creator in a recital of the Psalms. The Poles, on the other hand, spent their holidays consuming large quantities of vodka ('*yash*') and not a few celebrations ended in violent quarrels, fires and the shedding of blood.

In the summer season, Dowgalishok set aside its normal life of rustic calm. With the start of the vacation season immediately after the holiday of Shavuoth, masses of summer visitors thronged to Dowgalishok, filling every house and barn. The population doubled and tripled; the main and only street was teeming with men, women, and children of all ages – turning what had until then been a quiet and peaceful thoroughfare into a bustling ferment.

Although a large number of holiday-makers came from Radun, few of them, if any, were actually permanent residents of that town. They were mainly the families of the heads of the yeshiva and its leaders, accompanied by the elite of the students of the yeshiva. They had come to relax in those hot summer days, after having worn themselves out in pursuit of their Torah studies during the rest of the year. But one should not imagine that the Torah was set aside. Sounds of the Torah could be heard wafting on the wind in every corner, among the trees of the forest and along the paths where the yeshiva boys wandered, elucidating diverse questions of the Talmud.

8

This season of my childhood was the most wonderful of all seasons. For all the children of the rabbinical courtyard, the offspring of rabbis and heads of the yeshiva, with whom I played and studied throughout the year in Radun, this was vacation time. For me, it meant returning to the arms of my family, to my loving and beloved mother and my much-loved and esteemed father. There was no suitable Jewish school in Dowgalishok, and so I was sent together with my older brother Pinchas to study in Radun, and most of the year was spent in Radun, cut off from my parents, except for holidays and the Sabbath.

The house at the eastern edge of the village belonged to the Polish farmer Palsha. The courtyard and farm buildings seemed to be implanted in the pine forest, spreading out in all directions. During the summer, the house was given up by its owners and filled with endless Jewish holiday-makers. Every year, the lovely house and spacious courtyard, was taken over by descendants of the Hafetz Haim, that is, his son-in-law Rabbi Mendel and his family, and Rabbi Joshua and his family accompanied by an intimate circle of students of the yeshiva. In a single day, the rural countrified courtyard, turned into a rabbinical courtyard in all its outward aspects. *Mezuzoth* were placed on the doorways, one of the rooms was arranged as a synagogue, and the kitchen was made kosher, according to all the proper laws. The pigs which only yesterday could be seen roaming about the courtyard, announcing their presence with snorts and repulsive smells, were placed at a distance from which they appeared to be sheep, and the courtyard was filled with the clamor of playing children of all ages.

Different parts of the forest belonged to the village families. Dried timbers from its trees were used for heating in the winter and for cooking and baking in the village, throughout the entire year. The tall trees growing in the forest for many generations, would at times provide the villagers with an income, for in an hour of need, they would cut down some of them and sell the timber for a good price. It was in this same forest that we children would venture out to gather blackcurrants and mushrooms in the springtime. Here too, in the hot summer days, it would be filled by groups of holiday-makers from among the people of the yeshiva of Radun. Scores of hammocks were strung from the giant trees, which grew to great heights. Mischievous and playful children ran about, entwined in their branches, the sound of laughter and the vigor of youth echoed from their boughs, and everywhere one felt the joyousness. Here the twittering of the birds and the melodic repetition of the yeshiva students learning their Talmud blended together in one hymn of praise to glorify the Creator. And it was in this same forest, on Sabbath and on holidays, after the morning prayer and Mussaf, and after emptying the baking ovens and filling their stomachs with *cholent*, *kugel* (noodle pudding), and *kishke* (stuffed darm), that the villagers strolled along its pathways with their families.

My mother, Sarah Mina, and my father, Moshe David, dressed in their best clothes, would stroll along at their leisure, conversing of this and that, while we three children, Pinchas (Pinke), Avraham (Avremke) and Yekutiel (Kushka), would flit about them like butterflies, at times behind them or ahead of them. Here, when I was a little older, my father would take me with him to the edge of the forest, where he would stand on guard against robbers and thieves at the approaches to the village, for with the onset of the Second World War, these felons were on the increase. From then onwards, I learned what night-watching meant, and for many years, I was obliged to use what I had learned. It seemed that my father was instinctively guided to teach me to fear neither the darkness of the forest nor to be startled by the swish of the branches or the rustling of the leaves at night. It was as if he had foreseen those days when I would be forced to avoid the daylight and find peace and a haven among the boughs of those trees.

Yes, this was the very forest in which my father and other villagers took cover and found refuge in angry and disturbing times, and finally, just before the arrival of freedom and liberty, a hiding place from the Polish popular army known as

10

the White Poles (AK), who took upon themselves the role of the Germans. It was also on one of the hills of this same forest that my brother Pinchas is buried, with the *tefillim* he received at his bar mitzvah buried alongside him. The forest is unforgettable. It has many faces: the gaiety of children, the songs of the birds, the whispering leaves, the secrets of both life and death.

On the opposite side of the street, in the other house on the edge of the forest, lived Moshe and Esther Lipkunsky, an elderly couple of some 70 years. Esther, an upright woman of proud and determined bearing, still showed signs of the beauty, despite her 70 years. Her husband Moshe, a bearded, tall and easygoing man, who was ready to fulfill any of his wife's desires, would sometimes leave for America in order to make money and then return to his home and village. On his second visit to America, he was accompanied by his eldest daughter, a girl of 17–18, who remained there when her father returned home. A pair of ferocious dogs were tied near the entrance to the house. One Sabbath, on leaving after my visit to the elderly couple whose custom it was to offer me candies on this occasion, I was tempted to tease the dogs. Although I had been warned by Grandma Esther, I threw a stick past them and ran for my life, but I did not manage to get very far when one of the dogs broke away from his chain, raced after me, threw me to the ground, and sunk his sharp teeth into my new Sabbath pants, and even took a bite out of my bottom. It was only thanks to the old woman's alertness and shouts that the beast left off. From then onward, I learned not to tease dogs, and not to run away from them. Grandpa Moshe fortunately died in his own bed before the Nazi invasion, but the rest of this extensive family were all exterminated. Their son, Herschel-Zvi, was killed in the forests of Dowgalishok not far from their house. How fate mocks us at times and how many mysterious contradictions there are in our lives: Herschel, a sturdy, handsome young man, served in the Polish army only a few years earlier. His photograph in army uniform was proudly displayed on the wall of his home. He was prepared to defend his Polish homeland to the end, but he was killed not by the Germans but by the White Poles who were supposed to fight the German invader. Of this large, widespread family, only the eldest daughter Gittel remained alive: that same daughter who had traveled to America with her father on one of his trips, and who did not return with him to the valley of death in his Polish homeland. There are no traces of the other daughter Zviah and her family, and no one knows what became of them.

Since the days when I first heard the story of Reb Moshe Lipkunsky's visits to America, more than 40 years have passed, and it is 25 years since I put the story on paper. One fine summer day in 1979, however, there appeared in my office Jacob Levinsky, the son of Leibke Levin of Oran and Liebele Davidovitch of Radun, the daughter of Moshe and Dvorele, with the following account:

> I have just returned from the United States, where I was one of the delegation of diamond dealers to a conference in Hartford, Connecticut. At the reception arranged for us by the local Jewish community, I noticed a woman who closely resembled my aunt, my mother's sister and the resemblance so aroused my curiosity, that I suddenly found myself facing her and telling her about the likeness. In the course of the conversation that developed, when she heard that I hailed from Radun, she immediately announced that her mother had come to the States from Radun, and that her mother's name was Lipkunsky. Unable to believe my ears, I told her that I know someone from Radun whose name was Lipkunsky, who now lives in Tel Aviv.

She insisted that it was certainly a relative and she begged me to establish contact between her and the unknown relative as soon as I returned to Israel.

12

Jacob Levinsky pleaded with me, 'Avremele, you must write to these wonderful people immediately. They love Israel, so please write to them and tell them about yourself, for they are waiting impatiently for your letter and perhaps they really are family relations.'

I stubbornly refused to comply with all his entreaties, saying: 'Why should I write?' They would probably think that I was looking for American uncles and expecting gifts from them, as was usually the case during the first years of the State of Israel. I resolved not to write, but if they were to write to me, I promised to answer them. I pondered over why they suddenly remembered their family. Where were they during the difficult years when everyone had an uncle somewhere? In those days, it certainly would have done me no harm to have had an uncle, especially an American one. But now! It was only two years since we first went abroad and traveled the width and breadth of the United States, from coast to coast, as was the fashion among Israelis in those days, without any help from an American uncle. And now our financial situation was immensely better than in those days when we prayed for any uncle at all!

After a few days we received a letter from America, from our newly acquired relatives. This is not the place to go into the annals of our family and the depth of the roots we uncovered. The contents of their letter, that of Sidney and Ruth Cohen, offspring of the Lipkunsky family, uncannily resembled the story I had written about the elderly pair. From the letter, it emerged that Ruth was the granddaughter of Reb Moshe and Esther Lipkunsky of Dowgalishok. I had only to make a copy of what I had written many years earlier about the household of her grandmother and grandfather, and confirm that we actually came from the same village and that our names were identical. As we hailed from Dowgalishok and stemmed from the family of Lipkunsky, there was nothing more natural than to accept and embrace one another as family relatives. And so we did. We established connections and links that have become stronger and deeper from year to year. Since their first letter, they have visited us a number of times. Her brother, Irving Blasberg, was also caught up in the excitement of these family happenings, and he too has visited us, to hear at first-hand the rich source of information about this widely scattered family which no longer belongs to Dowgalishok. And I wonder whether Ruth and Sidney's children: Jonah (Jordan), Sarah (Susan), Moshe Isser (Mitchell), Esther (Cynthia), and Francie, Irving and Louise Blasbergs' only daughter, have derived something of their forefather's heritage.

On either side of the road, surrounding Moshe and Esther Lipkunsky's house, stretched the property of Rabbi Kaddish Rudnitzky, who had inherited it, even though he was not an offspring of the dynasty of the founders of the village. He had married Leah, one of the Lipkunsky daughters, and received the property of her forebears as dowry. Rabbi Kaddish was unlike most of his contemporaries among the villagers: those sturdy, manly young men. He was small and frail and the spectacles resting on the crook of his nose, together with his beard and his forelocks, hid most of his face, while the thick lenses blurred what one could glimpse of his eyes. It was obvious from his general appearance that he was not of the same stock as the local young men of the village, who still retained their native strength and whose eyes were not dimmed. But his frailty was compensated by his erudition and his understanding of the Bible, and he was considered a scholar alongside the rest of the villagers, who knew little of the portion of the week, the prayers and the *piyutim.** He was gifted with a sweet and melodious voice, which resulted in his being given the role of reader on the Sabbath and on the holidays. He was also very much in demand as a cantor, appearing before the Ark on the Days of Awe (the High Holidays), not only in Dowgalishok but in Radun and other nearby villages, for which he would receive substantial payment in addition to the honor and esteem which accom-

*Note: words or phrases marked with an asterisk are explained in the Glossary.

14

panied the role.

Reb Kaddish also visited America on a few occasions, and one can assume that he did not work there as a manual laborer but served in various ceremonial functions having to do with the synagogue. He would earn some money and then return home – to his family and the village of Dowgalishok. He was very proud of having seen much of the world, both at sea and beyond the seas, which served as the source for those wondrous and fantastic stories, the telling of which continued for many years. It was quite an experience to be standing by when Reb Kaddish met up with a Jewish tourist from America and had a conversation with him in English.

Reb Kaddish would hardly ever forgo an opportunity to test our knowledge, that is, my brother Pinchas's and mine, when we were back from Radun. He quizzed us on the portion of the week, in our understanding of Rashi* and the script. This, of course, was done in the presence of everyone in the synagogue, all of whom gathered around to listen to the interrogation. He would grill us as to the literal and the metaphorical meaning, for his erudition and knowledge was obvious to the ordinary folk, who would not dare to take part in the discussion. From the portion of the week, he would wander off to tales of the sea and the wonders of his journeys to America aboard ships armed with long knives and saws sailing on the high seas. They would slash away at the great fish – those whales who were craving to devour the ship (like that which swallowed Jonah in the Bible). And the ship would plow the waves, leaving behind it a long line of blood, coloring the ocean red in its wake.

Reb Kaddish's oldest son Leibke lived across the street. Apart from farming he also dealt in petty trading, supplying groceries to the inhabitants of Dowgalishok and gentiles from the surrounding neighborhood. The two daughters of Reb Kaddish were attractive and pleasant. Many young men who were always to be seen surrounding the girls, and we children learned some elementary lessons about the courting and wooing of young ladies.

When the Radun ghetto was wiped out, the two girls, Numke and Rochke (the eldest), fled to the forest. For a short while they found refuge with the farmers or in the woods of Dowgalishok, but because existence in the woods was so difficult, and even more so for young and pretty girls, they were forced to return secretly to the ghetto of Lida and join the rest of the Jews of Radun there. When the annihilation of the remaining Jews was reaching its height, they succeeded in escaping in the guise of village girls to the forests in the Dowgalishok region. For months they fought for their survival in the forest, and from time to time, they hid with farmers they were acquainted with, but eventually they fell at the hands of the slaughterers. Their beauty and charm was of no avail in the face of the guns and knives of the White Poles (the AK),* a short time prior to the Nazis' defeat in this area. Their parents and other members of the family were annihilated together with the Jews of Radun. Of this extensive family not a single person remained alive.

The house in the center of the village, on the eastern side of the road leading away from the village from north to south, belonged to Feivke Lipkunsky, His marriage to Blumke was the outcome of a brilliant matchmaking scheme which somewhat resembled the biblical story of Rachel and Leah. Blumke was a spoiled but intelligent city girl, a few years older than him. She came of a good family, close to that of the respected Akiva and Hassia Rogovsky and the latter's niece. Feivke was a handsome man, popular among the farmers of the region, and their opinion was naturally a decisive element in the choice of a bride. The intended bride was lucky, for she had a lovely younger cousin, the daughter of Hassia and Akiva, who also bore the name of Blumke, and the farmers were convinced that it was this beautiful young Blumke who was to be his bride, for they had had glimpses of her when visiting her father's inn for a drink, and it was not surprising that they encouraged and supported Feivke's assumed choice. The day after the wedding, however, they understood that

16

they had been mistaken for 'behold, it was Leah', and they had no alternative but to accept the situation. The farmers had great respect for Blumke's wide knowledge and education and would come to consult her and ask her advice when one of their children fell sick and there was no doctor to be had.

When Feivke lived in the village, he was in his thirties. His home was the newest and most modern in the place: the most attractive house in the village, displaying the most up-to-date innovations in its structure, both outwardly and within. Its handsome proportions were all the more marked when compared with his mother's house, that of the widow Mirel, which was shabby and rundown. This house, in which she and all her children were born and raised, including Feivke, covered a small patch of ground and looked like a square box placed alongside the street. Its wooden door hung on old and shaky hinges which groaned and creaked, while the doorway itself served not only as the entrance and exit of the house but also as the outlet for smoke – for unlike other houses there was no chimney extending from the roof. The window that looked out onto the street recalled the hatches on Noah's Ark, indicating what must have been a very gloomy interior; while the sloping thatched roof resembled nothing so much as a large hat on a small head.

Apart from farming, Feivke dealt in small trading and supplied groceries to the Jews of Dowgalishok and the gentiles of the region. Business was especially flourishing during the summer time, when scores of holiday-makers would fill every nook and cranny of the village. It was said that Feivke managed to save himself and his wife and children from the ghetto of Radun by going into hiding with a Polish farmer who had been a friend of the family – in exchange for all his possessions, of course. Due to all the secrecy that surrounded the situation, none of the Jews of Dowgalishok who had taken refuge in the forest knew his whereabouts. Alas, by handing over all his possessions as a legacy to the farmer who was to have concealed him and thus save his life until the war ended, he signed his own death warrant; for that same farmer who

17

was heir to Feivke's possessions quietly put an end to Feivke in order to come into his inheritance at once. Mirel's Feivke, his wife Blumke and their young children, suddenly vanished from the forest and no one saw them afterwards: it was as if the earth had swallowed them alive.

The western edge of the village was bordered by fields of pasture: wide meadows that stretched northward and southward, flanking the western edge of the river. The pastures and the meadows were divided up between the village families. It was an exhilarating sight to watch the scythes cutting the hay to be stored for the coming winter, the reapers advancing row by row in one measured beat. A great deal of skill and strength went into maintaining the rhythm of the work. After the hay was dry, it would be stacked in piles in the form of a dome, tied well and smoothed over, lest the rain should spoil it. To this very day, the intoxicating smell of the newly cut hay is with me still.

The stream that served as the border between the two villages of Dowgalishok and Pitzeluntze was a great temptation to children. The shrubbery along the sloping banks of the stream was heavy with berries and nuts. Not infrequently, we would skip school or go there when we had no studies. One such day would be 9 Av (August). It was a tradition that the fast observed by the adults on 9 Av would become a holiday and a day of excursions for the children, with or without the knowledge of their parents. They would leave the village walking quickly or almost running, for an hour and a half, until they reached that cool, enchanted site. Then they would stuff themselves with berries and their knapsacks with fresh nuts and return to Radun before nightfall, weary and happy.

The road from Radun to Dowgalishok ran through villages and estates owned by Poles. Normally the way was peaceful, and when I was alone with my brother, there was almost no antagonism towards us. Here and there we would be frightened that a dog would attack us, but the people were not hostile. Sometimes we would get a lift from a farmer with a wagon going towards Dowgalishok and back. Many farmers of the neighborhood knew us as the children of the black-smith, and they would invite us to join them on their wagons. But when we went with a group of Jewish children from Radun, quite a brawl would break out between us and the children of the village we were passing through. Most of the quarrels took place at the entrance to Radun, with gentile boys from the Radun outskirts. These skirmishes would sometimes develop into stone-throwing battles, which would at times end with our being the victors and at other times with us in full retreat, running for our lives.

At every crossroad and before every village there were crosses protected by little sloping roofs, with icons of Jesus or the Madonna beneath them. For some reason, we children were under the impression that Jews were forbidden even to glance at a cross, but our childish curiosity got the better of us and I would quickly and guiltily snatch a glance at the cross while repeating the short prayer 'thou shalt utterly detest it, and thou shalt utterly abhor it, for it is a cursed thing' (Deuteronomy 7: 26), spitting in the direction of the alleged cursed thing, but seeing to it that no one should see me doing so. Heaven forbid! Like the spitting after the saying of the prayer: 'It is our duty to praise the Lord, since he hath not made us like the nations of different countries, nor placed us like the families of the earth.' One wonders where this wayward custom came from, for neither at home nor in the *cheder*, and certainly not at school or in the yeshiva, were we taught it. And yet this was a deep-rooted custom which evidently stemmed from the suffering the Jews encountered in connection with the crucifixion of Jesus. The only reaction of the Jews to the brutality practiced against them because of their being Jews was disdain.

The house at the edge of the meadow belonged to the Polish farmer who had acquired the piece of land from one of the Paikovskys. Next to it stood the house of Reb Avremel Paikovsky, a tall and lean Jew with a small, pointed beard. He and his wife were childless and his house was spacious and always clean and in perfect order. One of the rooms served as a synagogue both during weekdays and on the Sabbath and holidays, for there was no regular synagogue in Dowgalishok. Prayers were held in people's homes, evidently according to a prearranged order or through the residents' offers. No one would forgo the prerogative to house the Holy Ark and those who prayed before it, for a certain period of the year. Reb Avremel's brother, Joshe Jankel, who was older by a few years, was not particularly learned or a brilliant scholar, but his honesty and simplicity, in addition to his pleasant voice, made him a suitable choice for cantor. He led the prayers on holidays and the daily morning services. People of greater status, such as Rabbi Kaddish generally led the additional services (Mussaf). Although Joshe Jankel was more than 70 years old, he was strong and tall, and he had lost none of his vigor. He once made a bet that he could lift a wagon loaded with wood, when a much younger man could not even lift a completely empty wagon. Naturally he won the wager! Despite his years, he would run and jump like a youngster, and who knows what wondrous age he may have reached, were it not for the fact that the White Poles put an end to his life in the Dowgalishok forest, where he had taken refuge with his son Simka, the tailor.

The house of Joshe Jankel's cousin and contemporary, Reb Joshe Paikovsky, stood across the road. In addition to farming, he was known as a builder of wooden houses. In my childish amazement, I frequently watched him raising his tremendous ax and bring it down with enormous blows and measured rhythm on wood that was being prepared for building. He was then in his seventies.

His ax was not like the other axes in the place: its steel blade was sharp as a razor, thin and flat, and longer than usual. The wooden handle too was long and had a peculiar form: it was wide and flat at the base, gradually getting rounder and thinning towards the middle and finally widening again. Its unusual shape and smooth surface made it possible to maintain a firm hold with one hand near the base, while the other hand would glide along the length of the handle as it was being swung down in an arc, thus giving a blow of great force. This very skilled craftsmanship would quickly turn the round log, crooked and gnarled by nature, into a straight plank, flat and oblong. On one side it was given a diagonal notch by the blow of the ax, to make it ready to take the dry grasses which would be stuffed between each plank. The skills of carpentry and woodcraft were also handed down to his son, Meir David, who was a well-known carpenter in Radun. He, in turn, passed on his know-how to his son, Haim Paikovsky, my contemporary and companion in the bunker we dug together in the forest, which was unfortunately discovered by shepherds. Haim pursued his family's traditional craft when he lived in Russia, and then later in the development town of Sderoth, in southern Israel, where he passed on his skill to his son.

2 Berl the Tailor

Along the road going eastward stood the farm of Kaschitz, a family of Polish aristocrats. They had acquired the property from Berl Lipkunsky – Berl the tailor – Berl of Dowgalishok, my father's cousin. Their homestead, and the outhouses attached to it, adjoined our own. It was as if one large field had been divided in two, for only two generations earlier, in Grandpa Yekutiel's time, the area had belonged to only one family. Grandpa Yekutiel had divided his property between his two sons, David and Pinchas Lipkunsky. The third son, Salman, left the village together with his children who emigrated to other villages and cities (some even went overseas).

David's son Berl, a tailor by profession and in his very soul, sold the farm and went to live in Radun, where he built himself a house. His older brothers and sister had left the village much earlier on. His brother Alter, who had served in the army of the Tsar, emigrated to England and changed his name to Gross. Their sister, the beautiful Hannah, married a man who was not Jewish – a man of considerable importance in those days, who was also very rich and the owner of much property. Some said that he was a captain of a ship and sailed the high seas round the world. They lived in Singapore.

There were many stories at the time going round about Hannah's wealth and beauty. One of them told of her appearance in the village (she had come to visit her family) accompanied by two guardsmen, whom the authorities of the district of Lida region had appointed to look after her, for she was dressed up to the nines and dripping with gold and diamonds. (The authorities feared lest she should be robbed, and they would be considered responsible and get into trouble as a result.)

On returning from this visit, she took her brother Alter with her, intending to take him to Singapore where she lived. On the train *en route* to London, her young brother informed her that he did not want to go to Singapore but preferred instead to stay in London. In her disappointment, and in the rage of the quarrel that ensued, hoping to prevent their parting from one another, she demanded that he return all the expenses that she had laid out for this journey, knowing full well that he did not have the wherewithal to pay her back. Alter, who was determined to remain in London, tore his gold watch and chain from the belt to which it was attached, and threw it in her face, saying, 'Here is all I have to repay you for what you have spent on me.' He then disappeared from the train into the streets of London. Contact between the two was interrupted for many years as a result.

Some decades passed. Alter served in the Tsar's army. Then in the 1930s, when Radun was part of free Poland under Marshal Pilsudsky's rule, Alter would turn up every few years, riding in his private limousine, with a chauffeur who was also his valet. He was considered enormously wealthy by the standards of Radun Jewry. The black car he had brought with him from London in which he rode about Radun made a tremendous impression there, for such a sight was indeed a rare one in a small town such as Radun. Alter was the soul of generosity, giving donations to charitable institutions and to the needy who appeared on his doorstep. Obviously, he helped to establish his brother Berl's financial situation. Berl's house was at the edge of the marketplace, at the junction of Klebanya and Mozeyka streets. Klebanya Street led in the direction of the church, which was at the far end of the street, already outside the village; while Mozeyka Street led to Dowgalishok. Berl was the best tailor in town, or at least the most successful. He had many young men working for him as apprentice tailors and he created an entire generation of tailors. Some of them emigrated to North and South America, and quite a number continue to earn their livelihoods as tailors today. His house was partly brick and partly wood, being one of the most handsome and spacious in the village. It was always bursting with life; boys from the yeshiva and other youngsters would come to hear good contrail singing in the evenings and listen to records on the phonograph shaped like a horn, with its red insignia of a listening dog (His Master's Voice). Eminent visitors from out of town who happened to come there for the Sabbath would stay in his house. Berl was a wise and successful man, and whoever was in need of advice or help would find it. He was one of the notables of the village.

Berl and his wife Hannah had three children. Sarahle, the eldest daughter, was a pretty and intelligent girl, who married Shimon Radiks of Brisk, one of the elite of the yeshiva, who had been ordained as a rabbi. Then there was a son, Shneike (Schneour), a boy of 12, and a little girl of 9, Teibele, the daughter of their middle years. A few months after the entry of the Germans into Radun, Berl was suddenly arrested as a result of slander that he was a communist. The Lithuanian farmer Rakoczsky from the village of Lilush, was the source of this slanderous accusation, as once a bicycle was stolen and placed near Berl's house, and when he asked for it to be handed over and was refused, he informed the Germans that Berl was a communist. It was quite enough that Berl was a Jew, but to be a Jew and a communist, gave excellent opportunity to settle accounts with a Jew at a time when the security of Radun Jewry was already threatened. After a few days, Berl was taken from his comfortable home and sent to the regional city of Lida, where he was to be tried. Members of the *Judenrat,** acquaintances and friends, did everything they could to save him. They paid out huge sums of money, and even managed to get the Polish mayor of the city to make statements in Berl's favor and give evidence with regard to his honesty and the fact that he had never been a communist. All this was of no avail and he remained in jail without knowing what was happening to him.

During the afternoon hours on a Sabbath during Hanukkah in the year 1941, a special unit of the German army arrived from the town of Lida. They took Berl's wife Hannah and their two children, Shneike and Teibele, to the edge of the ghetto on the incline of Lida Street and shot them in the middle of the street, their wounds bleeding over the white carpet of snow which covered the ground. The representatives of the Judenrat and the Jewish policemen of the ghetto, who had been forced to accompany them, were ordered to bury them at once. The gravediggers dug swiftly into the frozen ground, and when they went to collect the corpses in order to bury them, they were astonished to hear the murmuring of the little 9-year-old Teibele saying 'please don't bury me, I'm still alive!'

Hannah and her son Shneike died immediately on the spot and the little girl Teibele had fatal injuries to her head and chest. Despite the enormous danger of disobeying the orders of the SS, they tried to save the child's life. She was supposedly buried together with her mother and brother, but in fact they secretly transferred her to the house of a Polish farmer, and afterwards brought her to the house of her sister in the ghetto, who had been saved by having changed her family name to that of her husband – Radiks. Unfortunately, the Germans remembered that they had forgotten to take Hannah Lipkunsky's identity card with them, in order to submit it to headquarters as evidence, and they decided to look for it in the house where the little girl was lying fatally wounded. The *Judenrat* representatives who had to accompany them during the search were terribly anxious. The main representative, Noah Dolinsky, was so frightened that he hid; he simply disappeared from sight for a while. His aide, Berl Boyarski, who was chosen to escort the Germans, was also terrified as to the consequences that would ensue were the Germans to find the injured child. In his anxiety, he whispered to the Polish chief of police, Franciszek Lugowsky, who was a friend of the Jews, and the latter understood that he had to do something to prevent the Germans from searching that house, or else a further catastrophe would occur. Showing unusual resource-fulness, he invited the Germans to have a drink and snack with him and said that he would send some people round to fetch the documents. They accepted the invitation, and the band of murderers ate and drank vodka to their heart's content in the knowledge that the orders from above were being carried out. Under the influence of the liquor, one of the Germans recalled that he had seen the identity cards in the hands of Hannah, the mother, and he gave orders to open the grave and take the documents, and so the grave was opened and the identity cards retrieved. It was entirely due to the courage and resourcefulness of the people of the *Judenrat* and the Polish chief of police that there was no further bloodshed on that day.

The child Teibele succumbed to her wounds, and died a few days later, to the eternal shame of humanity. We learned later that on that same morning of the massacre the Germans had hanged Berl. In the prison in Lida. Thus they made sure that all the family were annihilated and wiped out on the same day.

Almost 50 years have passed now since these events, but the memory of them is with me still. They appear before my eyes in the form of written Hebrew letters which can never be erased.

The Polish family Kaschitz, who bought Berl and Alter's property, consisted of four people: the widowed mother, the older brother Kazuk, who stammered, was tongue-tied and good-natured, the middle son Franek, and the youngest son Wladek. We were on good terms with our neighbors, the Polish family Kaschitz. Though the snorting of the pigs and the smells that emanated from their courtyard were not pleas-ant, this did not affect our good relationship. Each family respected the way of life and customs of the other. Mutual help was given as a matter of course, especially in connection with working the fields, the common pasture, and the use of agricultural implements and beasts of burden – and even manpower, when the need arose at the height of the harvest.

When we returned from Radun during vacations, my brother Pinchas and I would play with the middle son, Franek, who was the same age as Pinchas. He was an intelligent boy who intended to become a priest, he studied theology and was especially interested in the sources of his religion. Quite often, a discussion or argument would develop about creeds and beliefs, the source of Christianity and Jesus Christ; about those elements the religions had in common and where they differed, and about the New and the Old Testament. It was amazing how we children understood how to bridge the gap over the chasms and competition between the two beliefs, to find what we had in common and to preserve our comradeship without either side either giving up its principles or beliefs. This friendship proved itself when Franek endangered his life and that of the entire family by giving us refuge in our hour of need.

It appears that the foundations of our house were laid by our Grandfather Pinchas's father, and here, after some 150 years, the isolated house became an entire village. Many of his offspring who had not found their place in the village were scattered around the world, in other countries. Our house stood on the western side of the main road that ran through the village from south to north. Southward, the village led to Radun, the distance of an hour's wagon-ride or a two-hour walk. Northward, the road went in the direction of Talkunca and the district town of Lida. The stretch of road that passed alongside our house was sandy and narrow; it also divided the farmyard, with the barn on one side and the cowshed, which was slightly behind the house, on the other. The road was close to the corner of the house and the cowshed was only a short distance away from the house.

In the spring and the summertime we would mainly come from Radun along this road by foot, but during the winter, we would take the same route riding along on sleighs. The road was very narrow and was just wide enough to enable one horse and wagon to pass. There were fences all along the sides of the road to prevent intrusion into the vegetable gardens. It was here that we would play and run about, for we knew every stone and shrub. We would run along this stretch of the road to Father's smithy (a short distance from our house), as long as it was possible. At times, we would pause at the single rock that protruded into the left side of the road and climb onto it, jumping from it again and again. Continuing to run further, we would stop underneath the pear tree which was right by the smithy, and test the pears for size and ripeness. Breathless, we would enter the smithy on the run and with bated breath would examine the enormous bellows which were rising and swelling, declining and contracting, blowing hard on the burning coals. We would stare in wonder and admiration at how Father and his workers would turn an iron bar into a horseshoe which fitted the horse's hoof perfectly, while the horse stood calmly on three legs, his fourth bent upwards to the rear awaiting the shoeing. Thick-headed, pointed and square nails were hammered with heavy blows into the horse's hoof. When his four hooves were shod in new shoes he would leave the place at a brisk trot.

We would watch as they turned a steel bar into the blade of a plough; as they made and attached metal hoops to the wooden wheels of a wagon; as a shapeless bar of metal became a living tool, which seemed to speak to one and invite admiration of its form. We watched the whitened metal and the sparks flying from it in every direction when the sledge-hammer came down on the anvil. The noise was deafening.

It was on this same stretch of road which we knew and loved so well, on the night of 10 Marheshvan 1942, that my older brother Pinchas's life came to an end. Pinke – the brother whom I so loved and admired! From this stretch of road, the bullets of the murderers who were hiding behind the walls of our house, managed to reach him, and the moon that was still not full, did not heed our prayers ('as I dance before you and cannot touch you, so may our enemies be unable to harm us'), and ignoring the wishes of his Maker, sent its rays to light the way for the bullets of the assassins. My dearly beloved Pinchas! The memory of you will be with me forever.

Our house had two wings with a single entrance. The older wing to the left, facing the road, was that of Uncle Jacob Leib and his family. Grandfather Rabbi Pinchas, who had taken the mother of Uncle's wife for his second marriage, lived there at one time. The newer wing to the right, which faced the court-yard of our Polish neighbor Kaschitz, was that of Father and our family. Grandfather Pinchas had died many years before I was born and I cannot even remember the way he looked in a photograph. But his character and personality is known to me from stories told by my father or by Grandfather's contemporaries in the village. Everyone spoke in praise of Rabbi Pinchas who was considered a learned and erudite man. There were those who said that the Hafetz Haim,* the modest genius of the time, when he came to Dowgalishok to rest during the summer holidays, would meet with Pinchas and they would discuss matters dealing with the Torah.

Our father, unlike his brothers, was not inclined to pore over his books. He preferred working with his hands to studying the Torah. Perhaps because of grandfather's weakness and ailments, he was obliged to deal with the farm, as his older brothers had left home and the village and moved to Dzivienishok where they had set up their homes. But when Father sought out a wife with whom to establish a family, he wandered as far as Eishishok, where he found Sarah Mina, the daughter of Esther Osna and Abraham Hirsch Rachovsky, who had been brought up among scholars, teachers, and students of the yeshiva.

Grandfather Abraham Hirsch and Grandmother Esther Osna had seven children, some with double names, evidently to ensure a long life, such as Jacob (Jankel) the oldest, who served as a religious cleric and earned his livelihood as a teacher. He taught the Torah to many of Eishishok's various age groups. But because his income was meager, he emigrated to America, as did many of Eishishok's Jews in those days. As long as his mother, Esther Osna, who in the meantime had become a widow, was still alive, he would regularly contribute to her upkeep and help support the poor family. When his mother died, the help ceased and their income dwindled, and their contact with him all but vanished.

Our mother was the fourth of the children, after two sons and a daughter, and according to what we were told, it was love at first sight, which explains why our future mother, who was a pretty girl of the town, was prepared to follow her beloved to a village. It was not easy for her to adapt to village ways – a fact which I learned from tales around the family table on the Sabbath or holidays in an atmosphere of humorous revelations.

They had five children: four sons and one daughter. The oldest son and the daughter died before I was born. Like my mother, I was also the fourth in line. From a rumor which reached my ears, I understood that I was born on the same day or week in which my older brother Hirschele died. Mother was reluctant to talk to us about it, but whenever Hirschele's name came up, tears trickled down her cheeks. Everyone who had known him, spoke with pain and admiration of the beauty and unusual qualities of this child. Perhaps her difficulties in adjusting to life in the village and the death of two of her children were Father's main reasons for changing their dwelling-place and trying his luck elsewhere overseas.

My memories since the end of 1929, from the time I was torn from my father's arms, were erased from my mind for two whole years. Nothing at all remains of this period, as if the machinery of my mind refused to record anything. Only after two years, when I was 4 or 5, does my wayward memory began to recall the events of childhood. And again, these are linked with tears and parting, the final farewell from the only grandmother I knew in my lifetime, my mother's mother, Esther Osna from Eishishok.

Here she lies, stalks of straw spread beneath her and a

white sheet covering her body. Candles are lit near her head and at various corners of the room. There are many people gathered round her, murmuring and weeping. I wander about alone among the many people, some of whose faces are familiar and others who are not. I look at the people and ponder over grandmother lying lifeless on her bed.

Only a few days earlier, I had seen her seated in her chair in the lounge, with her small eyes, sunken within a bed of creases, observing everything going on around her. Her mien was that of a queen, and everyone danced around her in awe and respect. What made this tiny, thin woman the object of so much admiration and why did she merit all this love and devotion? Was it because of the suffering and sorrow she had endured and knew how to bear with dignity. Her husband died when still in his prime after she had borne him seven children, and the little one, Reinke, scarcely knew him. A few years later the pride of her life, her son Mordkele, died. When still a very young man, he was appointed head of the yeshiva in the country town of Novogradok. The eldest boy Jankel sailed off to America immediately after his marriage. And so the little woman remained with five children, four daughters and one son: (Riva Malka) Alte, Sarah Mina, Beyla, Velvel, and Reinke.

Her little house on Millner Street also served as a grocery store, a sort of tiny general store for the many farmers who came to the market in Eishishok on Thursdays. The turnover on that day had to suffice for the entire family's support. The proud and energetic little woman also knew how to educate her children properly. The oldest son Jankel served as a teacher, a reader in the synagogue and also as a cantor. Her second son was head of a yeshiva, while her third son Velvel was a Hebrew and Bible teacher. All the girls, with the exception of Reinke, married during her lifetime.

3 Eishishok and Radun

Eishishok and Radun are two neighboring small towns, some 12–14 kilometers apart. Both are situated on the highway leading from Bialystok and Grodno in the west, and pass through them to Vilnius on the east. It is believed that Eishishok was founded in the twelfth century and if this is so, it would be older than Vilnius by 300 years. The Jewish community was also an ancient one, at least the elders of the community recalled having found gravestones some 600 years old. Eishishok was founded by a Lithuanian prince by the name of Eishish, and for centuries, there was rivalry between the Poles and the Lithuanians over its control. In the twentieth century, during the interwar period, the town was under Polish sovereignty, but in 1940 the Soviets transferred it to Lithuanian rule. It then became a border town between White Russia and Lithuania, with the frontier forming a line between Eishishok and Radun.

The Jewish congregation of Eishishok, which numbered some 3,000 souls, was a very rooted one and known as a center of Talmudic and Torah studies, producing many well-known rabbis and during the Haskalah (Enlightenment) many *maskilim** as well. The town was built in the form of a wide and spacious rectangle with a marketplace at its core, surrounded by residential and commercial buildings. The center of town and its main streets belonged to the Jews. Arriving in Eishishok, one felt one was in a Jewish town. It was an attractive and rich town compared with Radun, and until the rise of Hitler the Jews of Eishishok felt completely secure and feared no one. Its strong and valiant young men were often mentioned in stories of courageous behavior towards drunken farmers who were intent on harming the Jews or their property in the marketplace. These hefty young men would pull out the shafts or remove the wheels of the farmers' wagons and disperse the brawlers.

Eishishok was close to Radun not only geographically but also spiritually. The feeling of belonging to Eishishok was the same as the feeling I had of belonging to Radun. Not only was our mother born there, and her family still living there, but I spent a good part of my childhood in Eishishok. Actually, I felt that I belonged to three places: to Dowgalishok where I was born; to Radun where I lived and went to school; and to Eishishok, which was my mother's home town. Eishishok and Radun were like twin towns, with many interwoven family connections and mutual relationships influencing each other in matters of education and culture. Radun was small and poor in comparison with Eishishok's superior buildings and resources. On arriving there, one was immediately aware of the wealth and affluence; but when one came to Radun, one was enfolded in the spirituality and peace of the place. The yeshiva of the Hafetz-Haim and its hundreds of students filled every house in Radun, and in every nook and cranny one could hear the persistent and familiar intonations of children learning their Talmud.

Radun is situated some 50 kilometers northeast of Grodno, on the highway leading from Grodno to Vilnius and passing through Eishishok, or turning eastward to the district center of Lida. In both Radun and Eishishok there was a central marketplace surrounded by houses. Grassland spread out along the way from the marketplace eastward, with occasional old trees, and standing amidst them a cross, for the place was sometimes used as a Christian cemetery. Large stones were placed around the area as a fence and indicator of the boundaries of the cemetery. We children would sometimes play on the grass or take a short cut across it and not infrequently the priest or his acolytes who happened to be there would pursue and threaten us lest we dare to tread on the grass again. Residences, which also served as business premises, surrounded the marketplace and the cemetery. Most of them were wooden single-storey buildings, some were of brick, and a few were two-storey houses.

The marketplace in the heart of the town was mostly paved with cobblestones, as were the major roads, but the remaining roads were sand or earth. During the sunny summer days the roads were dry, but when the rains came in the autumn, or in the springtime when the ice began to melt, we waded through mud.

Some two kilometers westward towards Grodno, was the ancient Jewish cemetery where most of the inhabitants of Radun were buried. In the spring and the summertime, the youngsters and the children, as well as the yeshiva students, would stroll around the surrounding fields in which the corn grew to the height of a man, or they would play in the shadows of the young pine trees which had not yet reached their prime. Sometimes we children would venture into the cemetery and examine the ancient tombstones half-hidden by the wild undergrowth, trying to make out the town's past from what was written on them. There was a sort of harmony in the silence of the everlasting alongside the vibrant life about us.

Eastward, beyond the row of houses facing the old Christian cemetery stood the synagogue courtyard (*shul-hoif*), the very core of the spiritual life of the town. This courtyard covered a hill, and at its center stood the handsome and impressive building of the great yeshiva of Radun, the yeshiva of the Hafetz Haim. It was a large and expansive building, notable for its height. It was built of red brick, with tall windows set all along the upright walls. There were two entrances: one at the western end of the northern wall and the other at the western end of the southern wall. The placing of the entrances enabled people to enter and exit without disturbing either the students at their studies, the teachers, or the head of the yeshiva, while they were occupied in the eastern end of the hall.

Two rows of tall pillars extended from the east to the west in support of the high ceiling. The *maggid** of Radun and agile students would scramble up these pillars on Simchat Torah* or Purim and amuse the public with their antics. This sort of unusual mischief and daring was especially thrilling for the children.

The synagogue and the rabbinical seminary were situated alongside one another, about a hundred meters from the yeshiva. At the seminary, prayers were held all year round, for it was the seat of learned scholars of the Talmud and the Mishna throughout the day and night. Like an eternal flame throughout the night, there was always a persevering yeshiva student or a pair of students poring over their studies together by the light of a candle or oil lamp, or more recently, by electric light.

Those who came to pray in the synagogue were mostly the young people of the town, for prayers were held in the synagogue mainly on holidays and the Sabbath during the summer months. The cantor would stand before the ark and intone to the accompaniment of the choir. There were some who called this the 'cold synagogue'. Its outward appearance was not impressive but its interior was extremely attractive and pleasing to the eye. The gilded wood of the Holy Ark and the curtain on the eastern wall, embroidered with lions and every manner of animal from Noah's ark, were fine works of craftsmanship. Symbols of the tribes decorated the northern and southern walls. And on the western wall there were pleasing and moving murals depicting the exiles in Babylon on the banks of the river, weeping into their harps and chanting, 'If I forget thee, O Jerusalem, may my right hand forget her cunning.' The synagogue itself was small but there was a tremendous sense of majesty and dignity within.

The Hebrew school was situated to the south, and beyond it stood the Jewish bath-house that also included the *mikveh* (ritual bath) of the town. Some distance between the synagogue and the bath house were the public latrines, serving all those who came to the synagogue and the seminary, as well as schoolchildren. In their primitive way they were excellent, and anyone who had used them in an hour of need would not forget them.

There were nearly a hundred Jewish families and some 400 yeshiva* students living in Radun. They earned their livelihood in a variety of ways; everyone pursued a craft and everyone earned his living, and hence everyone had a nickname derived from his craft or from the father who sired him, or even on account of some event. At any rate, no one was overlooked and no one lacked a nickname. Berl the tailor, Notke the shoemaker, or Yudel the shoemaker (who was not really a shoemaker), Binke the stitcher, Berl the harness-maker, Avremke the smithy, or Avremke Yoshes (the son of Yoshe), or Menashe the smithy, Hatskel the glazier, Selig the carpenter, or Mishke the carpenter, Moshe the butcher, Bezalel the water-carrier, Haimke Pik, the communist, Feive the oven-builder, Kalman the chimney sweep.

(Cleaning the chimneys was essential for preventing fires in the town. The houses were roofed with wooden slats and also partly with straw. The winter in eastern Europe is extremely cold and continues for many months, and the enormous amount of wood burned to provide heat left an accumulation of soot in the chimneys. Not infrequently, the soot would catch fire and sparks would fly in every direction, at times to the point of creating serious fires.)

Bezalel, the water-carrier, was another unusual figure of the town. In those days, water did not flow through pipes in Radun; it was drawn by a rope or wheel from the well, which was generally in a central position along the roadway. A wooden shaft with two pegs on either side bearing two pails, would be borne on the water-carrier's shoulders, and moving to the rear, with a somewhat bowed head and bent back, Reb Bezalel would make his way forward, bearing the water carefully. During the winter, he had to maintain a delicate balance, for any water which spilled on to his clothing or shoes would immediately turn into ice. He was a healthy character both in body and soul, nor did he suffer from lack of appetite, which led to many stories in Radun.

An unusual custom, which became a tradition, was the production of *matzoth** for Passover. For a month preceding the holiday, the spacious house of Avremke Joshes, which stood on a small hill, was used as an improvised primitive bakery. Long tables covered in galvanized tin stood in the large living room, while many Radun girls and women would knead and roll out the dough expertly and swiftly lest the leavening process began. Rolling out the dough required expertise, for it had to be completely even in case it should burn in the thinner areas or be insufficiently baked in the thicker parts and so begin to rise as a result. After the flattening of the dough it was carefully transferred to another table in order to be punctured in close parallel lines by a tool with a wooden or metal handle and a wheel with tiny sharp teeth at its end. This puncturing was necessary to prevent the *matza* from burning on entering the hot oven. All this had to be done very quickly and in order to save time, it was done as if it were a conveyor-belt. Any uneven movement would tear the dough and the *matza* would be useless. The finished *matza* would be draped over a long, smooth, pole, some six or seven meters long, and quickly placed into the hot and blazing oven, laid out carefully in rows at its base.

There was a particularly festive mood during the making of the *matzoth*. Families and friends were recruited for this task. There were many preparations and for quite some time all were occupied in the proceedings. A holiday atmosphere prevailed many weeks before the Passover actually took place. Lightness and gaiety prevailed and friendliness reigned throughout, in gratitude for actually being able to bake the *matzoth* for Passover, a celebration of freedom.

There were also horse traders and dealers in grain in Radun. There were bakers and restaurant owners, water drawers and hewers of wood, teachers and rabbis, leaders of prayers and sextons, a slaughterer, a circumciser and a cantor. And just as the occupations and professions and livelihoods varied, there was much that they held and felt in common. They were simple and naïve people; God fearing and warm hearted to their fellow men. Though they came by their livelihood with difficulty, they shared their bread with any passerby and gave charity in secret. Not all of them understood the words of the prayers, but their prayers were genuine and devout. It was so small a town, so poor in resources, and yet so rich in spirit and in the variety of its inhabitants. Despite the limited population there was also every possible shade of opinion, party or movement among the Jews: Mizrachi and Agudath Israel, Bundists and communists, Hehalutz and Betar. There were recluses (yeshiva students who led a cloistered life) and agnostics. In Radun there was even a woman who was an apostate.

The courtyard of the synagogue served as the spiritual center of the town. Sometimes the town would be visited by lay-preachers and expounders of the scriptures, and the inhabitants of the town would fill the synagogue and listen intently to every word of encouragement they would utter. These were generally quotations from the Talmud and the Bible, and other sources, about the salvation that was near at hand; on the next world, the rolling of the dead and the resurrection that would follow in its wake; on the greatness of the Jewish people who were selected as the chosen people, and on the reason for their suffering; on the reward and expectations that would soon be theirs. And the entire assembly would be united and infused with great hope, leaving the synagogue with uplifted spirits and renewed inspiration to face the hardships awaiting them on the morrow.

This was not the case when one of the Zionist parties sent a lecturer to speak on their behalf. Then there was fervent excitement among the younger generation, and not infrequently such a gathering would end in a free-for-all and the meeting would break up in a scramble.

This was the Radun of my childhood and remained much the same Radun that I grew up in from the age of 2, when my father parted from us and went out to seek his fortune and future across the sea.

My first education and knowledge of the creation began when I started to speak. On waking, even before washing my hands or donning a cap, I was obliged to say the prayer on rising: 'I give thanks unto thee, O living and eternal king, who hast restored my soul to me in mercy: great is thy faithfulness.' From a very early age, I was taught to appreciate the value of life as a gift from God, and in turn, to offer those blessings and praise due Him for this gift that was bestowed on me. I was taught to be conscious and aware of life, for it had been given to me to look after until the end of my years and then once again to return to the guardianship of the Creator. By His will it had been given me and by His will must be returned. On going to bed, before closing my eyes, I was obliged to say: 'Hear, O Israel! The Lord our God is one God!', by which I pronounced that I acknowledged the one and only God also as my God.

At the age of 4, I was taken to the *cheder.** My mother took me by the hand and I dragged after her, stamping with my little feet. Almost running, we entered the inner courtyard of the synagogue, from which a narrow, creaking door opened, revealing a number of descending steps. We went down the steps and found ourselves in a long room which was partly basement. Its little windows were on a level with the ground outside; the light inside was weak and the air was warm and stuffy. Many little children were sitting alongside a long, dark, wooden table. The teacher (*melamed*), whose gray beard flowed as down as far as his chest, was dressed in a black coat (*capote*) from which the tassels of his small fringed garment (*talith*) peeked out from their four angles. The teacher was seated near the stove (which emitted an excessive heat), his staff in his hand, and a little child sitting on his lap. When he raised his hand, the children's mouths opened and a chorus of piercing voices chanted: '*kametz aleph – awh, kametz beth – baw, kametz gimmel, gaw*', in a single, excited melody. I loved being with the children, but I was very frightened of the rod in the teacher's hand and with which he was in the habit of using on the children's hands – not a very pleasant accompaniment to their alphabetical chorus.

I cannot remember our first dwelling in Radun, but I do recall the house we moved to when I was about 5 years old.

This was a small, old house standing at the edge of a hill overlooking the slope down to the street and the road that led to Lida and Eishishok, and near the courtyard of the synagogue. The house had two wings, with a common entrance. We lived in the left wing, while the family of Gershon the tailor lived in the other wing. He had two children: a son and a daughter. The son was called Itchele and he was aged 7, like my brother Pinchas. I was often in their home, where we would play and even do schoolwork together.

My childish curiosity was aroused by the sight of the sewing machine that was driven by pressing on a pedal, by the iron heated by charcoal, and by Reb Gershons' deft movements of his hands, weaving the needle in and out of the cloth – and all at once, there was a button sewn onto the lapel of a coat. Their apartment was the same size as ours, but for some reason or other it seemed smaller and shabbier, and there was dirt in every corner when the sewing was going on. Rows of cloth were scattered all over the place and the dust rose and fell and covered everything. There was an air of poverty and need in every corner. The collection of rags and crushed blankets, which were used as covers during the cold winters, roused all my childish compassion. The children were as pale as plaster and their eyes were full of sadness. It was said that Itchele had tuberculosis and that his life was hanging in the balance, all because of the constant dampness that penetrated into the walls and remained there permanently throughout the year, like troubles that had no end.

Because of our financial difficulties, Mother was forced to leave our former dwelling and move to this apartment, which was cheaper. We lacked nothing, but we felt the distress Mother experienced, realizing that we could not ask for such luxuries as the toys and games that other children possessed. We identified with the distress and were careful not to broadcast the fact. Mother would work day and night, constantly washing and mending our old clothes, lest – heaven forbid – we should appear in public with torn or dirty clothing. She would repeat to us again and again that there was nothing shameful in wearing old or mended clothing, but that it was not nice to appear in muddied or torn clothing, and she would generally add by the way, that it was also shameful to beg, steal or lie. Despite the hardships, she did not lose her faith or hope for a single moment, and her constantly repeated saying was: 'Whoever feeds and nourishes a worm under a stone, will also feed and nourish us.' Such was the strength and depth of her belief in the Almighty. Nevertheless, she did not anticipate miracles and worked endlessly, making use of her talents as a dressmaker, so that we should not lack any essentials and in order to make up what was missing when the money expected from Father overseas was late in coming, or was insufficient. The sewing machine with the Singer insignia that she had brought from her mother's house served her well. Once or twice a week, she would bake all sorts of cakes and *challot* which would be sold to the many farmers who came on market day to Radun or Eishishok, and on returning from school we would help her.

As a child, I felt profoundly the absence of Father as a protective figure, as a source of security: a father who would lift the children into the air or carry them on his broad shoulders, a father who would roar with anger, and a father who would accept and encourage one when this was needed. Having no alternative, I became accustomed to this situation and learned to deal with reality. But for Mother it was infinitely more difficult, for she had to fulfill the role of mother and father. She had to manage the household, to care for and educate three little children, all with very little means. Sometimes she would have to pawn her gold ring or the silverware in order to raise a loan. The bitterness in her heart she did not confide to a soul, and when we were still small and slept deeply without anxiety, she would find an outlet for her suffering in quiet prayer and tears that sometimes wet the pillows upon which she slept. She also knew how to bear her suffering in a manner which did not arouse another's pity. She was always properly dressed in clean garments, and we were clothed in a similar fashion. Her presence together with her three children always called forth admiration – her pride in her children was obvious. Her suffering increased in the course of those years when the situation remained unchanged and even letters were delayed. Gossip that reached her ears through the neighbors and friends of friends, that Moshe David had abandoned his wife and children, greatly troubled her spirit.

I went to school at the age of 5½. After a week had passed, I returned home and told mother that I did not want to go to school but that I wished to play with the children. The most popular game during that time of year was the turning of a wheel, generally the metal part of a bicycle wheel. Mother did not try to force or persuade me to go to school and let me have my way. However, it was not long before playing and wandering idly in the grass while other children were learning and spending their time together no longer appealed to me. So I told her that I wanted to return to school and she made considerable efforts to have me accepted in school in mid-term, promising that I would do all that I could to make up what I had lost by my absence. Indeed, during the second year, my school record in certain subjects was higher than the level of the rest of the class, and it was decided to advance me two classes further in certain subjects in the middle of the term. It so happened that I landed in my big brother's class. He was not pleased, and was indeed quite antagonistic towards me, unwilling to help me with my studies, and even refusing to let me use his books to prepare my homework. Mother preferred not to upset him and would wait until he was asleep and then extract his books from his school bag, quietly awaken me, and help me to do my lessons. This situation continued until my brother became accustomed to the idea and accepted the fact that his younger brother studied in the same class.

Father's finances improved in Argentina, and he began to send us money and letters more frequently. We left our little apartment and the dampness on the hill opposite the tailor,

and moved to a spacious and newer apartment in the house
of Reb David Jossel Berkovitch, Haim Itchke's father – the
gypsy. Whereas our former dwelling had been situated close to
the spiritual center, the synagogue courtyard, this one was close
to the business center, opposite the marketplace and behind the
house of Reb Moshe Davidovitch, the Lubaver (from the town
of Lubav) which faced the market. Our apartment was in the
inner courtyard and, in addition to the main road, there was a
small pathway leading to it through the courtyard of the
Lubaver, which we children liked to use as a short-cut, jumping
over the wooden planks strewn across the path to bar the way.
It appears that neighborly relations between Reb Moshe and
Reb David Jossel were none too friendly and one winter's day,
when everything was covered in a blanket of snow, and just as
I was making my way across the path, innocently jumping
across the wooden planks, Reb Moshe happened to be going
out of his house when he spied me. He started to pursue me,
shouting and warning me not to use this path again.
Frightened to death, and caught between the pursuing Reb
Moshe and the wooden planks, I managed to escape.

Ten years later, I met Reb Moshe in the woods of Karkodi a
number of times, where we were both hiding from the
Germans. It was there that I really came to know and respect
him, but the scene of the pursuit has still not left me until this
very day.

Life in the little town was peaceful. The presence of yeshiva
students as boarders in every home added to the livelihood of
the householders and also created a holy and spiritual atmosphere, an aura of Torah and learning. At every corner, one
would come upon a pair of students discoursing and arguing
over a question in the Talmud. Sitting on a bench, or lying in
the woods alongside the riverbanks, or standing in a corner or
strolling along, for as it is written: 'And thou shalt teach them
diligently unto thy children, and shalt talk of them when thou
sittest in thine house, and when thou walkest by the way, and
when thou liest down, and when thou risest up.'

(Deuteronomy 6:7)

In Reb David Jossel's house in which we lived, some two dozen students of the yeshiva sat down to dinner, and from time to time after the meal they would remain to hold a symposium. One of the students would speak on a certain question, and this was followed by a lively discussion. As a child of 6 or 7, I would observe and listen to the heated argument for hours on end, as if I understood what was being said. The stage, its performers, and the atmosphere of the discussion remain with me until today.

One summer's day, in the neighborhood of the synagogue courtyard, a group of excited yeshiva students burst into song at the tops of their voices, hands and arms linked, dancing in a number of concentric circles around the scrolls of the Torah which had been inscribed and dedicated to the Hafetz Haim. Together with other children, I mingled with the dancers, and so took part in the festivities celebrating the arrival of the new scrolls of the Torah.

It was also said that the Hafetz Haim wanted to go to the Holy Land, but the students of the yeshiva prevented him from doing so by deflating the tires of his car.

The days were quiet, but varied. Then a short time after Hitler came to power in Germany, the expulsion of the Jews to the Polish border near Zebonshin began.

The Poles refused to take the Jews in, claiming that they were no longer Polish citizens; while the Germans expelled them for being Jews, so depriving them of their German citizenship. The poor Jews remained on the borders for weeks on end, freezing with cold at the height of the winter, starving with hunger, without anyone extending a helping hand. As a child, I can remember the agitation that gripped the town. The Jews of Radun gathered at the synagogue, lit black candles, and swore on their oath and vowed and decreed a ban on all Jew-haters. The shofar was blown and a fast was called for, that the terrible decree might be withdrawn. I witnessed this singular prayer, accompanied as it was by the ceremony of lighting the candles while everything surrounding the rite was shrouded in black, I have never since seen the likes of such a ritual.

On a cloudy and dark day, the Hafetz Haim was called to the yeshiva of the higher spheres. The news spread through the townlet like wildfire, and thousands of people from all over Poland and the far corners of the world filled the streets of Radun in order to accompany the righteous man of his generation to the next world. The skies seemed to be weeping for him, as the rains did not cease for a moment, and a continuous procession of masses of people escorted him on his final journey to the cemetery. Sadness and gloom descended on the entire town. A sense of having been abandoned, together with tremendous fears for the future, possessed everyone. It was said that the Hafetz Haim was taken to heaven so that he should not witness the terrible events that would soon take place.

Father's last letters from the Argentine were all about uniting the family once again, and Mother had to decide whether she wished to come to Argentina, in which case he would send the necessary papers and tickets for the journey. If she did not want to leave, he would close down his business and return home to Poland. In another letter he explained that she should know that in the Argentine she would not be able to conduct the same sort of Jewish life that she did in Radun, and that it would not always be possible to keep the Sabbath and *kashrut* to which she was accustomed. Mother's suspicions that she would not be able to lead a Jewish life decided the issue, and without any hesitation, she told him to return home to Radun. At the same time, my little brother Yekutiel (Kushka) came down with a severe illness. He had a high fever, followed by convulsions, and there were fears for his life. In order to bring down the fever, he was wrapped in wet sheets from head to toe. It is difficult to describe mother's suffering. She sat at his side from morning to night, never closing her eyes. Her prayers and supplications tore at one's heart and resounded to the heavens. Kushka was a beautiful child, with rosy cheeks, blond hair, and clever bright blue eyes. From a very early age, it was clear that he was a talented child. When his illness became known to Father, he said to friends and acquaintances that he would never return to Radun were it not for the child's health. Nevertheless, Yekutiel's recovery hastened his return. He began to wind up his business in order to return to his family quickly and to see the little son whom he only knew from photographs.

In the springtime of 1934, we were surprised by a visit from Father's older brothers, who came from Dzevinishok: Yekutiel the elder, and Nachum Joseph the younger by some years. They were both hearty men, tall and broad-shouldered, with short thick necks, strong chins and jutting jaws. The fine fur coats they were wearing added to their dignity and sense of importance, while their personalities displayed self-confidence and responsibility. This was the first time that I laid eyes on Father's brothers, and I tried to imagine him as I gazed on them. There was a feeling of estrangement between us, accompanying the criticism that had crept into my heart. Why had they waited such a long time before coming to see us, since Father had left the house and gone overseas? Why had they shown no interest in what had happened to us until today? Hadn't they known of our difficulties? I do not know whether they had helped Mother in any way, but the children were given sweets and we were all photographed together. Uncle Nachum Jossel's charming personality helped to dispel the coolness between us. His interest in our studies, and the simple questions on the Bible which he put to us, enabled us to speak freely with one another, and my pride knew no bounds in having uncles of such obvious importance visiting us. The timing of their visit evidently had some connection with the arrival of their cousin Alter Gross (Lipkunsky) from London, who had come to see his brother Berl in Radun.

The spring of 1935 brought with it the anticipation of Father's return from the Argentine, and with it mixed feelings of joy and fear. The happiness was combined with pride – finally I too would have a father like all the other children, but at the same time I was anxious about the unknown factor I was about to encounter.

The events of the day of Father's return have slipped my memory altogether; for some reason or other, I cannot even remember the day he returned. His appearance, however, was another story. His head was wrapped in bandages which covered most of his face, arousing both pity and a certain degree of disappointment. Aboard the ship sailing from South America to Europe, he was attacked by terrible pain in his teeth and he was obliged to have a tooth extracted. This resulted in the development of a severe infection which made it necessary for him to have an operation on his gums. The father of my imagination was doubled up by dreadful pains and roamed about the house like a caged animal, finding little relief from his pain. The treatment in those days was the application of heated lentils, which kept their warmth for some time. Bags full of lentils were heated and pressed against the painful gums. Ever since that time, whenever I have a toothache or when someone speaks of toothache, my mind's eye recalls the image of Father doubling up with pain.

Various legal processes accompanied our return to Dowgalishok, but when these were finally accomplished, after a few months, my parents and little brother went off to Dowgalishok. My brother Pinchas and I remained in Radun in order to continue our studies at school and at the little yeshiva. We would return home to our parents in Dowgalishok for the Sabbath and for holy days, and during the school holidays. A room, which included our board and lodging, was rented for us with a family. Every Sunday we would return to Radun laden with enough food for a week. The landlady would look after us in a warm and friendly way, for in addition to the payment she received, she viewed this as a greater virtue than the monetary compensation, for were we not amongst the pupils of the little yeshiva, devoting most of our time to studying the Talmudic tradition at the rabbinical seminary?

Our separation from our parents at the comparatively early

ages of 9 and 12, did not create any special problems. It was understood that we had to continue with our studies at the school and the small yeshiva and that therefore we had to remain in Radun without our parents.

There was one thing I could on no account get used to, however, and that was the custom of 'eating days' (*essen tage*, in Yiddish), which meant being a guest of one of the town's householders at dinner on one day in the week. As many Jewish youngsters were sent to study at yeshivas in other towns, both near and far, there were Jewish families who adopted them temporarily. Every family which could afford to, would invite the yeshiva students to dine with them once a week, or for some particular meal. Their host viewed these invitations as special honour conveyed on him, and saw himself as participating in the virtue of studying the Torah. This was particularly the case when the host was someone who was not himself capable of studying. Every student of the small yeshiva was a party to this custom, whether he was the son of a wealthy family or a poor one, and shared the honour of studying the Torah with his host by sitting down at his table

I was childishly shy and would often walk around the house of my host a number of times without daring to open the door and enter. Frequently I preferred to go hungry for the whole day and forego the pleasure of being a guest. On those occasions, I would have to invent all sorts of excuses to explain my absence and avoid offending the householder. In addition, I had difficulty in getting used to the various dishes that were served, which were not at all like the meals my mother made. At times I would chew the food over and over again without being able to swallow it, and when I finally did, I had difficulty in keeping it down. I remember one instance when I just could not eat what was served, but could not muster up the courage to say that I didn't like the food. Luckily, the hostess left the table for a moment and I utilized this golden opportunity to dump the damp mess into my pocket and pour the liquid out of the window (which fortunately was open at the time). And thus I saved myself from choking.

The daily routine was full and tiring. School in the morning, and immediately after studies, at noon, with my satchel still on my back, I went straight to the rabbinical seminary, to listen to a class in Talmud taught by Rabbi Mendel of Sokolka, and then to higher grade of Talmudic studies held by Rabbi Mordecai Beer of Berdichev, head of the small yeshiva. Rabbi Mordecai Beer was small and wiry, and serious. Seeing him smile was a rarity for he was the embodiment of the spirit, with his sparse body, as if it had been created to contain only his soul and nothing more. On the other hand, Rabbi Mendel, the inspector, was tall and hearty, with a red-cheeked friendly face and a permanent smile hovering on his lips. His warm heartedness shone from his features and he was always ready to help. Indeed, he needed a great deal of patience to withstand our pranks and lack of restraint on our way from school to the yeshiva. Rabbi Mendel came to Radun from Sokolka, a small town in the neighborhood of Bialystok. He brought with him his two sons who were my age and who also studied at the small yeshiva. During the holidays and the long summer vacation, he would visit his wife and the remainder of the family.

This period of my life, from the age of 9 to 13, was the happiest time of my childhood. Studies at the small yeshiva filled my existence with a very special meaning and interest. I felt that I was growing and maturing from day to day and amassing knowledge from lesson to lesson. My devotion to Talmudic studies was marked; the casuistry and the philosophy, the analogy and the inference, the raising of a supposition and its refutation, had their particular eloquence which gave me incomparable intellectual pleasure. I competed with myself and enjoyed both the studies and the achievements. The feeling of fulfilling oneself that comes with the accumulation of knowledge was accompanied by a fundamental innocent and fervent belief in an omniscient God, the God of Israel and his doctrine.

At the age of 5, I began my Bible studies with Genesis, with the creation of the world, the heavens and the earth. At that age, I was still daring enough to ask myself: 'and who created God?', without asking others for an answer out of fear or shame. Later on, there was no need to ask, for it was self-evident that He was present and always would be, and that there was no other. The mere daring to suggest the question, even in one's inner thoughts, bordered on heresy. The faith had crept into every part of my body, all my thoughts and actions were guided by my belief in the personal and Divine Providence. The Ten Commandments had a realistic significance and were to be acted upon accordingly. 'Honour thy father and thy mother: that thy days may be long upon the land which the Lord thy God giveth thee' was a commandment to be observed as straightforwardly as it was written: that is, if one honoured one's parents, one would live long – and the contrary was also true. I would observe the most trivial precepts as I would the most serious, the precepts that were to be enacted and those that were forbidden. From my studies in the Sayings of the Fathers and the Talmud, I absorbed something of the wisdom of Israel and these served as signposts of behavior and a way of life. From the homiletic passages in rabbinical literature and the interpretations, I drew my hope and certainty of the utter salvation of Israel which would take place with the coming of the Messiah, however far in the future that might be. I was eager to read and hear about the war of Gog and Magog, the resurrection of the dead and the rolling of the bodies, and also about the great feast of the wild boar and the whale. I prayed with complete sincerity and devotion. With every good deed, I created a good angel and with every naughtiness, I created a bad angel, and everything would be taken into consideration by the Almighty on his scales of justice.

One day, I visited the great yeshiva during a sermon, and listened eagerly to the homily given by the head of the yeshiva at the time, Rabbi Mendel Zachs, who was the son-in-law of the Hafetz Haim. Most of the sermon dealt with various matters in the Talmud and much of it I did not understand. But what is a statement about belief? It is etched in my memory unto today. He stressed that the mere fact that the question had been raised, though the answer was convincing, was in itself a form of taint on complete belief. Utter faith does not require explanations and rational support. Our belief must be as much an inherent a part of our existence as are the limbs of our body. With devotion and perseverence, I would spend the late evening hours in the seminary, pouring over Talmudic subjects by candlelight.

Among the hundreds of boys who studied at the Radun yeshiva, the yeshiva of the Hafetz Haim, some were abstemious (Parush, or Pharisee), boys of the yeshiva who had foresworn the pleasures of this world in order to discover the inner meaning of the Law; strict observers of the Mosaic Law (and the rabbinical injunctions). Most of the day they were occupied with learning Talmud and studying books on morality that purified the soul. They only ate to keep alive, and fasted and prayed much of the time. They would withdraw into themselves and keep away from others and from any kind of idle conversation. Most of the boys at the yeshiva, however, were easy to get on with, well-dressed and smooth-shaven, though the latter state was not achieved with a razor. Here and there, some showed familiarity with other yeshivas, and one would sometimes come across them accompanied by a modest girl on walks among the cornfields at sundown. There were also others who could be found reading a liberal newspaper or secular book in secret.

Israel and the land of Israel were close to my heart. From tales of the Bible and the prophets, from legends and prayers, I identified with the heroes of the Bible. I was happy in their victories, and suffered with them in their defeats. In my imagination I was familiar with different parts of the country, and it was here that I fought many battles, beginning with the victory of Joshua bin Nun, through Judges and Kings. I grieved over the fact that the children of Israel deviated from the righteous path and were therefore punished and defeated by their enemies, and finally exiled from our land. In all innocence and full of purpose, I would pray, 'O that our eyes may behold thy return to Zion with mercy', or, 'O sound the great cornet as a signal for our freedom', and other prayers connected with Israel and the return of its people to that land. With special devotion I would utter the prayer, 'O let the slanderers have no hope.' It was inconceivable at the time that this prayer should be directed against informers among the Jewish people, for how was it possible that a Jew could be a slanderer and betray his own brethren to the gentiles to boot?

As a child, I once belonged to a group organized by the Betar* movement, and then again to a group called the Flowers of Agudath Israel,* or at times, to other groups. I could not tell the difference between one group or another, for their common feature was their interest in the Jewish people and the land of Israel. Bialik's poem 'To a Bird' which we learned to recite and to sing, shortened the distance between the land of Israel and myself, for in every bird chirping in the springtime I saw a greeting from Palestine and the distance between us merely the flight of a bird. Lag Ba'omer* and its activities took me back to Bar Kochba, the Maccabees and the Hasmoneans. I skipped over 2,000 years of exile as if they were tucked away into walks through the fields and the trees that were planted on that day. The stories and legends generated this emotional connection, and the games with bows and arrows together with the sports we indulged in provided an imaginative association between me and the soldiers of Bar Kochba. The folksongs sung by Mother, of blessed memory, in Yiddish mixed with Hebrew, were imbued with an air of sadness and longing for Jerusalem, the land of Israel, land of our fathers, and a great love for the Jewish people. At one time, I imagined Jerusalem as an abandoned rose in the middle of the desert, and at another, the Jewish people as a wandering dove or a lonely sheep amongst 70 wolves. I loved these sweet-sounding songs, and was prepared to hear them over and over again. They found their way deep into my heart and aroused a yearning and compassion for Zion and its people. These same melodies still echo in my memory today, though I am unable to sing them. This was the Zionism that I inhaled at home, at school, and at the small yeshiva.

Father's return from the Argentine to our home in Dowgalishok meant that we were a united family once more. For Mother it was a period of rejuvenation – her sadness disappeared, the color returned to her cheeks and spread over the dark tones of her skin. Her nostalgic songs made way for more joyful ones, and every corner of the house reflected light and happiness. Our financial situation improved from day to day. The farm began to develop and prosper, and the smithy that had been silent during all the years of Father's absence was once again active. The local farmers would visit the smithy daily, and its income grew rapidly. Mother, who had been accustomed to supporting the family, continued to ply her needle for the pleasure of it, though it also brought her some revenue. The house was filled with the very best of things and we lacked for nothing.

Every Thursday, preparations for the Sabbath would begin and would continue until the late afternoon on Friday. Ordinary *chollahs*,* plaited *chollahs*, cakes and cookies, were baked. The smell of *gefilte* fish* would fill the house and the courtyard, and meat and the stuffed *derma* were tucked away into the *cholent*.* *Kugel** and *strudel*, *zimmes** and *babka** – the house would be redolent with heady odours and the activity within would be varied and manifold, while we three children would be helping and playing alongside Mother, fascinated by all that was going on.

In the summertime, apart from the usual activity, preparations were advancing for the winter. This began with chopping wood for heating during the winter, making hay, collecting it in sheaves and drying it in the fields, and bringing it to the barn to be used as fodder for the cows and horses during the winter months. We had to dig up the potatoes and place them in special ditches dug in the earth for this purpose, in order to prevent them from being harmed by the frost. The dark cellar, reaching a few meters below the floor, was used to store potatoes, fruit and vegetables for the family's daily use during the winter. The huge cupboard which stood in the corridor of the house, was filled to the brim with bottles and jars of fruit and sugar: blackcurrants and redcurrants, berries and cherries, and all kinds of other fruits. The juice that accumulated from the fruit combined with the sugar became a sort of cordial with a heavenly taste. Frequently I would yield to temptation and on passing this cupboard, seemingly without noticing it, would sample this jar or that bottle, lick my lips carefully and quickly close the door of the cupboard. (This wayward habit and my weakness for sweets is still one of my traits.) Apart from preserves and other sweet things, barrels filled with pickled cabbage or cucumbers were prepared with the approaching summer. Every season had its particular activity. After Hanukkah, preparations went into motion for Passover. It was the time for killing geese and their feathers went into the making of pillows and eiderdowns while the goose fat fried with onions was preserved and put away for future use. On Passover, this fat was spread on *matza* and for making the *matza* balls for the Seder feast and throughout the holiday. The wine-making started a few weeks later. It was made from raisins and sugar, and the process lasted for a number of weeks, almost until Passover and the holiday atmosphere that went with it.

The quiet and simple life of Radun was disturbed at times by rumors of pogroms that reached us from different parts of Poland. Nazi propaganda against Jews and Judaism was growing, and this propaganda found fertile ground in the Poland of that time, with all its religious fanaticism. A single sermon against the Jews who crucified Christ, given by the priest in church on a Sunday morning, followed by the drinking of a bottle of vodka, sufficed to provoke an attack on the Jews, breaking their windows and overturning the Jewish stands in the marketplace. Debates among members of the Polish government against the ritual slaughtering of meat out of compassion for the animals also aroused anti-Semitism. Harangues against business dealings with the Jews in the name of Polish patriotism became increasingly common. The popular slogan was: 'Jews to Palestine', or 'Beat the Jews and save Poland'. In Radun, too, the peaceful existence was marked by early signs of anti-Semitism. There were increasing incidents of boys from the yeshiva being attacked on their way home late at night. Contrary to any rational thinking, at the same time that Poland's borders were being threatened by Germany, an increasing number of Polish people were being influenced by the Nazis. And these same Poles who defended Poland against the German invasion adopted the Nazi creed that a Poland freed of Jews would bring salvation to Poland, to its economy and security. Hatred towards the Jews grew and spread with the defeat of Poland by the Germans, and continued with even greater intensity throughout the occupation.

4 Under the Soviet Communist Regime

Towards the end of the summer of 1939 Germany's demands for territorial concessions from Poland continued apace, backed by the threat of war. In retaliation, Poland started to concentrate its army on its western border, and long lines of soldiers on foot and in cars passed through Radun on their way westward. The mounting tension of approaching war infected everyone, and every schoolboy would analyze the possibility of war breaking out and its probable outcome. Polish pride had reached its peak, relying on the army, propaganda and volunteers, and governmental organization of finances to support the war effort. All this was accompanied by battle slogans calling for a rapid victory. A large crowd gathered round the few radios existing in Radun in order to hear Hitler's threatening (and high-pitched) speeches against Poland, intermingled with incitement and threats against the Jews and world Jewry.

As a child, I had heard many stories about the First World War: about armies that had passed through Radun; about battles between artillery and cavalrymen, the firing of cannons and acts of robbery and plunder; the brutality of soldiers; and the hunger and distress that was endured. Despite all the horrors of war indicated by the stories, I did not understand the meaning of war, and in my childish curiosity I wanted to see it first-hand: to see the armies in conflict and to be involved in adventures that did not occur in the normal course of affairs. And, naturally, to see Poland victorious and Germany defeated.

War broke out with the Germans invading Poland on 1 September 1939. In the 'blitzkrieg', they had already taken over large parts of Poland before the Polish army managed to reach its destination on the border. Warsaw fell on 19 September. Thus Poland was defeated even before its army had succeeded in fighting a single defensive battle. The Red Army also participated in crushing Poland. Even before the Germans marched into Warsaw, the Red Army crossed Poland's eastern frontier on 17 September in accordance with the secret agreement between the Germans and the Soviets to divide Poland between them. Their argument explaining this move was that as Poland had ceased to exist, the Soviet Union was merely taking back those areas that had previously belonged to Russia.

The Red Army entered Poland almost without any fighting at all, for the Polish army was concentrated at the German border. With the breakdown of the Polish government, and before the Russians entered the town, Radun was left for a few days without any authority in control. Fearing plunder and robbery by the negative elements of the town, a militia was chosen from amongst the citizens, most of whom were Jews, in order to maintain civic order until the arrival of the Red Army. Some days passed, and an advance unit of the Red Army entered Radun from the east via Lida, taking control of the city. In the wake of the advance unit, other units of the Red Army arrived, in huge numbers in Radun a few days later.

Radun became the barracks of a garrison in the center of town, in the marketplace, in the courtyard of the synagogue. Everywhere one turned, soldiers were stationed. The Red Army arrived in Radun as the authority in charge, they came in cars and in armored vehicles and tanks, accompanied by large guns of various kinds. This was the first time I had seen so much military equipment of such a great variety. Unlike the Polish army and its soldiers, who we did not dare approach in peacetime, the soldiers of the Red Army were friendly and the children and adults even mixed with them. The language problem was almost non-existent, for the adults had still retained their knowledge of Russian, and those who spoke

Polish did not find it difficult to understand the soldiers as both these languages are Slavic. Every unit had its mobile kitchen and stores, and the storekeeper responsible for them was the sole 'king'. Each soldier would be allotted his share and they would sit around in a circle eating their meal, while we children would be standing alongside, peering at them.

At this point, before we were aware of the meaning of war, peace reigned in the whole area. There was no shortage of food, for every family had some reserves stored away and business continued with the farmers of the region on a barter system. The Russian soldiers also took part in the bartering and were ready to purchase anything, particularly watches, women's clothing, textiles, dresses, underwear and night-gowns. Quite often one could see a Russian woman dancing at a party in a colorful nightgown instead of a dress, or pyjamas instead of a suit. Their oft-repeated slogan was; 'We have everything – matches, sugar, salt, but we have no God!'

Slowly and persistently, the Russians began to establish their authority, and communists who had been prisoners of the Polish regime, were called on to occupy ruling civilian posts, among them two Jews who had been imprisoned for a while. The authorities quickly adopted their particular attitude to religion, to traders, and to the affluent in general. The yeshiva building and the summer synagogue, as well as the Jewish school, were taken over and became storehouses for grain and corn, and other needs of the Red Army and its administration. Heads of the yeshiva, seeing what the future had in store for them and the yeshiva, quickly abandoned the place and moved to the Lithuanian border, to Eishishok and Vilnius, together with most of the students.

The frontier ran between Eishishok and Radun, some ten kilometers from Radun and about four kilometers from Eishishok. The district of Vilnius, which had served as a source of historical conflict between Poland and Lithuania, was designated as belonging to Lithuania and hence the border fell between Radun and Eishishok, with the latter in

Lithuanian territory, while Radun was annexed to White Russia. Radun was suddenly emptied of all its yeshiva students and its cultural and spiritual ambience. Instead of the young yeshiva students, the streets were full of Russian soldiers. And instead of Talmudic intonation, Russian chatter was to be heard. We did not feel the horrors of war, but we did feel the darkening of our Jewish spiritual world, as if all the lights had been put out and life lacked interest and excitement. The synagogue courtyard, which had been the spiritual center and bursting with Jewish life, changed its format and lost its charm. Fewer people came to pray at the old synagogue (Beth ha-midrash), and most of the buildings belonging to the community and used for religious purposes had been taken over by the Red Army. The prayer shawl and the white surplice did not fit in with the red flag, and so relinquished their status.

My brother Pinchas, who was then 15 and about to start his studies at the great yeshiva, crossed the border into Eishishok together with the yeshiva, and I joined him to live in the former home of my grandmother Esther Asna, of blessed memory, with my Aunt Reinke and Uncle Velvel, as we were very attached to them. After a number of weeks had passed, I was overtaken by a desperate longing for my parents, and there was no alternative but to return me home to my parents before the frontier was finally closed. And so I returned to my parents and my little brother Kushka in Dowgalishok. Kushka had started to study at the Russian school in a nearby village and was the only Jewish child amongst the gentile children. I remained at home with my parents for some months, without schooling and without friends, for there were no other Jewish children of my age group in the village. My parents were not pleased with this situation and they began to discuss what should be done about it. My father was of the opinion that I should attend the Russian school, if I was not to remain an illiterate who could neither read nor write. One had to accept reality as it was, and that this was the fate of all Jewish children. Mother, on the other hand, could not accept the idea that her sons, whom she secretly anticipated would perhaps be rabbis, should become gentiles and not learn the biblical and Talmudic studies that was the tradition of her family. It was more than enough that she had to accept the fact that her little son studied with the gentile children, but as he was a child of 9, one could have a Jewish tutor to teach him at home privately. Where I was concerned, however, having already attended the small yeshiva and gained certain credit in the process, this was no solution. At home, the discussions and arguments over my future were heated. However, my parents were unwilling to make any decision without hearing my opinion on the subject.

As I had already reached bar mitzvah age, having received a set of phylacteries (*tefillin*)* from mother, and my parents having said the prayer relieving them of their responsibility for me, I suddenly felt answerable for my future and my actions, for I was already accountable for my behavior. This was the first occasion on which I had to decide on and commit myself to a way of life. If I wanted to continue studying at the yeshiva, I would have to cut myself off from my parents' home indefinitely and cross the border into Eishishok once again. The alternative was to remain in my comfortable home and go to the Russian school together with all the gentile children, and (God forbid!) become one of them. It was difficult to make a decision, and a number of months passed before it was taken. In the meantime, the winter was at its height, and there were some older people who said that they had not experienced such a severe winter in decades. The freezing weather was terrible, reaching minus 30 degrees centigrade.

During this winter, Radun served as a transit point for Jewish refugees who had succeeded in escaping from German-occupied Polish areas in order to reach Lithuania, which was then considered an independent state. From there, they would try to reach the Western world. Both the Russians and the Lithuanians strengthened their border patrols, and there were rumors of brutality against Jews who were caught.

Some were shot and killed crossing the border; while others froze to death in the attempt, buried by the snowstorms and disappearing without a soul knowing their whereabouts, what had happened to them, or who they were. The days passed, and rumors succeeded rumors, while I sat idle, knowing that my brother Pinchas and the friends I had studied with were only 20 kilometers away, and my heart went out to them. With daylight, I was longing with all my heart to be with them, once again to live in the aura of the seminary and the yeshiva. I was filled with regret that I did not have the strength to have remained with them and that I had returned to Dowgalishok. During these moments of self-reproach, I would mentally summon up the courage to return to them. But with nightfall, with the angry winds whistling round the windows as if they would raise the roof and send it spinning in mid-air – at those moments I was full of fear of the dangers that were to be encountered on the way, and the parting from my parents, and then fear and trembling would invade my whole being. After a considerable struggle with myself, I decided to ask my parents to help me cross the border. Father turned down the idea altogether, viewing it as suicidal. He insisted that I attend the local school. But I had some inner resistance to going to the Russian school with all the gentiles and could not get used to the idea. So I placed my trust in God, and stated decisively that I wished to return to Eishishok.

The preparations for crossing the border were made in utter secrecy lest some harm befall my parents, as this could be interpreted as an indication that they were against the regime and its enemies. Finally a farmer was found whose house was near the border, and who took on himself the task of taking me across the border – for a goodly sum of money, naturally. Mother was absolutely against the idea of entrusting me to a gentile, however good and trustworthy, and she decided to cross the frontier with me, to look into the conditions in Eishishok, and at the same time to see how my brother Pinke was getting on, for he was a weak child and there was some fear for his health.

So on a Wednesday, market day in Radun, in the early evening when all the farmers leave the marketplace after selling their produce, we set forth dressed as farmers returning homeward. We sat in a horse-drawn sleigh, which began to plod along in the waterlogged snow on a road that did not resemble a road, in a strange and threatening neighborhood, accompanied by a snowstorm all along the way. The prayer for travellers, which I had said before setting out from the house, went: 'Let us arrive in peace at our destination, and save us from any enemy, and ambush, and robbers and malicious animals.' This prayer was repeated all through the journey, lest we should encounter trouble.

We finally arrived at the farmer's house late in the evening. The floor was strewn with straw and we lay down to rest for a while before crossing the frontier. Despite the fact that we were tired and worn out from the exhausting journey and the emotional tension of the long day, we did not sleep a wink. The winds continued to blow wildly, and the snow was piling up in high mounds that covered the roadway. Even a mad dog could not be seen abroad on such a night. Excitement, mingled with fear of what lay in store for us, best described my state of mind. Mother's presence gave me a feeling of security. Perhaps this was the propitious hour to cross the border, when the guards would be freezing at their posts; perhaps heaven had provided this weather especially for us. The farmer, however, would on no condition agree to leave the house, for he claimed that on such a night to attempt the distance of ten kilometers without the benefit of a road was suicidal. We were forced to wait for daylight. All kinds of doubts began to trouble us about the trustworthiness of the farmer who was to take us across the border. Did he have evil intentions and would he fulfil his promises? At any rate, we did not dare to close our eyes that long and weary night.

At last the dawn came, and to our surprise and delight, the wind had subsided. The dry snow beneath our footsteps was as soft as cotton-wool and quiet to tread on. The farmer took us out of the house and pointed in the direction of the frontier. Being reluctant to endanger himself, he told us to continue on our own. We had little choice, now, for we could not return home.

So we set out on our way with fear and trembling in our hearts, and put our trust in God. All that could be seen was a white expanse, and there was not a living soul on the horizon. I repeated the traveller's prayer three times and held Mother's hand, its warm touch dispelling my anxiety. Once again, I felt secure. Without looking to the right or to the left, or glancing backwards, we continued to make our way through the snow without knowing where we were going. We did not know whether the frontier was ahead of us or behind us.

After about half an hour – a distance of approximately one kilometer – we saw a tall soldier standing to the right of us, and further on, a series of tall wooden posts painted in various colors. We made a detour in order to avoid the soldier, and without glancing his way, continued in the direction indicated by the farmer. Fearfully, we marched forward through the white and infinite expanse. With set lips and an open and subdued heart, I laid my prayer before the Almighty: 'Please God, help me arrive at my destination in peace, do not fail me, lest my dear mother suffer as a result, for it was only to promote your greatness and study your teachings that I am doing this.' At the end of this pure and sincere prayer, that of an innocent child who had only just turned 13 and who with awe had taken on the burden of a bar mitzvah, I placed my trust in God and felt relieved. After a few hours of walking, we arrived in Eishishok at the warm and light-filled house of my mother's brother and sister.

This was the first international border I crossed surreptitiously, but it was not to be the last. It was merely the beginning of innumerable border crossings and something of a lesson in tramping and treading across white snowy expanses – a sort of introduction to crossing other frontiers in days and nights to follow. How different all these later crossings were – for it was not for the love of studies that they were made but for the sake of survival.

After resting for a few days, we went to the Lithuanian police station, in order to register and arrange our stay in Eishishok legally. The tall Lithuanians were reluctant to believe that I was 13, as Mother declared, for they had thought that I was about 10. After investigations and examinations, and the intervention of others, together with ample bribes, everything was officially settled. I remained in Eishishok and Mother returned quite legally to Dowgalishok, for she had told the police that due to illness, she was obliged to remain at the home of her brother and sister and now that she was well again, she wanted to return to her home.

I returned to my former life within the seminary walls, in an aura of study and Judaism, as well as yearning for my loved ones across the border and my home. Less than a year went by and the Russians decided that they had had enough of an independent Lithuania, and once again we were caught up within the communist regime and the frontier which had kept us from going to jail. We returned to our home in Dowgalishok quietly, like thieves in the night, and not a little frightened of informers. The slightest whisper against us could have sent the entire family into exile in the depths of Russia, condemned there to hard labor. It was only due to the excellent relations that father had with both Jews and gentiles that we succeeded in becoming citizens and were able to go out openly into the streets without being pointed out as people who had run away from the enlightened and advanced regime. Father's occupation stood him in good stead, for he earned his livelihood from farming, from the smithy and frame-making, that is, he lived by his own toil and not by selling and trading.

Who could have foreseen that the fortunate fact that we were not exiled and sent into the depths of Russia would actually be our misfortune? Who could have known at that time that

Germany would sweep into Russia at such a pace, or that the cultured land we assumed Germany to be would turn overnight into a mad creature and that we Jews would be the main victims of its madness?

Sitting at home in the peaceful and quiet village was dull, especially after the adventure of stealing across the border and the separation from Mother and Father. The isolation we imposed on ourselves out of fear, however, had its good points. Once again, we enjoyed those hugs and caresses we had missed so intensely. We absorbed deeply the warmth of the house; we had time to take in the ways of a village home, and frequent opportunities to listen to and enjoy the sweet songs that mother sang while working at her sewing machine – the same songs that told of holy Jerusalem, of Palestine, of the Temple that had been destroyed, one in Hebrew and two in Yiddish.

The way of life we had become accustomed to was completely destroyed without there being anything to take its place. We could not be enrolled at the Russian school, partly because it was the middle of the school term and also due to our age. We were afraid of being seen in public and left the house quietly in order to help father at his work in the smithy. We would also work in the fields, harvesting and threshing the wheat in the barn. Rather than make plans for the future, we began to get used to the situation and accept reality. Our little brother Yekutiel, who was an excellent student at the Russian school, helped us to learn to read and write Russian.

From time to time, the farmers of the area would be assembled in Dowgalishok, to be initiated into the workings of the new regime and the building of a new society by the professional propagandists, the agitprop.

Youths of 16 or 17 who were not studying were sent to technical schools in Russia, and we were frequently afraid of being caught and sent somewhere far away in the Soviet Union. For the time being, however, everything was quiet and the main news to be had was of the immediate surroundings and the region itself, and tended only to be concerned with financial and agricultural matters. This news appeared in the official newspaper and was also broadcast from the radio via a loudspeaker situated in the center of the village.

This was the quiet period, the lull before the terrible storm that was to follow.

5 *Under German Occupation*

One fine day it was announced on the radio that Germany had declared war on Soviet Russia. And on the morrow, together with the Soviet statement that they were at war with Germany, the advance units of the German army reached Radun. Although it was a distance of hundreds of kilometers from the new Russo-German border, the German vanguard managed to penetrate deep into the Russian army's rear before the Russians had an opportunity to reorganize the army for a proper withdrawal. It all happened so suddenly, and the result was chaos. The Soviet army was at a loss to understand what had occurred, nor were they aware of such a possibility. After the events, they did not know how to react or what they were to do.

The German advance units reached Radun and Dowgalishok from two sides, from the east towards Lida and from the west towards Grodno and Bialistok. Entire armies were cut off, without receiving instructions to fight or withdraw in order to reorganize, nor did they attempt to halt the enemy. There was a mad rush eastward and all sorts of good and new weapons, including cannons of all sorts, were abandoned at the wayside and in the forests around Dowgalishok. Farmers collected these arms for many months and put them away for the future, when they would be called to serve in the army of a free Poland. It was a terrible sight to see so large and strong an army, equipped with the most modern weaponry, disintegrating in the course of a few hours.

They vanished and escaped just as they had arrived in 1939. Overnight, their multitudes disappeared from the face of the earth. On foot and on anything that ran on wheels, they made off eastward. And when their fuel ran out, they abandoned their cars along the wayside and continued on their way by foot. One cannot forget the scene of a group of Russian soldiers, who had remained in the rear a few days after war broke out and the front passed them by. They reached our village of Dowgalishok hungry and thirsty, barefoot and worn-out, asking for clothes and food, and advice on what roads they should take in order to escape to the east (for the Germans had already reached Radun but had still not arrived in Dowgalishok). The adults were afraid to approach them and speak with them, lest it was later revealed that they had given food to Russian soldiers. However, we children brought them loaves of bread, a bit of soup, milk and water, so that they could quench their thirst and stay their hunger. Afterwards, we advised them to leave for the forests, for the Germans could appear at any moment, and then, heaven help all of us.

Accompanied by our pity and sorrow, they left us and we saw no more of them. Just a few days back, they had sat in a circle around the huge tanks singing happily, while passing sweets to the children and whoever was standing by. And now here they were, sitting along the roadside, unshaven, worn-out and helpless, with parched lips and bruised feet from endless plodding, hungry for a crust of bread and a sip of water. Were these the same valiant soldiers, radiating confidence and the belief that they could conquer the entire world? 'Did you meet the Germans and did you fight them?' we asked with childish naïvity 'We never managed, nor did we receive orders to fight,' they answered sadly.

We Jews were shocked to witness the Red Army in this state. Even those who had contemplated escaping with the Red Army to the east had to abandon the idea, for nothing was left of what was called the Red Army. The army bases in the rear suddenly found themselves surrounded by the German army and did not succeed in withdrawing to the east. Most of them changed their uniforms for civilian clothes and stayed behind to work as farmhands for the farmers in exchange for their keep. The Germans were aware of this but preferred to ignore the matter and did them no harm. It was only a few months later that the German high command issued an order that these Russians had to report to them and be registered. Most of them reported to the army and they were shortly afterwards taken to labor camps in Germany. Only a small number managed to hide on the farms or in the woods. These same soldiers were eventually to play an important role in the partisan movement in our area, which was first formed by the Jews who succeeded in escaping from the ghetto in Radun when it was being destroyed.

The Jews of Dowgalishok, who lived in a rural region surrounded by farms owned by Christians, saw no difference between their own village and the neighboring ones. Each continued to work the land on his own plot, each continued to gather potatoes from the earth and bury them in ditches before the winter frost set in. From time to time, some German officers from fighting units would appear at our farm, eager to have eggs and milk, and we 'politely' provided them with these provisions while they reimbursed us as they pleased. At times, they would interest themselves in our origins. When they learned that we were Jews they would nod their heads and look at us as if we were the condemned and in need of pity. The situation of the Jews of Radun, a distance of some seven kilometers from Dowgalishok, was very different indeed. As soon as the first German soldier appeared on the scene, the Jews were ordered to wear yellow Stars of David on the back and front of their clothing, and every Jewish house was obliged to display a sign stating that Jews lived there.

On their first day in Radun, the Germans took a group of Jews to work on repairing the bridge on the eastern side of the town, on the road leading to the district center of Lida. When the work was finished, a German soldier approached the group of workers, saying: 'You have done a good job. Now you have to be paid,' and lifting up his stick, paid them all by beating them on their backs. This was the opening scene of the terrible tragedy of Radun: a modest forecast of what was to follow. The injuries and oppression increased, but we consoled ourselves with the fact that one could still live with them, for we did not want to believe that it could get worse.

Life took on a different pattern. Every morning, the Jews of Radun went out to perform various kinds of manual labor, lined up like soldiers, with the yellow Stars of David on their breasts and backs, and escorted by one of the local Polish soldiers. Things were not too bad as yet. Every day after work, they would return to their warm families and homes, as if nothing untoward was occurring. A few weeks went by, and the news from Radun was none too good, pointing as it did to an even more dismal future.

A number of Germans broke into the synagogue during prayers and began to fire bullets in every direction. By chance, there were not many people in the synagogue at that hour and most of them managed to get away through the windows into the fields. However, two elderly men who did not have enough strength to escape were caught, and were cruelly beaten and then shot. The first victim was Bezalel the tailor, who lived on Kleibenia Street, a Jew some 70 years old. He was dragged around by his beard, and finally killed. The second victim was 'Forelocks', as he was known in the village. He was an orthodox Jew who observed all the precepts, no matter how difficult. Devout in his ways, he was the possessor of lovely, curly forelocks. He had come from a nearby village called Sabaknitza and was a carpenter by profession who made only a poor living. Despite this fact, he was always content with his lot and constantly thanked the Almighty for all that he was given. He was one of the 36 saintly men, as well as one of the ten idle fellows that every Jewish village boasted. After the Germans abused him, he was shot and seriously wounded. All this occurred during prayers and naturally put an end to praying in the synagogue. Poor 'Forelocks' lay wounded for some months before succumbing to his wounds.

In this way, the Jews of Radun learned to accept blow after

blow, pausing to breathe for a spell and reconcile themselves to the situation. They were deluding themselves as well as accepting the 'righteousness' of the judgment against them, not only towards the Almighty but also in terms of the mundane world, by claiming that this was an exceptional act, a plot connived at by a number of brutal soldiers who acted on their own behalf without receiving orders from above, and that if they had not encountered the two elders, the whole sad affair may not have occurred at all.

The Germans were systematic: they humiliated and terrorized the Jews, whilst simultaneously spreading calming rumors, in order to dim their victims' desire to rebel and defend themselves. After every abusive or murderous act there were always promises that this would not happen again and that it was done only by isolated individuals who happened to be passing through the village and over whom the local authorities had no control.

The Germans chose to rule the Jews via the Jews themselves. They issued an order to set up an independent Jewish authority, the *Judenrat*, with a Jewish police force to support it in order to carry out those orders given to the *Judenrat*. The Germans had certain motives in choosing to set up the *Judenrat*. Firstly, in order to pacify the Jews from the psychological point of view, the mere fact of establishing an independent Jewish authority indicated planning for a long period. Secondly, they could rule over the Jews more easily in this fashion and impose economic and other decrees at any time it suited them. Fellow Jews, who knew only too well how the Jewish mind worked, its intentions and weaknesses, would act on their orders swiftly, for they knew just what was happening on the inside. Thirdly, they could be held as hostages to carry out the Germans' orders, if need be. And so the order to set up the *Judenrat* was accepted by the Jews of the village willingly and as a sign of peace, not only because they would then not have to stand face-to-face with the Germans or accept orders from the anti-Semitic Poles. Everyone was certain that the *Judenrat* was set up in order to act as the Germans' intermediary, to satisfy their needs, and to execute their plans in the most effective way.

The members of the *Judenrat* were chosen by the heads of the community, and to a certain extent were more or less forced to take on these positions, as it was no great pleasure to meet with the mad and brutal German command. Having no choice in the matter, they accepted the decision to represent the community in facing up to their enemy.

The six who were chosen were Noah Dolinsky, Avremke Joshes (Jankelevitch), Leibke Eliashevitz, Berl Boyarsky, Hirschel Engeltzin, and Reb Abraham Warshavsky. Lipa Skolsky was appointed head of the police, and other members of the force were Leibke Rogovsky, Yankele Kovalsky, and Leibke Hefetz.

Noah Dolinsky was chosen as the head of the *Judenrat*. He was one of the few men in the village whose outward appearance was that of a modern man and he had connections with the Polish intelligentsia. He was considered to be one of the town's wealthy citizens. Together with his brother Shmuel David Dolinsky, he owned the mill and the only generator for electricity in Radun.

Avremke Joshes was a blacksmith, a sturdy and healthy-looking individual and simple and modest in his ways. He was also a warm and compassionate Jew. His wife Mina, of robust appearance and rosy cheeks, was also goodhearted. The Russian accent in her speech hinted at her origins. Apart from looking after their large home, she was also responsible for the women's ritual bath (*mikveh*), a role she inherited from her mother-in-law Frieda, who was very exacting concerning the purity of the Jewish women of Radun. Her simplicity and warmth and fastidiousness was the source of innumerable droll stories told by the wits of the village about events in the *mikveh*.

Leibke Eliashevitz was in his late thirties and thought of as a solid householder and the happy father of two fine children. A driver and mechanic, he was part-owner of the only bus in Radun, which was no small matter in those days.

The fourth member of the *Judenrat* was Reb Abraham Warshavsky, called Abraham the Orler. (He had come to Radun from the little town of Orlah.) He was a learned and scholarly man who knew his Bible and the precepts, and was devout in observing them. Despite his closeness to the heads of the yeshiva in Radun and his obvious knowledge of the traditional literature, he lived modestly and earned his livelihood with difficulty.

The fifth member, Berl Boyarsky, was one of the town's elite and a member of its intelligentsia: a sensitive and modest Jew, well-liked despite his superior status in the village and the fact that he was the manager and partner of the only bank in town.

Hirshel Engeltzin, who was appointed as an employee of the *Judenrat*, was a student and scholar at the yeshiva, a genteel and modest man who married Liebele, Shmaya Mendel's only daughter. His young wife Liebele, apart from possessing beauty and charm, had a noble character; her faith was strong and constant and her unusual qualities enabled her to withstand the most difficult conditions.

It was an ideal *Judenrat*, for these people were the first of the townspeople to suffer. They did not try to exploit their status or enjoy privileges, or even save their own lives, but accompanied their people to their very end.

The Jewish police force attached to the *Judenrat* wore armbands with the Star of David on their sleeves in addition to the yellow patches which every Jew had to wear. Lipa Skolsky (who came from Oren in Lithuania,) was appointed commander of the police.

Leibke Rogovsky, the elder son of Itzchak Rogovsky, and brother of Niomke, Haike and Mashele, was the owner of the ironmonger's store in Radun, and he was appointed Lipa's assistant.

Yankele Kovalsky, the son of Menashel (owner of the smithy and grandson of Reb Hefetz of the sewing workshop) and Leibke Hefetz of Eishishok (who was married to Leibke Kagan of Radun) were policemen. All the policemen, except for Leibke Rogovsky, were among the first to set up a Jewish underground movement in the Radun region. In the spring of 1942, immediately after the Radun ghetto was wiped out, they fled to the woods, and formed the nucleus of the Jewish–Russian partisan movement.

6 The Annihilation of the Jews of Eishishok

The month of September was coming to a close. We said many penitential prayers. Now, more than ever, there was a special significance to these prayers, to our penitence and entreaties directed inwards to purify our hearts and upwards towards the heavens, entreating Him to open the gates of heaven and listen to our prayers and take pity on us and on the innocent babes.

The Days of Awe arrived, and with them the terrible news from the Jews of Eishishok. Jews were not permitted to travel and doing so could be fatal. But farmers of the neighborhood began to tell terrible stories of what was happening in Eishishok, adding that there were plans to kill all the Jews. No one believed that such a thing could happen; no sensible person could imagine an entire village being wiped out – men, women, and children – about 3,000 people in all.

A few days went by, and the first refugees from Eishishok began to arrive in Radun by whatever means they could. Yeshiva students who had remained in Eishishok ever since they had fled from the Russians in Radun arrived in Dowgalishok. They remembered the Jews of Dowgalishok from before the war, when they would come to spend their summers there and they knew that they would give them refuge and food. And indeed, every household harbored as many refugees as it could, and perhaps more. I remember our mother, Sarah Mina, daughter of Esther Asna, of Eishishok, working day and night, cooking huge pots of potatoes, in order to provide some hot food for the many hungry people who found a safe haven in our house. And we children, together with father, helping her in serving round after round. Despite the absolute ban on taking in strangers, and despite the fear of informers to the Germans, we opened the doors of our home and welcomed whoever was in need of refuge and food, and how glad we were to be able to help the escapees! We were not alone in this – all the Jews of Dowgalishok behaved similarly, and whoever managed to reach Dowgalishok found a haven. There were many stories of atrocities, every refugee had a personal account and a family sorrow, and the overall picture of what had happened to the Jews of Eishishok was almost impossible to take in. It needed some time to digest, and understand, were this even possible.

From the accounts which reached us from the little town of Oran and its neighboring villages, all these places had been emptied of their Jewish inhabitants, most of whom had been publicly executed. Only those who managed to escape were still alive. The Jews of Olkenik and its environs, some thousand souls in all, were supposedly transferred to Eishishok, but in fact were duped and taken to stables near Eishishok. On their arrival, the Germans, in a humiliating and mocking manner, declared that the Jews were not wanted in the town, which served as a sign to the cruel Lithuanian collaborators and anti-Semites that they could do exactly as they liked with the Jews without any interference on the part of the German soldiers.

As yet, the Germans had not harmed the Jews and only demanded a supply of wine, cakes, eggs and butter from time to time. But it was not long before a border patrol reached the village, together with the Lithuanian police, headed by the terrible Ostrovskas. The abuse and maltreatment of the Jews increased from day to day. A group of Jews were forced to go into the river in their clothes, and then to roll along on the roadway in order to clean it by means of their wet clothing. One day, the Germans and their Lithuanian aides assembled 250 bearded Jews, and ordered them to tear out one anothers' beards. Sticks and whips flashed in mid-air and fell on the heads of the poor souls, lest they perform this task ineffectively.

News of the wiping out of the Jews of the neighboring

villages reached us through the Polish farmers with whom we were acquainted. The Jews of Eishishok, however, were unwilling to believe their ears, deluding themselves that although their property would be expropriated, it was not possible that their lives would be taken from them. Thus many Jews of Eishishok handed over part of their property to friendly farmers on the assumption that it would returned on a day of judgment after the war. Some, however, saw the situation as it really was, and dared to warn people of the danger and urged them to treat the rumors seriously and face the fact that perhaps all would be killed. The rabbi Reb Shimon Rozovsky called together the heads of the community, and warned them not to hand over any property to the gentiles, for this was the way to turn them into enemies.

When the rumors of the wiping out of the Jews of Oran grew from day to day, a reliable gentile was sent to find out if they were indeed true. When he returned, he told them that the streets of Oran were still filled with the bodies of dead Jews lying neglected and unburied. The rabbi again assembled the heads of the community saying: 'You see that our end is approaching, the Almighty does not want us to be saved, our fate is decided and we must accept it! But if we are to die, let us die honorably. Let us buy arms with the little money still remaining and defend ourselves to the last soul. Let me die with the Philistines!' Opinions were divided. Yossel Weidenberg, a wealthy and influential member of the community, said: 'You wish to bring disaster on the town, any day may bring about a miracle and we shall be saved. I'm telling you that it is our property that they crave and they would not kill all of us, such a thing is impossible.' So the meeting dispersed with no decision being taken.

In the meantime, Commander Ostrovskas informed us that if he were given a thousand gold rubles, he would defend the town from its anticipated destruction. Once again, hopes and illusions were awakened and jewels and gold were quickly collected. Gold coins had already been taken by the Germans, and fearfully and with little hope, the ransom money was handed over to the would-be murderers.

On Sunday, New Year's Eve 1941, an order was received from Wolf, the district commander in Vilnius, that the Jews of Eishishok were to deliver up to the police, all their money and jewelry and clothing of any value. Any house in which money or clothing was discovered would result in the death of every member of the household. The committee members understood that this was the end, and they went from house to house advising each family to take flight and escape to wherever they could find refuge, each on his own and each to his own fate.

Itchele Sonenson, who was then a child of 10, recalls that at 2 p.m. his father Moshe came home and said that the situation was very difficult and that they had to escape. He told Itchele to take his little sister Sheinele, then 6 years old, and to go to a gentile neighbor named Yuzik, who was a friend of the family. Then he told his wife Feigele to get herself and their baby ready, while he made some arrangements in the town. On his return, he would collect her and the baby, pick up Itchele and Sheinele on the way, and leave town.

According to Itchele, his father Moshe went to the rabbi together with others, and asked permission to set fire to the town, but the rabbi refused.

There were many attempts to escape, and it is estimated that some 500 souls fled from Eishishok on that day. However, most of them were caught and killed by the Germans, the Lithuanians, and the farmers of the neighborhood. As told by some few survivors and farmers of the region, the following facts emerge. On that New Year's Eve, all the Jews of Eishishok, the old and the young, the men and the women, were ordered to gather together in the two synagogues. Whoever remained outside the synagogues would be shot on the spot, it was decreed. The local Lithuanian police, supported by additional units of the police and Germans brought in from elsewhere, went from house to house checking whether there was

78

anyone remaining in the houses. They saw to it that not a single Jew remained outside the synagogue. All were within the synagogues of Eishishok, some 3,000 Jews of Eishishok and a further thousand from Olkenik and the surroundings.

A heavy guard surrounded the buildings and no one entered or left. Thus they remained, enclosed and imprisoned, without food or drink, for the two days of the New Year: two days and nights in which even their personal needs had to be done on the spot.

It is impossible to forget those extraordinary Days of Awe in the Eishishok of my childhood. How all the people would enter the synagogues dressed in their finest, as befits appearing before the Almighty; bowing before him in prayer and song and joyousness. The children would have supplies of delicious foods with them, and we, too, would pray and frisk about in the courtyard of the synagogue. At the time, I still did not know the meaning of the words Days of Awe.

Now they were subjected to ridicule and scorn before their Maker, humiliated and crushed before their Father in Heaven. Can one imagine the feelings of a father embracing his starving and thirsty children, with no answer to their cries? Is it possible to picture the pain of a mother embracing her baby in her arms and unable to save it?

A Jewish community of more than 20 generations, of 700 years almost since the founding of the town, was being torn up by the roots. Its voice was strangled and could not be heard. Its cries did not open the gates of heaven, and its groans did not stir the revered throne.

On Tuesday, after New Year's Day, the doors of the synagogues were opened and the imprisoned were aligned in rows of four, and taken to the cattle market in Radun Street. Leading the death march were the Rabbi Shimon Rozovsky and the Cantor Tabulsky, who chanted the confessional prayer before death along the way. The marketplace was surrounded by German and Lithuanian police units who stood by for a day and a night. Escape was impossible.

At dawn on Wednesday, one could see from afar, in the

direction of the old cemetery, groups of peasants digging. At 8 a.m. the Lithuanian police commander Ostrovskas chose 250 of the most husky men, leading them away. An hour later, another group of 250 were led away. In order to quieten suspicions, a fraudulent letter written in Polish, supposedly from Leib Milikovsky, was read out, in which it was stated: 'Do not fear, we are preparing a ghetto for you', and to his wife he wrote, 'I am awaiting you.' The letter once again aroused hopes in many hearts, and there was no opposition to the death marches. Late in the afternoon, not a soul was left alive: they had all been murdered in the old cemetery.

On the following day, it was the turn of the women and the children. The farmers of the neighborhood recalled that Ostrovkas wore a white coat and white gloves, shooting down the children himself, and then throwing them into the ditches while they were still alive. On his orders, the rabbi had to be present at the cemetery, so that there should be a witness to the annihilation of his bretheren and he suffered this torture until a bullet fired by the murderer put an end to his own life.

Thus ended the trials of the honest and simple Jews of Eishishok. This was the end of the splendid community of Eishishok and the beginning of the comprehensive annihilation of endless Jewish communities.

In the neighboring villages beyond the fictitious border between Lithuania and White Russia, nothing had changed, but the peacefulness was fraught with tension. The Jews tried to quell their fears by believing that what had happened in Eishishok and other villages was due to the fact that this had occurred in Lithuanian territory: the Lithuanians had instigated the killing, and the Germans had only helped them. The Germans themselves did everything they could to reinforce this belief.

In the meantime, the Jews of Dowgalishok quietly went on with their lives undisturbed, and continued to prepare for the winter. There were a variety of rumors regarding German intentions, but no one really knew what they were. One can assume that they were aware of the refugees from Eishishok who had arrived in Radun and Dowgalishok, and intentionally ignored this fact so as not to cause panic or opposition, waiting until they were sufficiently prepared to undertake another murderous campaign.

From day to day news of the massacre of the Jews of Eishishok loomed larger. We were dumb with shock, suffering their pain, and fearful of what was to come. Mother's brother and sister, Velvel and Reinke, had lived in Eishishok, as had other relatives, both near and far. Uncle Velvel had been a teacher of Hebrew, Bible, and Jewish history. When we would come there for holidays or summer vacations, we would meet him, for he would also return to Eishishok at the same time, for he would be teaching elsewhere. Velvel was a gentle man with a pleasant manner, and despite his profession, he would not ply us with questions in order to test our knowledge and not to spoil the absence of school by reminding us of our studies. Perhaps he himself needed the rest. He liked to talk with us, however, about all sorts of things, and involve us in family affairs. He would speak of his older brother Yaakov Rachovsky who had emigrated to America, and who since the death of Grandmother Esther Asne had ceased to write or send money to help the family. He also spoke of his second brother, Mordecai, who was head of the yeshiva in Novogrodek, who had died young; and his sister, Riva Malka Alta, who had married in Oshmiano; and also his sister Beile who lived in Radun with her sick husband (she had financial troubles). He would tell us about our mother Sarah Mina, and how our father fell in love with her at first sight; about his younger sister Reinke, who lost her father when she was a young girl, and how his feelings of responsibility for her were great and how he himself could not marry until she had found a husband.

I remember Aunt Reinke well from my childhood. She still comes to mind from time to time, even today. I still remember her laughing face, her sparkling eyes, the golden tooth that was revealed when she smiled, and her lean and upright stature. But more than anything else, I still recall her warmth, her hugs and caresses all over my body until I fell asleep in the late hours of the night or on a Sabbath afternoon.

Reinke became an orphan at a very early age, when still a girl. She ran the household on her own and also kept the small store, which was a sort of mini-market for groceries, haberdashery, and other goods which the farmers of the neighborhood needed. She grew up and became almost an old maid, still without finding the man of her choice. And just when the Soviet army returned once again to Eishishok, she found a man to suit her. The news that reached us from over the border was that the man was handsome and kind, an excellent tailor, and that he earned well and respected and adored her. News of Reinke's happiness reached us from across the border and our household was overjoyed. Some time passed and we were informed that she had given birth to a son and that her happiness knew no bounds. We praised the Lord for his care of widows and preservation of orphans, for he had repaid her many times over for her orphaned state.

It was difficult to believe that Reinke and her little son of less than a year were no longer among the living, that their blood had been spilled in broad daylight. Velvel, who had come to visit us a few weeks before the New Year, was saved from the slaughter in Eishishok. We mourned the death of Reinke and her young family, and drew some consolation from the fact that Velvel was still alive.

7 Life in the Radun Ghetto

Life in Radun seemingly returned to its familiar pattern. Refugees from Eishishok and its surroundings managed to escape from those areas under the Lithuanian regime. They reached Radun and registered with the local authorities, received identity cards as inhabitants of Radun, and these served as a sort of temporary insurance of survival, as anyone caught without this document, was immediately shot or imprisoned, and his life would depend on the decision of this or that German and the latter's mood at the time. The situation was bearable in general, but the anxiety concerning the future engendred by the wiping out of the Jews of Eishishok went deep into our souls. The relative calm which reigned for a number of weeks, gave rise to an element of hope that here, in a Polish–Russian region, the same thing could not happen that had occurred in a Lithuanian region. There were also some who believed that the respect due to the Hafetz Haim would serve to protect them.

While still licking our wounds, it was decreed that the Jews of Radun were to be enclosed in the ghetto defined and set aside for them. The boundaries of the ghetto were determined by the authorities, extending to the northern side of the town, that is, the houses opposite the marketplace. On the other side of the northern boundary there were stretches of green, some fruit trees, and pasture. To the west, the ghetto began at the corner of Tatarsky and Grodno Street, and continued until the middle of Lida Street.

The ghetto area covered less than 20 per cent of the area occupied by the Jews of Radun before they were obliged to move there. And, not only all the Jews of Radun had to live here, but also the survivors from Eishishok, the Jews of Dowgalishok and Jewish refugees from many other places. The population increased four- to five-fold and reached some 2,500 souls. Four families were crammed into an apartment intended for a single family.

In an order published by the Germans it was stated that all the Jews had to move to the ghetto by 10 a.m., and that any Jew found wandering in the street would be shot on the spot. Every family marched with their belongings (whatever they could carry in a bundle on their backs) to the ghetto. Some of their property they deposited and gave as gifts to Polish friends, but most of it was left in the abandoned houses, to be taken later by gentile neighbors or pounced on by nearby farmers. A number of Christian families who lived within the periphery of the ghetto left there in good time, particularly as they were promised much more spacious dwellings. The order to occupy the ghetto came as a complete surprise, and the time allowed for its execution was so limited that one could not even think about the possibility of transferring food or property to the ghetto area. The new situation was a tremendous shock and aroused fears concerning what the future had in store. The fate of other ghettos was known, and now that everyone was concentrated and crowded into one small area, it was a simple task to supervise every movement that took place there.

The Jews of Dowgalishok still believed that they would not be moved from the land they had cultivated for hundreds of years, for they grew the food needed by the Germans for the war, and they were very productive. In addition, who cared or knew anything about the existence of a handful of Jewish families living peacefully and in harmony with their gentile neighbors? In order to feel more secure, Father began secretly to transfer some of his movable goods to friendly farmers. All this had to be done in great secrecy, lest those who did not receive a share of the property that had to be left untended were jealous and informed the authorities. All the Jews of Dowgalishok did likewise. They reckoned that this property could eventually serve as a guarantee that in a moment of need, the farmer would perhaps help them out with food, on the quiet, in exchange for the goods he had received.

The thing the Jews of Dowgalishok feared most, and did not dare to believe would happen, came like a thunderbolt one bright day, in the form of a decree. They were ordered to leave their village, never to return. They were permitted to take some personal goods and movable chattels – enough to make up one wagonload – some food and clothing, but no domestic animals or valuables. The decision as to what to take and what to leave behind was a very difficult one, for food and clothing were an immediate necessity, particularly as the winter would come soon, and without these essentials they would freeze to death. Books, especially, sacred books, could not be left behind, for the gentiles might make use of them in blasphemous ways.

The heaps of goods to be taken grew and grew, and time was running out. Most difficult of all were the farewell glances at every corner and item, in the knowledge that they were never to be seen again. Unconsciously, my eyes fell on the portraits of the family's forefathers and sages of the generation and a view of Palestine, Rachel's tomb, hanging on the walls. And I looked at the oven from which so many tempting dishes had emerged on the Sabbath and holidays.

From the window facing north, I could see the see the cow shed and the cow chewing its cud, standing alongside her little calf born only a few weeks earlier: I wondered who would milk her and who would drink the warm frothy milk. Across the street was the vegetable garden where we would hop over the fence and pick a carrot or green cucumber to munch on.

With dawn coming up there were usually the sounds of life coming from the smithy: resounding clangs which rang out from the whitened metal being hammered on the anvil. How would the smithy look without father and how would father, feel away from it? The first rays of sunshine touched the tops of the tall pines of the wood where we had played so often.

Our neighbor Kaschitz's horse and wagon approached the

doorway of our house. Bundle after bundle was thrown onto the wagon, until there was no space left. The *mezuzoths* of the house were taken down, one by one. We wondered whether to close the door behind us.

The cupboard for jams and preserved fruits was no longer to serve as a temptation. One more step, and I was outside, near the already moving wagon. The horse turned to the right at the corner of the house, followed by the wagon, to the dirt road leading to Radun. The wagon made its way between the house and the barn, past our cowshed, and continued along the road to the Radun ghetto. And we trudged after it, our faces full of sadness and our heads bowed. This was the last time our family walked together. Mother and father at the front of the wagon, and behind them the three children Pinchas, Yekutiel, and Avremke, from time to time helping the horse pull the wagon when it encountered a pothole in the road or watching out for a falling bundle.

This painful and humiliating march was not recorded by any camera but is engraved on my mind until this very day. We were not 'alone' on this sad journey. In front of us were Joshe-Jankel and Joshe-Luya, of the Paikovsky family, and following in our wake were Feivel Lipkunsky, Kaddish and others. Without tears or lamentations, a Jewish tribe was torn away from its land; farmers who had worked their land for six or seven generations were now exiled to the ghetto.

This is how the Jewish farmers of Dowgalishok were uprooted from the source of their livelihood, where they were born and had lived for generations. This too is how the noose was tightened around their throats, little by little, with persistence and planning.

It was a Friday, a short, autumn day; the rays of the sun that were to be seen in the early morning were soon to be swallowed by clouds and the sky darkened as the day wore on. With sad and fearful hearts, we entered the outskirts of Radun. We passed the house of Moshe and Zippi Ribak in Mosaika Street; the spacious house with the large courtyard, which was always filled with farmers who came to sell their produce and buy provisions, now looked abandoned and orphaned. How glad they were that only one daughter, the mother of Shlaimke Ribak (whose family had a butcher shop for meat and sausage), had remained in Radun. They had five sons and three daughters, who luckily sought their futures away from Radun, across the seas. Yoshke had left America for Palestine; Froike reached Palestine and lived there until he died; Leibke emigrated to Argentina; while Sheike and Nochke went to America.

Some ten meters further, at the corner of Mosaika and Kleibenia street, we passed the house of Berl the tailor (see chapter 2). It was a handsome house which had been enlarged not long before with the help of his rich brother Alter, the generous and warmhearted brother from London. Usually when one passed this house or on entering, one could hear the singing of the tailor's apprentices accompanied by the humming of the sewing machines – a delightful combination. Conducting the work and the orchestra was sturdy little Berl, with his smiling face and clever eyes which were at the same time cunning and playful. The needles, with thread trailing away behind them, dipped into the fabric along the lines marked by tailor's chalk by the professional hands of the maestro, and then rose, like the bows of violins, sometimes with swift strokes and sometimes slowly and rhythmically.

In the evenings, and particularly on Saturday nights, this 'chamber' music would become vocal music, with the large gramophone placed in the center of the table, and the wonderful voices of the best cantors of Poland and the rest of the world, would entertain the guests sitting around the table, sipping tea and enjoying their strudel and *babka*.

We arrived at the marketplace, and advanced towards the *Judenrat* in order to receive an apartment, unpack some of our belongings, and settle down as best we could before the Sabbath. We had returned to Radun, but it was not the same Radun. This was a Radun enclosed in a ghetto, and we had come like unjudged prisoners who did not know why and for what reason they were being held, or when the judgment would be carried out.

The apartment allotted us was on the slope of Lida Street, in the house of a Pole. It to have gentiles living among the Jews. Thus it was possible to supervise every movement within and close the ghetto from without, isolating its Jewish inhabitants from the rest of the town. The apartment consisted of a single room. On entering, we found a family of four refugees from Eishishok already occupying the place: the husband Velvel, his wife Haya, and two charming teenage girls. There was also a girl on her own from Olkenik called Rivka, who had succeeded in escaping the annihilation of all the Jews of Olkenik together with the Jews of Eishishok. In the course of a conversation and an account of her background, it appeared that she was a relative of our mother's. We were joined in the ghetto by our Uncle Velvel, who had been staying with his sister Beile in Radun until then, so it was that all eleven of us crowded into this one-room apartment, without sanitary conditions.

A certain talent for improvisation was needed in order to find room for everyone, and tolerance and goodwill was even more essential. When we arrived, there was one bed in the room occupied by Velvel and his wife Haya, and there was no room for any other. So a bench or a table served as a bed, and even a small piece of floor in a corner would do in order to rest one's weary head, after a tiring day on an empty stomach.

We found some consolation on top of the oven built into the corner of the room, which was bricked up on three sides. Normally, this would be the favorite venue for slumbering cats but now it became a respectable bed, and even at times a dressing room. For us children, it was also a place to play and to whisper our secrets to one another.

With the outbreak of war and the entry of the Germans into Radun, there were those who consoled themselves with the thought that with the coming severe winter and snowstorms, Hitler and his armies would meet their end in the same manner as Napoleon's army. To our sorrow, however, the Germans prepared for the coming winter well in advance and deprived the population, especially the Jews, of their warm furs and woolens, sending them to the front. And not only did they not retreat as we had hoped, but from day to day we heard of the German army's further advance into the heart of Russia and its victories over the Soviets. The news arriving from the front was that the Germans had taken Kiev and that they were advancing towards Moscow. We despaired of a sudden and swift salvation by way of the natural course of things; now we could only hope for a miracle.

Life in the ghetto assumed a regular pattern. Every day we went out to work, including teenagers and youths: some to chop wood and others to clear the roads of snow. Battling against strong winds, frost and snow, we marched a distance of some ten kilometers to work every day. The daily rations for a worker was 100 grams of dry bread, and one had to fulfil a certain working norm. The foreman, a Pole from the neighborhood of Radun, would supervise our work, pressing us to complete our work quota — either out of fear of the Germans or because he thought the Jews should work even harder, there was no need to pay them.

With all the pressure, suffering and torture, we did not actually starve, for in every household some foodstuffs had been stored and some warm clothes retained for the winter. Secret contact was made with farmers, who would steal food into the ghetto in exchange for goods which had been hidden there or for money and valuables. There were also workers who were sent to work outside the town, to chop wood for the Germans in the woods of Meizanze. Every Friday they would return to Radun and another group would take their place. Outside the ghetto, there were greater possibilities of contacting the farmers, and a regular barter trade developed: food for clothing or other goods, and at times, they even succeeded in smuggling some food into the ghetto.

At times, we would be lucky, and one of the Polish foremen

would know a member of the workforce, and he would try to placate us by allowing us to visit and warm ourselves in the home of the neighborhood farmers. This would be possible only if we fulfilled our work quota quickly, before the time allotted for it. On a severe winter's day, some 20–30 degrees below zero, the snowstorm would be so strong that the blinding snow would lash and sting that part of one's face that remained uncovered, so that this was a golden opportunity to warm up and rest a bit, and even more important, to receive a piece of bread and sometimes a glass of warm milk – a luxury we were no longer used to. At times, we would be given a thicker slice of bread which we would hide in one of our pockets in order to take home to our families.

When we were first told that we had to leave Dowgalishok and move to the ghetto in Radun, I still did not know what a ghetto was. Now I knew that a ghetto was an enclosure, like a sheepfold; that in a ghetto, one lives in a one-room apartment together with 11 or more souls. In a ghetto one cannot bite into a piece of stale bread even when one is hungry, for your co-dwellers' eyes are riveted on you and your bread. In the ghetto, when a mother was preparing food for her children, she knew that the hungry eyes of the neighbor's children would be following every bite her children were taking.

As Father was a professional blacksmith and fitter he worked for the Germans under a special license in the smithy outside the ghetto. Every day, he would leave the ghetto for his place of work, where he would come across many of his farmer friends and acquaintances of old, who would bring him food for payment, or at times even out of friendship. Our fellow apartment-dwellers also benefited from this, for it was obvious that we would not eat while our closest neighbors peered at us with hungry eyes. These same moral standards were almost universal in the ghetto: despite the difficulties the communal sense of unity and responsibility were beyond belief.

Not everyone living in one room together had the same opportunities, or the possibility to acquire food. Those who remained in their houses were in a better situation than those who had had to leave their homes and property and move to the ghetto with little or no possessions at all. The worst off were the refugees who escaped with their lives from the neighboring villages, and who had nothing of value, such as silver or gold, for which they could barter for food.

In the reality of the ghetto, when one is less hungry and living together with others who are more so, the result is tension and jealousy, and even hatred. In the ghetto, families who are strangers to one another are forced to live in close proximity, the married and the unmarried alike. When a single girl is combing her long hair, preening herself among the married men, for lack of anything better to do, the older women would stare at the poor girl, and at their husbands, both enviously and angrily. And when the girl needed a man's help in some domestic chore and used her charming smile to get it, she received the required assistance to the accompaniment of a poisonous look from one man's wife.

There is no doubt that one of the Germans' intentions was to debase the Jews in their own eyes, to create circumstances in which Jews would tread on each another by cramming them together in such a crowded and limited space; to make them work like slaves with no compensation and supply them with so meager a diet that their state of perpetual hunger could barely keep them alive, and thus destroy their humanity.

Radun was a small, poor town. From time to time, the Germans would request that the Jews of Radun supply them with all kinds of items, in quantities and of a quality that perhaps did not exist there at all, so that when members of the *Judenrat* and the Jewish police went from house to house to collect these articles, the Jews would open their doors and ask the *Judenrat* officials to look through the houses in order to discover whether they possessed such items.

Lipa Skolsky of Oran, head of the Jewish police, claimed that the Radun ghetto differed from ghettos in other towns. Despite the poverty and the shortages in Radun, and the fact that the ghetto contained so many Jews, including refugees from other towns who had arrived penniless and with nothing on their backs, there was no instance of actual starvation. Mutual help was commonplace, and all the needy would receive daily food rations, contributed and distributed voluntarily by the Jews of Radun.

Liebe Shlosberg organized a group of girls who would do the laundry for the single boys, particularly the boys of the yeshiva. It needed a strong desire to help and a generous heart, to undertake the attempt to deal with so much dirty linen that encompassed as many lice as in an Egyptian plague.

Lipa Skolsky, who attended meetings of the *Judenrat*, recalled that at one of the meetings it was decided to put a rabbinical ban on whoever would slaughter a cow or even a chicken, as the slaughtering of animals put people's lives in danger. In the neighboring village there were instances of Germans finding meat in Jewish households and killing many Jews as a reprisal. (The proclaimed punishment for slaughtering or possessing meat, milk, or other fats, was death.) Lipa, as head of the police, was asked by the rabbis to see to it that the ban was observed and from then onward the slaughtering ceased.

After some time, when the food situation had deteriorated, and working was obligatory, they cancelled the ban and Lipa was again asked to keep an eye on the Germans, lest they carry out surprise raid, to find meat and other forbidden foods. From that time onward, the slaughtering took place in the same building as the *Judenrat*. During one of the searches, they succeeded in getting rid of the meat in time and hiding it in the snow outside. On another occasion, Lipa was obliged to stuff a piece of meat into his pocket while accompanying the Germans on their rounds.

'Normal' life would become difficult from time to time, as a result of various decrees, but as long as these dealt with questions of money, gold, or other valuables, and no people were harmed, we could accept our situation. Fate was not so inclined, however.

The sudden arrest of Berl Lipkunsky because of slander, and his execution in the Lida jail, together with the annihilation of his family in Radun, was a great shock and a source of anxiety for the future. Suspicions were aroused that the slander would be followed by further slander and blackmail. The efforts to raise a large sum of money to pay the ransom was pointless, for the money was taken, but it no longer availed.

The Germans in charge locally used the Polish police commander to calm the population by saying that they were not the ones responsible but that slander caused this trouble, and that the order came directly from the district headquarters in Lida. After every such occurrence, the Germans tried to pour oil on troubled waters and made vain and deceitful promises; in addition, would extort money for saving people. In this manner they managed to subdue any desire to rebel or escape.

The cruel truth was that it was convenient to believe what they were saying, for we knew too well that the likelihood of escaping from the ghetto was well nigh impossible at that time. The war was at its peak and the Germans were advancing on all fronts; it did not seem that the war would soon come to an end. Considering the circumstances, there were not many farmers who would endanger their lives in order hide a Jew, even for a large sum of money.

Victory over the Germans was not even vaguely visible on the horizon – on the contrary. The slightest whisper or suspicion would end in the execution of the Jew in hiding, together with the farmer's entire family, or the burning of his house with the family within. The other alternative – of escaping to the woods in the winter, with a temperature of 20–30 below zero, and lacking the prior preparations – was quite impractical. The chances of survival were nil. Snow was the great and most dangerous 'informer', for every footstep left its imprint until a new snowfall.

The rural population, even if it had not yet submitted to hatred towards the Jews, did not display any great affection for them. Certainly people would not come to their aid while endangering themselves. A very small number were prepared to help. And the fact that this was done for money did not alter the matter in any way. But if there was one Jew-hater who would instill his terror into the neighborhood out of blind hatred of the Jews, or for money promised him for informing on a Jews, it was enough to cause havoc in the entire region. In such circumstances it was easier to accept the Germans' promises, and it appeared to be safer in the ghetto than outside, especially to those who had little children or women or the elderly depending on them.

In the evening, it was forbidden to leave the house, and one's life was in danger if one disobeyed this order. In spite of this, I would steal out of the house together with my brother. We would run from house to house until we reached the dwelling of Reb Mordecai Beer, head of the small yeshiva of Radun, in order to study Talmud with him and to listen to tales that would warm our hearts during the cold evenings, and we were encouraged by his predictions of the future promised by the Almighty.

8 The Murder of the Jews of Lida

A few weeks of comparative peace and quiet passed among us; the days of Hanukkah also went by without much celebrating but also without any untoward events. One morning, we heard the loud purring of motorcycles coming from the slope of Lida Street and moving towards the market-place alongside the ghetto. Radun had taken in a number of Jewish families, some 40 people in all, who had succeeded in joining their relatives there after escaping from the Lida ghetto, where a terrible hunger reigned. Apparently a German unit was checking every house, leading the refugees outside the town back on the road to Lida. We assumed that they were being taken back to the Lida ghetto, but some 20 minutes later we heard the sound of shots, and we understood that Jewish blood was again being spilled. Some moments later, I saw these angels of death returning to the center of town; whether they were returning to have a drink or to indulge in further atrocities, I did not know. When I saw Jews carrying shovels, running in the direction of the woods outside the town, I also joined them. I learned from them that the Germans had commanded the *Judenrat* to send people to bury the victims quickly, in order to return to the ghetto while the day was still with us. We ran as quickly as we could, thinking perhaps that there were wounded who would need help and perhaps could be saved while they were still alive.

What confronted me were heaps of bodies strewn about, some still warm with fluttering pulses, others face down in the snow, and others staring at the sky, unbreathing. Many bodies, lying across one another, stretched out across the white blanketing snow. A child alongside its mother; father and son embracing one another; women and men, all sleeping the sleep of the just on a white carpet flecked with their red blood. That scene is still with me today – it was the first time I had seen so many victims. It was a scene out of one's darkest fantasy – the fantasy of a battlefield.

The winter was at its height and the ground was too hard to dig graves in the frozen earth. These were the hours of the late afternoon and the sun was about to sink into the horizon, which was also turning blood-red. We had to return to the ghetto while it was still light and, having no alternative, we hid the bodies in the snow and also covered the bloodstains with snow, lest they be seen by man and God. It was only on the following day that the *Judenrat* placed them in a proper grave.

Our lives were now in constant danger. We lived with a sense of despair and acceptance of our fate, and did not believe that there was any hope of salvation. The question was only who would be the first to go and who would come afterwards. Everything was seen through a haze of apathy, for what could one do? And as long as we did not know who was next in line, we all waited helplessly for the next decree, without trying to change the situation. On the contrary, we feared that any action on our part could intensify the retribution, and bring about the end sooner. We felt that the cord strangling us was getting tighter and tighter but we saw no way out – for where would we go in the middle of the winter with the snow betraying our footsteps? Where could we hide and for how long? The front was deep in the heart of Russia and we thought that any movement of the front to Germany's detriment would hasten our destruction. Gershon the Dolger (he was from the town of Dolge in Lithuania), who was also called the 'one who was shot down', would say: 'We are all shot down' – his comment after he fled from the slaughter in his town in Lithuania, and afterwards from the train taking him to a concentration camp. In our heart of hearts, we hoped for miracles: miracles at the front, or from heaven. There were rumors going around about German losses at the front, but most of these were all only wishful thinking.

Jankele Menashes, the blacksmith (Jacob Kovalsky – the son of Menashe the smith), a lad of about 17 or 18, while in the Jewish police, noticed a girl of his own age from the Lida ghetto – Michele – and her sister Taybele, and their young brother Joseph. They were the grandchildren of Reb Judah, the shoemaker, of Radun. He took a chance and succeeded in extricating Michele and her brother from among the condemned Jews of Lida, hiding them among one of his Polish acquaintances. He undoubtedly saved their lives. He also tried to get Taybele out, but she refused to go with him out of fear or some other reason, and this young woman's life ended on the white snow. Michele and her brother managed to get out of the ghetto when it was burned down. She escaped to the woods, and became a partisan, together with her savior Jankele. When the war was over, Michele married Haim Itske, 'the Gypsy', who was also a partisan. After the war, the three of them emigrated to America, where they settled and raised a family. Jankele Kovalsky eventually managed to reach Israel and also became a family man.

One day, I noted that in a corner of the old Christian cemetery in the center of the town, opposite the ghetto, a large gate was being constructed. Two tall wooden pillars were sunk into the earth, at a distance of some five to six meters from each other, and another beam was placed along the tops of the pillars. I was curious as to the purpose of this construction. Was it to serve as a gate of honor for some visiting notable at some future festivity? My curiosity was not satisfied, and a number of days went by without a solution to the puzzle.

One Sabbath morning during the Purim holidays, the riddle was solved. As I was leaving the house, I glanced in the direction of the gate and saw people crowding around it. There was snow on the ground and higher up, three large dolls were dangling in the wind. As I came nearer, the dolls slowly took on the forms of human beings. At first I did not grasp what I was seeing, I thought it was some optical illusion or acrobatics, but I soon became aware of the tragic aspect of the scene when I saw the faces that had turned black and the bulging eyes. The bodies were swinging in the wind over the heads of the indifferent spectators.

I awoke from my apathetic state and tried to make out which Jews had been fated in this way, but to my surprise, these were two Poles who had been caught stealing, and the third was a Jewish girl who had become a Christian, so they said, and had been caught at the home of some gentiles, and informed on. This spectacle was intended to show what would be done to those who disobeyed the orders of the German authorities.

Being a small and young lad, I was not sent to work on clearing the roads regularly, and thus I had an occasional opportunity to bring Father some warm food while he was working in the smithy outside the ghetto. Later on, Father managed to get a work permit for me as an apprentice, as well as a permit to go to work outside the ghetto. A work permit and an artisan's skill was a sort of life insurance. Firstly, because it was believed that the Germans needed skilled workers, and that they therefore would not be harmed, or at least would be the last to suffer. Secondly, the mere fact of being able to leave the ghetto made it possible to meet up with farmers, to get food from them, and bring it into the ghetto, or to eat a satisfying meal from time to time.

On one of the occasions that I visited Father, I saw that he was working very hard and that he was tired – I rarely saw him in this state. I begged him to let me help him, and took the heavy hammer from him and started to hammer away at the whitened metal lying on the anvil. I was trying to show him that I actually had the strength to use the great hammer at the necessary pace. During one of the blows on the anvil, I felt a sort of electric current and twinge in one of my spinal vertebrae, and since then, when from time to time, I recall the scene of my father at the smithy outside the ghetto, I again feel the electric current and pain running through my spine.

Once again, life in the ghetto returned to its usual routines.

Every day, we would go out work and receive our inadequate ration of food, supplementing it by the food we would bring in from outside. The crowding and privation was growing, but no one in the Radun ghetto was starving or died of starvation. One blessed every day that passed in peace, and awaited the morrow in the hope that it might bring some good news, for we had become accustomed to hoping that 'God's salvation is immediate'. The winter was coming to an end. March was with us and with it the Purim holidays; a month which had seen the salvation of the Jews from its enemies. Perhaps a miracle would also occur in our times.

9 The Ghetto is Surrounded

The German command in Radun suddenly ordered the Jewish artisans to make all sorts of furniture for them, as well as wagons and carts, with the greatest possible haste. Rumors began to circulate that perhaps the Germans were on the move. The situation was unclear; something might have happened at the front, for the war had already lasted almost a year. The rumors reached their height on 7 May 1942, when it was said that the Germans were indeed packing their bags. Some said that they were getting ready to flee for evidently the German front had been smashed. The more pessimistic thought there was no truth in the rumors, and that even if they were true we should be prepared for further trouble, for the Germans would not leave Radun quietly and that they would finish us off before that. The town was in a stew all that week, we were prepared for what was to come, and waited hopefully for a miracle.

The riddle was finally solved. When we awoke on the Friday morning we could not leave the house. The entire ghetto was surrounded by the local Polish police force, complemented by Lithuanian and White Russian police, brought in from other places. In addition to the local German forces, a special German unit arrived to supervise the mission. At that very moment, we knew that our fate was sealed; we merely did not know at exactly what moment they would execute their plan and in what manner it would be done. Everyone began to weigh up the options: was it worthwhile to take the chance of escaping immediately or was it preferable to wait for nightfall, or even to wait until the intentions of the Germans became clear.

The difficulties were immense. Here you were, closed up in a cage together with your children, your wife, your parents, everyone who was closest to you, with the knowledge that in a few minutes, you would lose them and never see them again. The little children clinging to their parents listened to them discussing plans to escape. Time passed in the meantime.

One had to flee at once, before it was too late. But how? When? Where to? And if we succeeded, who knew for how long we could manage? The chances of remaining alive were minimal. On second thoughts, perhaps it would be better to let fate decide, instead of undergoing pain and tribulations, and if we were to die, would it not perhaps be better to die together with the family and the entire village, rather than fall victim to torture and endless suffering later on?

To this very day, I still remember Father's terrible dilemma, when he told us that each of us would have to try to escape separately and take our chance, for in any case we had nothing to lose. We must flee to the woods and hide with friendly farmers whom we knew. Everyone had to try his luck and in this way, perhaps some of us would be saved. We could not succeed in getting away together, and if we stayed together and wait, we would all be killed.

We children were afraid to go out alone, understanding that we had to flee, but we wanted to do so with Father and Mother. Again Father explained to us and to Mother, that we must separate and that each of us had to go on our own, or at most, only two could make their way together, and only later would we meet up with one another. If we went all together, we would all be caught. I can still hear Father's pleas to the children: 'You go first and I will afterwards help your mother out of here,' for she utterly refused to move alone. She also hesitated to let us go, but she finally agreed that if we would leave, she would also leave with Father.

This same woman, who some years earlier knew no fear or anxiety, who risked her life and that of her children, and dared to steal across dangerous borders for the sake of learning and righteousness, now lacked the strength to save her soul. Father, as head of the family, said that he would have left first, crawling on his own, but he could not leave us and

Mother, lest people would say that he had saved his own life and abandoned his family.

Father had been a soldier in the First World War and therefore believed that under cover of darkness, he could evade the guards. He did not delude himself and knew that our fate was no longer in our hands and that we had nothing to lose. He even tried to bribe the police to enable us to leave together, but on the other hand, suspected that if we left together, the policeman would take the money and hand all of us over to the Germans. On Friday, throughout the day and night, he battled with his problem.

The Germans announced that they intended to take us out of the ghetto and transfer us to labor camps. Following this announcement, there were some who stated that it was worthwhile waiting to see if they would return the workers in the woods to the ghetto, for if they did send them back to the ghetto, it was a sign that they intended to finish us off, but that if they left those workers where they were, then it might be possible that they would also send us off to work. And so hour after hour went by and the zero hour was approaching.

Rumors and hints reached us via farmers friendly to the Jews that the situation was grave and that we had to try to escape from the ghetto whatever the cost. But how? No Jewish father would agree to run off and leave his wife and children to their fate. The close family ties of the Jews prevented many from trying to escape. Nevertheless, there were attempts throughout that Friday night and from time to time, we would hear shots and many were shot at and killed, but some succeeded in hiding and save their lives.

There is no doubt that if the Jews of Radun knew that after they managed to get through the guarded confines of the ghetto, they would have places to hide and take cover. If they had known that the non-Jewish population would help them, or at least not attack them, then many would have managed to save their lives. The chances of getting help outside the ghetto were extremely small while the enmity towards the Jews, and the satisfaction the gentiles derived from the situation, was great. There was therefore little sense in leaving the family, suffering mental and physical pain, and afterwards getting killed among some gentiles in an unfamiliar place. In these circumstances, it was preferable to die honorably, together with one's family and the entire village.

By Saturday morning, we were worn-out by sleeplessness and shattered nerves. Quiet prevailed and the attempts to escape ceased together with the shots – as if nothing had occurred. Carefully peeking outside, we could see the armed guards standing opposite every house and corner and we began to see through our delusions and vain hopes. But to try to flee during the day was tantamount to suicide, and so we had to wait until nightfall, assuming we lived until then.

My little brother Yekutiel (Kushka), aged 12, with his blond hair and blue eyes looked like most of the gentile children in the neighborhood, and he was fluent in Polish. He was also familiar with the ways and customs of the gentiles. We decided to clothe him as a Polish shepherd and in this way to get him out of the ghetto. With a shepherd's crook in his hand, he left for the ghetto's boundary. Father gave him instructions as to where he should go and it was agreed that if he should succeed in getting out, then on Saturday night, father would take mother and the two of us, and try to leave the ghetto. His attempt to flee the ghetto succeeded but when he tried to reach the outskirts of town, the local Poles unfortunately suspected that he was a Jewish child, and he was arrested by the Polish police. Though he put up some serious opposition, nothing helped. They took off his pants in order to see whether he was a gentile like themselves, or whether he was circumcised and Jewish. He was not harmed, but was sent back to the ghetto.

Kushka's failed attempt to flee the ghetto, and the manner in which he was identified by the Polish police, somewhat lessened our wish to leave the ghetto. We knew only too well that not only the Germans were after our lives, but many others as well. Many elements of the local population would be only too willing to assist in our undoing, if not by their own hand, then by gladly informing the Germans of our existence and having us jailed. Physical and mental weariness prevailed, despair and helplessness reigned, and to a certain extent, also acceptance of what was to come.

The Sabbath had come to an end. The sun had set and the day departed; twilight was with us, and the decree had still to be executed, while we lived in its shadow. Another night had been granted us and in its darkness lay our hope. The stars kept their watch on high and were not dimmed by the watchfulness down below. In the corner of the room, we lit the Habdalah candles and said the benediction at the conclusion of the Sabbath with trembling voices: 'Blessed art thou, O Eternal! King of the Universe, who distinguisheth between sacred and profane, between light and darkness, between Israel and other nations', and between life and death.

One's eyes were fastened to the doors and window openings, and one's ears were attuned to the slightest rustle. Perhaps we would find a way of escaping under cover of darkness and the night. The attempt to bribe the local Polish guard so that he would ignore us for a few minutes and not shoot at us when we tried to flee did not succeed. The bribe was taken but he threatened to shoot us if he did not receive more money, and with the disappearance of the money, our hopes also vanished, for our intentions had been revealed.

The moon rose and slowly made her way in the heavens, accompanied by the stars shedding their light on the watches below. Our spirits fell and our hopes subsided on seeing that even the stars and the moon in the firmament were against us.

Each inclined towards the other, worn and wearied by yet another night of watchfulness, and the night passed without our trying to escape and without our knowing whether we would have the opportunity the following night. Dawn was on the horizon and the world outside was silent. The shooting had ceased, and with it the barking of dogs. Only the early birds could be heard outside, as if adding their song to our prayers to the Almighty.

10 The Jews of Radun are taken to the Death Pit

A new day appeared, the first day of the week, 23 Iyar (10 May) 1942. In the early hours of the morning, the Germans and the police burst into the houses in the ghetto, and according to some criteria of their own, chose some hundred hearty men, among them Father, handed them shovels, and led them away westward, towards Grodno.

Thus we were left without the head of our family and his authority, and we were helpless. We did not know where the men were being taken, or for what purpose. Once Father had been taken away, Mother's spirits fell and all her desire to live seemed to vanish. The spiritual force needed to survive left her. She saw no sense in living, nor did she see any possibility of an existence without Father, especially outside the ghetto. In reality, she accepted her fate and did not try to influence it in any way. From that moment onward, she did not try to keep us near her, nor did she advise us as to what we should or should not do.

Her opinions and thoughts had had a great deal of influence in the past, as had her fervent belief in divine providence. Quite often she had expressed her sorrow at the possibility of one of her children remaining alive among the gentiles. She would rather have the child die as a Jew than live as a Christian. This outlook was common to most of the Jews of Radun – all of whom were ardent and confirmed believers in the Jewish faith.

Vigilance over the ghetto was increased and we sensed that at any moment something would happen. The fact that they had taken away the men with shovels at a time when the ghetto was surrounded by policemen and Germans was a clear sign that something terrible was about to occur. We felt like the condemned awaiting execution.

About an hour later, we heard series of shots from automatic rifles coming from the direction in which the men had gone, that is, from the direction of the town's cemetery. The intensity of the shots, and the direction from which they came, left us in no doubt that the men had been shot down. Had they been led out of the ghetto in order to kill them? And were the shovels given them to serve as a pretext to make us believe that they were going to work as usual?

Had they all been killed? Perhaps they had rebelled and tried to escape, and been fired at. So there was a chance that some of them had indeed escaped and might still be alive.

The Germans had preferred to take the young and strong first, in order to isolate those who were capable of rebelling against them at a certain stage, and also those who were physically capable of hard labor, such as digging.

After hearing these shots, we were in no doubt that this was our last day on earth and that our hours were numbered. Knowing Father's way of thinking we were certain that he would try to escape no matter what was facing him. What had prevented him from escaping until then was his responsibility for and attachment to his family: he was not morally capable of escaping on his own and leaving the family behind to its fate. There was also no possibility of succeeding in fleeing together with his family. Now that he was alone and his conscience was clear, there was no doubt that he would try to escape at any price. This slight possibility that he may still be among the living spurred us on to find a way to flee, to try to escape whatever the outcome, for there was no longer anything to lose.

Some time later, the policemen returned to collect more people to go to work with shovels. Without thinking or hesitating for a moment, my brother took hold of a shovel and I did likewise, volunteering to be taken to work. We secretly believed that if we could only succeed in getting outside the town into open country, among trees and bushes, we might perhaps have a chance of escaping. And if we did not succeed, it would be better to be shot in the back while escaping than to go passively to our death.

Pinchas was taken with the second group, but I was turned down and dismissed, on the grounds that I was too small and did not have the strength to work. 'Too young to be given the right to live, and too weak to be a danger', I thought to myself, and having no alternative, I returned to mother and my little brother Kushka, and my Uncle Velvel from Eishishok.

Back to Mother, perhaps orphaned of my father, perhaps abandoned, cut off from my brother to whom I was so attached throughout all of my childhood. Back to Mother, who had lost her warmth and vitality and who could not protect her beloved son. She had become reticent and inaccessible, and only the sadness of her face showed what was happening in her heart. She received me without a kiss or a hug, and heard my story with indifference, as if to say: 'You are big enough to find your way in life on your own: you no longer have a mother to lean on.'

I was engulfed in loneliness. There was a choking in my throat and I could not weep, but suddenly I sensed that I had grown up and that the burden of responsibility for my future weighed heavily on me, and to a certain extent, the fate of those close to me as well. All at once I was a man.

On realizing that there was no possibility of escaping, I helped the whole family to climb up to the attic, the only place in the house that had some hidden corners. The house was built in two wings with a wide connecting corridor, and only one exit. Some 25 people ascended the ladder to the attic and I covered them with all sorts of rags and wood that I found lying about, in a final attempt to save our lives.

Things moved quickly. Outside the atmosphere was strange and forbidding, as if the angel of death was hovering above. Until this very day, I cannot explain why it was I who thought of this possibility and not someone else, or what drove me to this action. Was it the result of all the thoughts that had been going through my mind or was it instinctive? Was it the fact that I was the older son and had assumed the responsibilities of the head of the family that motivated me?

This was the last act of love that I could offer my mother and little brother. I descended in order to get rid of the ladder that was leading from the attic and to find some hiding-place for myself. But before I could manage to get rid of the ladder, I heard the wails and wild shrieks of masses of people, accompanied by shooting and the noise of motorcycles. While seeking cover, I peered outside and saw that all the Jews from the nearby houses – children and the elderly, women and babies – were being led to the center of the town. I understood that the last moments were approaching. I did not manage to find a hiding-place and the armed Germans burst into the house and started to strike out with their rubber truncheons, shouting 'Raus, Raus' (Out, out). A German was standing in the doorway with his thick rubber truncheon in hand, and everyone going through the door would be beaten over the head until they lost their balance and were thrown outside on trembling knees.

Like an animal escaping from its pursuer, I quickly jumped to the door and raced through it bent over like a frightened monkey and managed to get through without a blow, much to the German's amazement. Some moments later, lonely and solitary, I found myself among masses of people, women and children, all pushing one another for fear of further blows for those who lagged behind.

The moving stream of people pushing and shoving like a whirlpool drove me forward. Some hidden force then held me back and the stream of people passed me by and I was left behind. I wanted to know what had befallen Mother and the others. Had they remained in their hiding-place undiscovered, or had the Germans found them? I feared that I would encounter them among the people being herded forward, and this was unfortunately true, for I recognized them from afar. I joined Mother and my brother, I to her right and

Yekutiel to her left, and Uncle Velvel alongside them, surrounded on all sides by relatives, friends and acquaintances. An impressive family parade among the masses of people.

Families and more families, assembled together and separated, around a father or a mother, women and men, the elderly and the little ones, babies in arms and still suckling, hordes of people pushing and marching toward the market square. While we were walking, my brother told me that the Germans had discovered them in their hiding-place and had beaten them violently. Mother walked with bowed head, suffering and pain stamped on her face, while her lips were repeating: 'Hear, O Israel! The Lord our God is one God.' From time to time she would turn to us, saying: 'Children, say '"Hear, O Israel" and we shall die like Jews, as martyrs.'

Thus were we led, with the entire town saying '*Shma, Yisrael*'; like sheep being led to the slaughter in holy sacrifice, in union with the Divine Presence. 'Hear O Israel'– my lips were repeating the prayer without accepting its meaning; I mumbled the words after her, but inwardly I rejected them, and was even opposed to saying these final words. Without understanding the logic or reason for my feelings, I could not accept these last words of confession.

My thoughts were with my father and my brother Pinchas. I wondered if Father had succeeded in escaping the shots we had heard, or whether he had been shot down and killed, and what had been the fate of my brother. My small stature enabled me to observe what was going on around me without getting beaten for it by the German guards, for I was hidden by those around me. The Germans and the policemen closed in and surrounded us on all sides, each a few meters from the other.

At our side, marched the family of Shlomo Koralnichik, friends of the family. He had married Sheinke, the eldest daughter of Reb Joshe Luya, the builder, from Dowgalishok. Shleimke was a gifted tailor and they had two talented children. He had been in Cuba for a number of years in order

109

to earn some money, and it was not long since he had returned, only to be killed together with his wife and children. The entire camp moved forward quietly without weeping or wailing – even little children did not weep – only here and there one could hear the crying of an infant. There was no mass hysteria, nor individual instances of hysteria. There was no physical resistance, for there was no moral resistance. Peacefully and silently, they were ready to accept their fate. One heard only the hysterical shouting of the policemen and the Germans, armed with automatic weapons, who surrounded us completely. One Polish policeman, known as 'The Bastard', who had grown up in the vicinity of the synagogue, found this an ideal opportunity to exercise his cruelty and beat the weak and those who were lagging behind the others. The rubber truncheon and the butt of his rifle was constantly being used on the heads and backs of those feeble creatures who were unable to keep up with the rest. Every once in a while, we would hear shots which had been directed at an old man who could not proceed and was left lying dead in the middle of the road.

We arrived at the corner of the marketplace, opposite the burnt-out shell of Itzchak Rogovsky's house. The entire crowd was ordered to get down on their knees, bowing their heads. Anyone who tried to raise his head, was forcefully beaten on the spot. This had its effect, for everyone was very obedient and there was no sign of opposition.

A community of Jews, on all fours, but not praying to God. The Polish spokesman appeared before us and made a short speech, the gist of which went: 'Everything that is happening to you today is due to your historical sin, the crucifying our Lord Jesus. And therefore you must be punished for it today.' The speaker was himself a priest – a messenger of God. This sermon was intended as our last confession, to atone for the acts of our forefathers in the distant past. These were the words of a preacher, an instrument of the Almighty, uttered in the name of the religion of pity and forgiveness.

These words echoed throughout the marketplace and

hovered over the heads of those who had been condemned without a trial. I still hear them but they have not penetrated my soul. My thoughts at the time, the thoughts of a Jewish child, carried me away from these messengers of a God of slaughter, from the murderers and their preaching, to my own living God.

The sun setting in the west lost none of its brilliance and warmth, and beat down on our heads from behind as we were bowed down on our knees, our heads bent to the ground. When we were ordered to stand up, we stood with difficulty, swaying uncertainly like drunkards. We did not see what was happening around us and no one tried to escape or rebel. We had been led for a distance of some two kilometers on the highway leading to Grodno, until we digressed leftward on to a dirt road, and we came to the town's cemetery.

Row after row, family after family, the entire Jewish community of some 2,000 souls, were kneeling on the ground with bent heads. Anyone attempting to raise his or her head, was shot on the spot. I was kneeling on the ground at the center, among the last section of the crowd, and surrounded by masses of people, like young trees planted in the earth, fixed to their places, without a word or a sound or a cry. Peacefully and with unusual self-discipline, they awaited the moment when it would all come to an end – their hopes of life as well as their suffering.

And like a plant deep in the earth, unable to uproot itself, I sat with my legs tucked under me, but my young, curious eyes sought out every corner to see what was going on around me. Beyond the heads of the crowds, there was a pit of enormous proportions. Alongside it, on the huge mound of dirt that was created by the digging of the pit, were stationed machine guns surrounded by Germans and armed police.

Line after line and group after group moved forward: the old people and the little ones, men and women, were led to the edge of the pit and stripped of their clothing. (Clothes were taken from their wearers in order to be certain that there was no money or gold hidden on them.) The clothes were placed in heaps, for their living and breathing wearers, created in God's image, now had no further need of them.

A round of shots rang out, and the ring of naked Jews standing on the edge of the pit, fell into it while they were still breathing, before they surrendered their souls to their Maker. Here a father holding his child's hand, and there a mother clasping her infant to her breast – fell upon one another into the dug-out hole. On top of the mounded earth, the heaps of clothing piled up, while below, the heap of warm and pulsating bodies grew higher. All this was happening in broad daylight, with the sun setting in the west, as it does each day. The rattle of the machine guns and the rifles continued apace, like a conveyor belt. Group after group, family after family, went up to the mound alongside the pit. Freed of their clothes and all else, remaining only as they were created, they fell into the pit one after the other.

Suddenly, there was a moment's respite, and the machine guns went silent. A young Jewish girl was screaming and struggling with her captors. She was not fighting for her life, which was well nigh lost, but for the respect and modesty she was not willing to forgo. Out of sheer modesty, she could not undress and the guards were trying to tear her clothes from her by force. The struggle continued until a bullet relieved her of the hopeless contest.

The rattle of the machine guns and rifles resumed, and the slaughter went on.

11 The Escape from the Death Pit

My eyes followed the horizon, beyond what was happening around the pit, and I saw on some figures rising from the pit, going over the mound and going forward towards the road. 'Pinke's alive, Pinke's alive,' I whispered to Mother, 'I can see him among those who were taken in the morning, they must have left him among the living to serve as an essential worker.' The Jews who had dug the pit in the early hours of the morning moved in a retreating line towards the road, away from the valley of death, and there, among them, was my brother Pinchas.

'Goodbye Mother, goodbye Kushka', and without waiting for a reply, I took to my heels like a whirlwind, abandoning my place in the crowd, stepping over the heads of those sitting nearby, I fell, took another step and crawled towards the road. I was still alive! They had not shot me, and here I was near the ditch alongside the road!. Stretched out on my stomach, with my head buried in the earth, my eyes were closed and I could not see a thing. Was it possible that I was not seen? Were they blind? perhaps they had not reached me. All was quiet about me.

I heard the sound of footsteps approaching from the direction of the road. Suddenly, they stopped and standing near me was Zelig the carpenter. He was an excellent craftsman and worked for the Germans. With a document from the head of the Gestapo, he was trying to extricate his wife from among those meant to die. As he left the road, a German approached him, grasped his collar, and shot him in the back. Zelig's face went black on the spot but he continued to contend that he had received permission and that he had documents from the high command. The German paid no attention and did not listen to what he was saying. He shot him again and Zelig fell nearby, at the edge of the road. He had dared to try to save his family, and had paid with his life.

With my eyes tightly shut and my head close to the ground, awaiting the bullet aimed at my head or some other part of my body, I was certain that the German would notice me and undoubtedly shoot me as well. I did not move or tremble and remained as still as a statue. It was strange to await a bullet that did not arrive. As if he were suddenly blinded, the German passed me by without being aware of my presence.

Like a trembling caterpillar, I crawled along centimeter by centimeter and then meter after meter, until I reached the road. Another few centimeters and I had reached the tail-end of the group of diggers now on the road leading to town. At that point, a German came over to me and asked who I was. Despite my shuddering, I did not lose control and answered at once in a shaky voice that I was a good worker, a professional smith, and showed him my permit as evidence of this. Without saying anything, he left me alone and went off to seek other victims. I continued crawling, now within the group, until I reached my brother Pinchas.

Brotherly love and the strong emotional ties between us, which had become a powerful and mystical magnet, had drawn me away from the masses condemned to death towards my brother Pinchas. And these lines, too, are being written under the influence of that same brotherly love. The group, which had dug the pit, my brother and I among them, was made up of some hundred men. We lay down some distance from the place, towards the town and behind us lay the valley of death. We lay face down, immobile, stuck fast on the road, unable to utter a sound. My thoughts were confused and fragmented – had I not seen human beings slaughtered? Were not my mother, my brother and cousins among them? Emptiness and shame ran through me –- I had abandoned them in their worst moments and escaped with my life. I was torn in two, physically and emotionally. Perhaps their dying was better than my being alive. I consoled myself with the thought that everything was now over for them: their struggle had ended. But what now was to become of me?

12 The Destruction of the Ghetto

We were given the order to stand up and move on. We marched without shedding a tear or turning our heads, hurrying towards the town, as if to distance ourselves as quickly as possible from the scene of violence where the angels of death reigned, and to flee from the place lest our captors change their minds and turn on us.

Accompanied by the police, we returned to the ghetto. The entire group was registered and we were ordered to appear the following morning in order to receive work permits, which would at least allow us to stay alive for the time being. Like two lost lambs returning to the fold, we returned to the house, to see for ourselves that it was not just a nightmare but reality. We approached it hesitatingly, preferring not to disturb the threatening silence all around. We entered with knees trembling, for our beloved ones had lived and breathed here only a few hours earlier. Now the shadows of death capered about on the walls and we began to grasp what had happened to us. Emptiness and fear enveloped us; we had awoken from a nightmare and felt that reality was in fact worse.

We quickly fled the house as if the earth beneath us was on fire. We sought a house where there were some Jews still alive. We could not live with ourselves and our loneliness. At twilight, in the corner of a room, we sat down on a tattered mattress and wept. The book of prayers we had taken from home helped. We addressed our prayers to the Almighty with choking voices, ashamed. We prayed and wept, wept and prayed, until the tears came to an end.

Lonely and orphaned, weary and worn, we fell asleep

embracing one another. Like brands snatched from the fire, like birds whose wings had been clipped, we had returned from the deadly pit, each with his own story, his own sorrow, his own orphaned state, while the overall tragedy united the few who had remained.

We were in a state of shock and could neither understand, nor appreciate nor feel, the extent of the tragedy. Only on the following day, in the full light of day, we saw how bereft and alone we were. Only yesterday, these houses were teeming with people. Despite the distress and crowded conditions, there was a joy in living, for there was still hope. Now all the houses of the ghetto were empty, with death dancing in their shadow. Emptiness dominated beings, and fear of life overcame our fear of death. We wanted to escape from the house, from the ghetto, and from ourselves, lest we see blood or the smell of death and the bodies strewn about. But where were we to go?

On Monday, 11 May 1942, the morning after the slaughter, when the Germans learned that many Jews had managed to hide and even escape to the woods, they issued an order that whoever returned within a day and registered would stay alive, and that whoever did not return to register would be killed. (Actually, the Germans extended the deadline and allowed people to return and register for a few days longer, in order to inveigle the Jews who had escaped from the ghetto to return. This news was published in the villages near the woods and most of the Jews returned to the ghetto and were registered.)

Having nowhere to go, the Jews preferred to believe the Germans. There was no leadership among the Jews at that time, or any organization to advise and guide them, and thus 900 Jews returned to the ghetto, with the idea that as long as it was possible, it was safer to live in the ghetto than elsewhere. At the same time, every Jew who returned to the ghetto affected the will and thoughts of those who were planning to escape. As more and more people returned to the ghetto, there were fewer who fled to the woods. The question no longer arose as to whether it was possible to annihilate masses of people, and despite the clear knowledge that the day would come when the entire population of the ghetto would be wiped out, people preferred life in the ghetto under conditions they were familiar with to the possibility of survival in unknown conditions outside.

Most of the survivors had found hiding-places at the very last moment; some in attics and others in cellars no longer in use. Only a few owed their lives to the fact that they had tried to escape on the very last night or a few moments before the gendarmes came to extinguish the ghetto. Everyone had a story, everyone their fate, but the general story emphasized the helplessness, the sheer inability, to contend against the cruel force of our enemies.

Sixteen people had crowded into one attic, among them the Sonnenson family of Eishishok. Their home there had been situated at the corner of the marketplace, near my grand-mother's house on Milner Street. I remember their house from childhood, when I would accompany my Aunt Reinke when she paid them a visit. But I knew Feigele and Maishke Sonnenson and their two children, Itchele and Sheindele, more closely, when I studied at the small yeshiva of Eishishok. For a certain time, I ate at their house once a week and it was the only place I liked to come on the *essentage*, which was, as I have already said, a custom I particularly disliked. This may have been because of Itchele, for though he was somewhat younger he was a good companion at games. Or perhaps it was due to the family relationship. But more than anything else, it was because of the mother, Feigele, who was both pretty and charming, and whose face always had a friendly expression. I could never forget the warmth with which I was welcomed as I stepped through the doorway, which gave me the feeling that I was really wanted. The house had been full of light and gladness, and the figure of Feigele is still etched in the memories of my childhood.

With the annihilation of the Jews of Eishishok, 10-year-old Itchele and his sister Sheindele, aged 6, were sent by their parents to a Polish acquaintance named Yuzik. He lived beyond the garden of the Chuchinsky family. Their father Moshe was to have returned from the town in order to fetch his wife Feigele and their baby, and then collect them, in order to escape from the town together.

At the same time, the Germans and the Lithuanians began to take the Jews out of their houses. Feigele, carrying a baby, could not escape and did not manage to hide, and so was taken together with her child, and with all the other Jews to the synagogue. Itchele and Sheindele, who had reached the house of Yuzik in the early evening, heard the shooting from the direction of the town. At the same time, Yuzik entered and said to them that the situation was bad, and that not far away, there were police who were looking for escaping Jews. He took them to another Christian named Yashke of Malishkevitz, who lived at the edge of the woods.

Sheindele wept bitterly throughout the night and demanded to go home. Her father Moshe succeeded in escaping from the town, and arrived at five o'clock in the morning, telling them that he did not know what had befallen his wife and baby. The Christian accompanied them until they passed the slaughter-house and Moshe begged him to do whatever he could to extricate his wife from the synagogue, and they crossed the river, entering the village of Leibednik in Byelorussian territory and stayed there for the night.

Fearing to keep them, the Christian advised them to hide, and so they left and reached Radun. When the refugees from Eishishok arrived in Radun, rumors went round that any refugees who were caught would be returned to Eishishok. Moshe Sonnenson, who had learned from experience that one should not ignore rumors, took his two children and fled to a nearby village by the name of Vasilishok, which was also outside Lithuanian control, and stayed with a Jewish acquaintance. The Jew demanded that Moshe go to the police to register, and when he did, he was arrested and sent to prison because he had come from Lithuania without an exit permit. Finally, as a result of pressure on the part of the Jew from Vasilishok, and a considerable bribe, he was released.

Feigele, who had been taken to the synagogue, and from there to the cattle market together with all the Jews of Eishishok, succeeded in escaping with her baby with the help of Zoshka, a Christian who had been their laundress. The latter entered the market and took them away, declaring that Feigele was her sister, and, within sight of the drunken Lithuanian guards, crossed the border. Shortly afterwards, one of the policemen became suspicious and started to pursue her. When Feigele realized the danger they were in, she threw the baby under a haystack alongside the road and hid herself under another haystack. Luckily, the baby did not cry and when the guard found no one there, he returned to his post. Feigele emerged from her hiding-place, took her baby, and reached Radun. When Moshe learned that his wife and child were safe in Radun, he took his other children and went off to Radun, and the family was united once again.

In her book *The Annals and Destruction of Eishishok*,[*] Sheindele tells how while they awaited their end, the baby suddenly started to cry. The mother tried to feed her but the poor baby would not calm down. One Jew said that she had to be 'quieted', and that the lives of 16 Jews were more precious than the life of one baby. When the mother froze and could not answer, the man threw some clothing over the baby and the crying ceased! They were all petrified and the mother fainted.

The Sonnenson family was in hiding for 26 months with various farmers in exchange for payment, and when they could no longer stay with the farmers, they took to the woods. They survived to see the defeat of Hitler, and had another child. But cruel fate had not yet finished with them. On returning to Eishishok, they were attacked by Polish partisans, the AK, who killed Feigele and her child. The partisans had

---

[*] Sheindele Sonnenson, *The Annals and Destruction of Eishishok* (Jerusalem, 1950).

succeeded in doing what the Germans had failed to do: 'to eliminate' another two Jewish souls from Polish soil already awash with Jewish blood.

Moshe was arrested in Russia at the end of the war for trying to take revenge for the Jewish blood that had spilled. He was condemned to ten years hard labor. Sheindele, the daughter, reached Palestine immediately after the war ended, together with her uncle, Shalom Sonnenson, who was a Palestinian citizen. Now called Jaffa Eliach, she is a professor of history and a founder-director of the Holocaust Center in Washington. She has published many important books, a number of which deal with the Holocaust.

Sheindele's brother reached Israel later, via Cyprus, together with Benjamin Rogovsky, in August 1947. He now lives in Haifa with his family. His father Moshe was freed from a Russian prison in 1956 after Itchele wrote to Malenkov, the Soviet head of government at the time, requesting his freedom.

Niomke Rogovsky was one of the few who dared to escape from the ghetto. Early on the Sabbath eve, he jumped out of the window and started to run through the woods, reaching the forests in the region of Mezanze and Karkodi.

Jossele Zelver, who was from a small Lithuanian town, had been a yeshiva student in Radun, and was well-known for the fine voice he used to intone the pages of the Talmud. He had also served in the Polish army, and in Radun he lived on his own, without a family. He escaped about half an hour before the gendarmes arrived from Lida. He ran across the fields from the end of Lida Street in a zigzagging fashion, and though the policemen and the Germans fired at him they did not pursue him as they were unwilling to leave their posts lest other Jews took the opportunity to escape as well.

Reb Maishel the Leibaver, Moshe Davidovitch, was also among the few who tried to escape with his entire family under cover of the night. On the Sabbath eve, when he was convinced that the Germans intended to eliminate the ghetto and its entire people, he took his wife Dvorele and his four children, Zelatka, Chaike, Liebele, and Estherke, and explained to them how they should behave. He showed them how to crawl on their stomachs until they were out of the danger zone. When they were at a distance of some tens of meters beyond the barn belonging to a Christian, there was a Polish policeman on duty, calling out 'Who goes there?' And when he received no reply, he fired some shots in their direction. Maishel began to run away as the shots were being fired. Zelatke was wounded by a bullet and fell. When Moshe saw that she was badly hurt, he shouted to the rest of his family to leave her where she was and to continue running. The policeman continued to shoot at them, and wounded Liebele in the leg. At that moment, Dvorele grasped the policeman by his hand and shouted at him 'we will pay'. The policeman's comment was 'a pity', but she paid the bribe she had prepared beforehand to deal with any unforeseen trouble.

Maishel continued running and ran smack into another policeman, who had heard the shots and was hurrying to see what was happening. The force of the impact of the collision brought the policeman to the ground and Maishel continued fleeing. A few minutes later, he heard four shots, which made him suspect that his wife and the three remaining children had been killed. Dvorele, together with her three children, were not aware of the fact that it was the policeman who had fallen, and thought that Moshe had been killed. They continued hurrying on their way through the forests of Mezanze, after paying the first policeman the ransom money. At the same time, Liebele ran all the way with her injured leg and only on the following day, managed to see to it. Maishel met up with them on the following day at the farm of one of their acquaintances in the area of Yewonza. They lived and hid in the woods and the forests of this region for 26 months.

Reb Moshe Davidovitch succeeded in saving his own skin and that of his family, and brought them to Israel. The daughters married, produced children and lived to see their grandchildren and great-grandchildren. Like the rest of the Jewish population of Radun, Reb Moshe was a keen observer of the precepts, and when they lived in the forest he struggled with his conscience and with the conditions there, in order to continue to observe them. His approach and philosophy towards everything that concerned his beliefs helped him to maintain his observance and live as a Jew even under the circumstances that prevailed in the forest.

Reb Moshe also immediately returned to the ghetto after the slaughter in order to register, for he believed that life in the ghetto was more secure than it was elsewhere, for the time being. But after a few days he escaped to the woods once again.

Jews who had fled from the ghetto of Radun continued to emerge from their hiding-places even after the deadline set by the Germans, and after the registration of those entitled to remain alive, as it were, for they did not know that the list was already closed. They were miserable to find that they were not included in the registration list and tried by means of bribery to get on to the list of those registered to live in the ghetto.

Those not included in the list were shot on the spot. On the day after the slaughter, we were ordered to appear for work, which seemed to indicate that we were indeed essential workers, and that our lives would therefore be secure. During the first few days our main task was to collect the bodies of the victims, which were strewn all over the town.

One group of Jewish workers was sent to cover the mass grave with earth, which only the previous day had been filled with hundreds of corpses of the Jews of Radun and the neighborhood. I began to work as a fitter and blacksmith, the profession I claimed when lying on the ground during the mass murder, and thanks to which I probably saved myself at a fateful moment, when a German asked me to identify myself. Since then I have always been very fond of this trade.

From my father Moshe David I learned many details about the first group that was taken to dig the mass grave in the morning of that fateful day. When they were given the order to turn off the road and go forward in the direction of the cemetery, father let out a shout 'Hurrah! Hurrah!' and a group of them who had conspired during their marching fell on the Germans and the police, attacking them with their shovels, and then ran off. The Germans and the police started to pursue them and were firing at them. Some of the group were killed on the spot, while others lay down on the ground and did not try to escape. The Germans joined them to the second group taken to dig the pit.

Only 17 men succeeded in getting away as a result of this revolt. Meirke, the smith, was a healthy and manly youth, who had reached Radun with the refugees from Eishishok. He worked and lived with Menashe Kovalsky. He was one of the leaders of the revolt, and fought with the commander of the gendarmes, who pursued him riding on his horse, while firing at him with his revolver. Meirke's only weapons were the stones he found on the way, which he flung at the horse and its rider, while racing across the woods. He succeeded in escaping to the forest and did not return to the ghetto. He was among the first to set up a Jewish partisan force to fight against the Germans.

Menashe Kovalsky, the father of Jankele, the Jewish policeman, owned a large smithy in Radun. He too was among those who revolted. He was badly wounded during the struggle and arrived in the nearby village of Popishok in a sorry state. The villagers refused to help him and handed him over to the Germans.

This uprising led to German suspicions of further attempts of this kind. They therefore tried to assemble all the young people still in the ghetto and announced that they were needed for special work in the ghetto of Lida. They also promised that they would receive better food and clothing there, and that those with families would afterwards be able to have their dependants join them.

On the basis of these lies, the Germans managed to placate the young people, and sent them to the ghetto of Lida. When they arrived there, however, they learned that young people were not missing from Lida, but that the Germans were assembling all the young people from neighboring towns in one place in order to keep an eye on them.

A few days had passed since the Jews were led to the pit in Radun that was dug by their brothers and sons. Those who were still alive, either by virtue of a miracle or the hand of fate, or who had found a hole into which it was possible to crawl like a hunted animal, were saved for the time being.

These same survivors, still in a state of shock, when awakening from their nightmare, came face to face with the threatening emptiness that prevailed all around. They began to understand what had happened to them, and what they could anticipate in the future. Nevertheless, only a few dared to leave the ghetto and try their luck elsewhere.

Some of them tried to hide with farmers whom they knew in the region, in exchange for payment, or valuables, or whatever useable clothing they still possessed. Some had transferred property to the farmers before entering the ghetto and tried now to get help from them.

Others went straight to the forest in groups of twos and threes. With whatever money or possessions they still had, they bought food and managed to maintain themselves in this way at first. And those who had escaped by the skin of their teeth had to live by begging and depended on the kindness of local farmers and former friends in order to receive some bread and sometimes milk and potatoes which was just enough to keep them alive.

Guarding the depleted ghetto was an easy matter. It was also comparatively easy to leave, but only a few individuals did so, for the simple reason that there was nowhere to go. Life outside the ghetto was even harder than in it, and the danger in the short run was greater. Few were willing to risk their lives by hiding in the forest.

13 The Escape from the Ghetto

On the third day after returning from the pit, where we had left our closest and dearest forever, we made up our minds to escape from the ghetto no matter what, for we were on our own. No one would be concerned about us and we had nothing to lose except our lives, which had little value at the time.

For all that, a spark of hope and encouragement entered our hearts with the thought that Father was still alive. We knew that he had been taken to dig the pit, and we also knew of the uprising. Also, we were aware that a number of men had managed to escape and as he had not been identified as one of the dead, it was possible that he was among them.

This prospect encouraged us to flee the ghetto and seek our freedom in the neighborhood of Dowgalishok where we had many friends and acquaintances among the local farmers. Thus, after work on Wednesday afternoon, we returned to what had been our house in the ghetto before the slaughter, and collected some silver items that had remained there. We hid them among the roof planks and beams, with the thought that they might come in handy in a moment of need. We made up a small parcel of our clothes and some dry bread we found on the premises to sustain us on the way. The prayer books were hidden in pockets close to our bodies in order not to lose them, in case we would have to discard the parcels while trying to escape.

Out of fear of the night, and the possibility of losing our way in the darkness, we left the ghetto while it was still light, though the sun was well on its way westward. We crossed the marketplace and made our way along the street of the pigs.

We passed the post office, penetrated some 200 meters further, and there beyond the houses were the meadows.

At that moment, we encountered a Polish policeman from Radun who recognized us as Jews and led us away to the Germans. It was clear that these were our last minutes. Run, we said to ourselves, run as fast as you can, for there was nothing to lose. Another thought that entered our minds at that moment was that there was no reason to escape, as we had lost all that was dear to us and we wondered whether we should try to save our own lives. We almost envied those saintly men who had lost their lives as martyrs.

On our way to the German headquarters, and still being led by the Pole, we met up with another Pole who happened to have known my parents. While greeting us, he turned to our captor and said: 'Let them go, I know their father, who is a good Jew. In any case, they are goners!' The last words were the most convincing, not only to the policeman but also to us, for we knew that our fate was ordained. We merely did not know when the sentence would be carried out.

The policeman took our papers, lest we try to escape and hide in the ghetto, and brought us to the Polish police, handing us over to the man in charge. The two of them discussed whether to deliver us up to the Germans or to let us go. They took our papers, gave us a few kicks in the ass as if we were stray dogs, and threw us out with the warning that we should not try to escape again. Our documents were not returned to us, though they were aware that anyone caught without them would be shot, evidently thinking that they could extract a sum of money from us or at least receive something for their generous spirit.

So we ran off back to the ghetto. We looked for a house in which some Jews still remained, to crowd in amongst them like errant and frightened sheep. In the narrow and unpaved lane of Jacob Moshe (Yankel Moshe, the soda-maker), in the house of Haimke Pik, the carpenter's father, we found some Jews who had survived. We sought out a corner of a room, and put our heads down on our poor belongings.

Wearied by the drama of the past few days, shaken and confused, shocked and frightened by what had just happened, we were also without the documents needed to remain alive. We pondered over the profound loss we had witnessed and feared what awaited us on the morrow. To mourn and weep over our parents and the rest of the family who had been murdered was no longer possible, for the source of our tears had dried up. We were left with our prayer books and the psalms and poured out our hearts in prayers and pleas before the Creator. These were the pure and sincere prayers of lonely and abandoned children: prayers that could rend the heavens apart. The skies remained frozen and unhearing, giving no sign or response. Our prayers returned as they had gone out, penetrating straight into our frozen hearts, which had now thawed and the tears began to flow. We spoke to and about ourselves; looked at one another, and saw that no one was listening.

Like a streak of lightning, an inner voice accompanied by some hidden force took hold of us for a moment and delivered us from the wasteland of the valley of death, and we decided to flee again at once. Like two shadows, we stole out of the ghetto and the town, without giving a thought to what might occur or whether we would be caught again. Fear and anxiety seemed to have vanished and we were now in the hands of fate.

Our second escape plan was different. This time we went down the slope of Lida Street, making our way directly towards the marshes and the river. The nearer we approached the town's environs, the stronger the beating of our hearts, but as we moved further from the town, our pace gained ground.

The sun sinking in the west was on our left and the loathsome town of Radun was slowly left behind. We did not dare to look back, lest we be punished like Lot's wife. For two hours, we trampled through the marshes, the same marshes that would be covered in yellow flowers in the springtime, where we would gather bouquets of flowers to take home with us.

The sun set slowly and it was twilight when we reached the village of Mozaika, the same village we would pass through *en route* to our beloved Dowgalishok, at times on foot and at other times on a horse-drawn wagon. Now we did not dare take the highway and we made a detour around the village and went through fields and bushes. From time to time, we would stop and take in our surroundings, and sit amongst the bushes to rest a while. We kept a sharp watch in every direction, our ears were attuned to the slightest rustle. We read a few psalms and finished with the prayer for the road.

We reached Dowgalishok in the early hours of the night, unconsciously, without knowing why or wherefore. Our legs had carried us along roads and lanes to which they were accustomed for many years, ever since our sweet and happy childhood. On entering Dowgalishok, we awoke from our dreaming state and stopped. A shudder ran through my body while holding my brother's hand, as we realized that it was dangerous to enter the village, in case we should encounter the inheritors of our former home and property who might attack us and try to kill us. We observed the sleeping village with affection but also fear. We made a detour around it in the direction of a neighboring village: Pitzeluntze.

Like a calf trailing after a cow, I followed in my brother's footsteps through plowed fields and woods, without knowing where he was leading us and where we would land. This was the first time I encountered a misty night in a hostile neighborhood. Every rustling leaf would frighten me, every tree took on the aspect of a man, and every bush seemed to be a beast of prey. In my fevered imagination, a branch swaying in the wind appeared to be devilish spirits, such as those described in fairy-tales. My thoughts went for a moment to the edge of the forest of Dowgalishok, to the night-watches in Father's company, when I accompanied him to guard the entry to the town from possible thieves and robbers, who had greatly increased during the period between the overnight collapse of the Polish regime and the as yet impermanent establishment of the Soviet authorities. This short experience, though undergone under Father's wing, as it were, now came to my aid and gave me the courage to overcome my fear. Now I was under the protection of my brother, who seemed to me to have grown older than his years, for he fulfilled the role of both father and mother to me. Without him I would have been lost; without him I could not have survived our first evening. My brother, who noted my lack of knowledge of the area, as well as my lack of confidence, treated me with fatherly concern, showing no signs of fear whatsoever and marching ahead confidently along the vaguely discerned and dusty lanes as if they were paved roads.

After a long and tiring trek, we finally came to a lonely house standing in the midst of a field. We stopped and looked around for a few minutes and heeded every sound for possible suspicious noises and quietly approached the house. We knocked at the door gently and waited with baited breath for someone to answer.

The door opened slowly and I instinctively moved back, while Pinchas took his courage in his hands and approached the farmer who stood in the doorway. He greeted him with 'a good evening' as was the custom, and started to talk to him. I came closer and listened to the conversation. At this point, we learned that our father was still alive and that he had visited this farmer two days earlier.

'I do not know when he will come again,' the farmer said. He suggested we go and spend the night in the barn, and sleep on the straw. However, he said we must leave before dawn for the nearby woods without being seen and hide there for the rest of the day. He also promised to try to let us know where father was and that he would inform him that we were alive. Exhausted and weary, we lay down on the straw as if it were the softest eiderdown, but aware of every sound and barking dog we were unable to fall asleep. We were afraid that we might have been followed. The happy news that Father was alive was immensely exciting, and we were impatient to see him and be certain that it was really true. The mere thought of him was encouraging and gave us new hope and desire to continue living.

Dozing rather than sleeping, the thoughts of what we had experienced raced through our minds: the pit which had claimed life and death; the abandoned streets of the ghetto with the shades of death dancing in every corner; Mother's lovely features when sadness overtook them; and her last words: 'Let us say "Hear, O Israel" and die like Jews.' I brought to mind the face of my little brother Kushka, with his chubby, rosy cheeks and his bright, innocent eyes; the young girl fighting to protect her honor on the rim of the pit, unwilling to be undressed and reveal her nakedness; the masses of Jews gathered together, with bowed heads who knew what awaited them.

The news that Father was alive centered my thoughts on the future instead of the past. I would tell him what we had experienced since he was taken from us, and how we were saved – and how I was saved! I imagined how happy he would be to learn that at least two of his children were alive. We would no longer be forsaken and he would be proud of us, of our courage in daring to escape and find our way to him. Was it not for this reason that we had been saved? And in our hearts there was the silent gratitude that at least some of the family remained.

The events of the past flowed through my mind to the days of my childhood and the home that no longer was there. Everything had been cut off so suddenly. I had been orphaned in one moment from a beloved mother who had worked so hard and wearily for our sakes in the days when we were alone and without Father. Her whole life had been centered on her children: their education, their clothing and their spiritual values. Alas, even in saying kaddish for her, I cannot repay her.

Dear God, have pity on us and keep watch over Father,

that no harm should come to him. With your great compassion, see to it that we meet very soon and that we should no longer be lonely and abandoned, for we have already lost our mother and our brother! A single lonely tear rolled down my cheek. I licked it and swallowed it.

It was a long night, unwilling to end, and I thought perhaps it would be better were it not to end. For who could tell what the day would bring. How would the forest receive us and where could we hide? These were but two of the frightening questions that troubled us.

Through the chinks in the walls of the barn, I managed to get a glimpse of the clear and unclouded sky. The stars slowly disappeared from the infinite expanse, but the dawn was yet to come. We crept out quietly to the nearby woods in order to find a hiding-place for the day. At night, the darkness was frightening, but we also feared the daylight, lest we should be discovered.

Not far from the edge of the woods, which bordered on to a ploughed field, we found a natural cover beneath the branches of an ancient tree. Its long branches and thick foliage were bent right down to the ground by their weight and spread out to form a protective shelter. We slipped under the branches, which served as a natural hideout, and all we could see was the sky moving between the branches.

In the not too distant past, we had used the branches of the fir trees as covering for the *Sukkah** during the Feast of Tabernacles, in memory of the tribes of Israel dwelling in their booths during their flight from Egypt. I recalled the decorated *Sukkah*, with everyone in holiday garb, and the intoxicating odors of food being served on the festive china reserved for holidays and the Sabbath.

And now, had we fled from Egypt? Now that we had escaped from our pursuers and persecutors, where were Moses and Aaron? Where was Aaron's rod and why did those same miracles not occur now, for whom were these signs and wonders intended? Now the branches of the fir trees were serving as our cover, protecting us from our pursuers and persecutors, hiding us from the daylight and from both people and God.

We lay beneath the trees and did not move throughout the day. The prayer book, which also contained the Psalms, was our salvation, for the saying of prayers and portions of the Psalms dispelled the depressing loneliness to a certain extent. The recitation of the Psalms with all one's heart and soul, followed by an endless flow of tears, was sustenance in those days. We were not hungry as yet, for we were sated with tears and loss, sorrow and fear. And so our first day in the forest passed, the fifth day of the week, and five days since we left Mother and our brother, and the rest of the Jews of Radun, in the pit dug by Jews of Radun – my brother Pinchas among them.

Towards evening, we came closer to the edge of the forest, from which we could see the house and courtyard of the farmer. Stretched out on the ground and hidden by the branches, we watched people coming and going and what was happening in the courtyard. As it was getting dark, when the farmer was herding his cattle and sheep into their pens, we quietly stole over to him and asked him if there was any news of Father. His reply that he still hadn't made contact with him was disappointing and it saddened us immensely that Father still did not know that we had survived and would undoubtedly be troubled about the fate of his family. From this conversation with the farmer, we learned that there were other Jews from Dowgalishok who had succeeded in escaping from the ghetto and that they were wandering about in that neighborhood. At the same time, he warned us against an armed Russian who was also roaming about in the area and who killed whoever he came across, including Jews, and added that he chased after a Jew from Dowgalishok and shot him. This story naturally added to our fears.

14 The First Days in the Forest

During the next few days we began slowly to emerge from our hideaway and to acquaint ourselves with the forest and its environs. For many a day we wandered alone in the woods. For ten days and ten nights, we did not meet a soul. We lived on dry bread and some bottled water, and our prayers.

Having no choice, and out of a sense that the forest was actually our only true friend and protector, we became accustomed to this new situation and familiar with the secrets of the forest. We learned the language of the trees swaying in the wind and seemingly conversing with one another, or praising the Almighty in song. We learned to listen to the rustle of the branches and the secretive murmuring of the leaves. Our fears were somewhat quieted and our self-confidence increased amidst these woods.

As permanent dwellers in the forest, we began to know and sense our immediate neighbors, the biting horseflies and the blood-sucking mosquitoes. It appeared as if all the insects of the forest were united in an offensive war against us; the ants creeping up and invading our clothing, reaching every hidden crevice in our bodies. The troublesome horseflies left us no peace while the mosquitoes bit our eyelids and the lobes of our ears, leaving no exposed spot on our bodies neglected. They even penetrated into our ears, buzzing and revealing their secrets. This war of the few against the many was a lost cause and we were bitten everywhere, in every exposed and hidden area all over our bodies. We were swollen from the bites and exhausted by the insects' offensive against us.

Like two rabbits, we lay under the trees with our ears anticipating every sound, and our eyes fixed on the horizon in every direction in order to pinpoint any imminent danger in time. The hours of waiting for the evening were long and drawn-out, and the days became like years, not wanting to come to an end. One's imagination began to flourish, imagining all kinds of horrors, such as that something had happened to Father, or suspicions regarding the farmer's integrity and that perhaps he was hiding something from us and plotting against us.

Looking forward to meeting Father now occupied all our thoughts. Throughout the day, we waited impatiently for the evening in order to hear some news from the farmer about him. Out of caution and a certain degree of suspicion, we stopped visiting the farmer every evening and changed the times of our visits altogether. We also started to visit other farmers who had been friends of the family, particularly those who had been Father's friends in the past.

Early every morning, we would thoroughly search the area from our look-out, to see whether there were any strangers about, or whether Germans or policemen were in the vicinity. At nightfall, we would carefully approach a house, trying not to arouse the dogs with their sharp teeth. We would tap on the door or window lightly. My brother, as spokesman, would introduce us as the sons of Moshe the blacksmith and ask if Father had perhaps visited there by chance. Thus he would inform them that Father was still alive and ask them to tell him, should they encounter him, that his two children were looking for him. These farmers who had been Father's friends would give us bread and milk still warm from the cow, and also bread for the following day.

The neighborhood did not have an abundance of virgin forest. It was a rural area with poor, sandy soil, and the main crops were potatoes, rye, barley, and oats. The area had been covered with pine and birch trees, but in the course of time, parts of the forests had been converted into agricultural land, so that every village was encircled by woods or forest.

The natural roots of every village lay in the forest. Immediately after the thawing of the snow and the first signs of spring, the herds of cattle and sheep, accompanied by a shepherd, would graze in the woods throughout the long day. There was not a single spot or part of the forest that was not familiar to the shepherds and their charges.

The houses of the village were built of wooden beams hewn from the trees of the forest, and the roofs were mainly covered with straw. Some had wooden tiles. These wooden houses with their roofs of straw were easily set on fire, and frequently fires broke out which burned entire villages to the ground. These conflagrations were mostly due to the use of fire for domestic purposes, for cooking and heating, as well as for lighting. But quite a few of them were deliberate: the result of enmity between neighbors.

In more recent times, colonies of single houses were set up, each with its own plot of land. Generally, these houses would be built at the edge of a forest or wood. They were dispersed and at quite a distance from one another, unlike a village where all the houses were concentrated in one area. The reason for this may have been to prevent the spreading of fire from one house to another.

After a week and a half, some ten whole days since we stole into farmer's barn during the night, Father appeared, having waited in the barn to greet us. We gazed on his face as we would on that of an angel, for we could not believe our eyes. We fell into one anothers' arms with kisses and caresses and wept and wept, crying like children who had held back their tears.

Father also wept. This was the first time we had seen him cry. We were witnessing an outburst of joy, bereavement, and happiness. But the moments of joy were short-lived, the agonizing moments of happiness dissolved quickly with the dreadful message we had to convey. Our very existence without Mother and our little brother Yekutiel revealed that they had remained behind and that we would never see them again.

Father did not ask after them or where they were, as if everything was clear and self-evident, and how this had happened was set aside and postponed for a few minutes to enable the happy meeting to exist for the moment. We did not take our eyes off one another, and gazed with surprise and amazement at what we were taking in. Was it really true, or perhaps we were seeing things or daydreaming. My compassion was stirred by the sight of our father, a strong man built like a rock, succumbing to his feelings and weeping out of sorrow or happiness, or both.

In honor of Father's arrival and our meeting, the farmer had prepared a hot meal for us: a feast for kings. Potatoes cooked with a great deal of salt, and swimming in onion and dill. The appetizing aroma wafted across the entire courtyard, penetrating into the haystack and our nostrils. The stew was served in unlimited quantities, together with bread and butter. Fresh, sweet milk, taken straight from the cow, and homemade sour-milk, were also brought to the table. The meal reminded us of the days at home in Dowgalishok, but now we dared not even dream about them.

We talked for most of the night, telling Father about all our experiences from the Sunday when we were taken in the early hours of the morning to dig the pit. We were curious as to how he had survived, and if there were other survivors. He told us that when the group was approaching the cemetery, on turning off the highway, he shouted 'hurrah, hurrah', at which point, the men fell on the Germans and the policemen with their shovels and with stones and then ran off. He was able to flee too, and went directly to the neighborhood of Dowgalishok.

With sunrise, we went to the forest with Father, wandering around looking for hiding-places in the woods and among the trees. At the end of the day, when the night was falling, he took us to farmer friends and acquaintances, and introduced us to them while informing them that we were all he had left of a family. He had a dual purpose in doing this: firstly he wanted us to get to know these friendly farmers, so that we could ask for help when it was needed, or food and clothing, or a place to spend the night; and secondly, to examine the possibility of hiding in their homes in exchange for payment.

They welcomed us in a friendly manner and even promised him to help us and provide us with necessities whenever we asked for them. None of them, however, would let us hide in their homes or on their land, for they feared that someone might inform the Germans. The fate of a Christian family giving refuge to Jews was determined in advance – all the property and the home and family was destroyed by fire.

Astonished, and with an intense disappointment that was difficult to bear, I listened to Father's decision that we had to separate. He had reached the conclusion that it would be better that he should go about on his own while we two remain together. 'But,' we cried out, 'we do not know the farmers and they do not know us, and we are afraid to stay in the forest without you. The dark nights in the forest put the fear of God into us, and wandering through the open fields, seeking pathways and going astray along the unfamiliar lanes is frightening, not to speak of the barking dogs, with their snarling and showing their sharp teeth whenever we approach the house of a farmer to ask for a crust of bread. We're just not ready to part from you. We don't want to be alone and we don't want to live without you.'

Father tried to explain the reasons for his decision: 'I intend looking for places to hide among the farmers, and I will have difficulty in finding one who will agree to hide all three of us. For each of us separately, however, I may succeed in finding a hideaway.' He added, 'There is greater danger if we stay together, we can be wiped out in one blow. But if we separate, and the gentiles know that I am alive and am staying in a specific place, they will not dare to harm you, nor inform on us to the Germans, for fear of my revenge if they do so and your revenge if I am harmed.'

The weapon available to us was fire. Even the most anti-Semitic gentiles feared this. One match and an entire household would go up in flames. This longstanding fear came to our assistance when we needed a crust of bread from a gentile unwilling to give it.

Father's decision was hard to take, and painful. Even his rational and convincing arguments did not reduce the disappointment at the fact that we would not be together. I could not understand his reasons. At the very time we had succeeded in evading death and had lost our mother and brother, we were to separate.

I did not try to change his mind or make his life difficult by pleas and crying, for I was ashamed to display my cowardice, and also, because in my heart of hearts I accepted his decision. However, the memory of that disappointment has never been erased, and I can recall it to this day.

15 Life in the Forest

On leaving behind the deserted ghetto and the blood-stained, bereaved Jewish town, the first few days were spent together with my brother Pinchas on the edge of the forest near the grounds of the farmer Shamashke. We were still in a state of shock from all that we had witnessed. We still lived under the impact of the mass murder of the Jews of our town; still seeing the huge pit of death devouring the living and the dead. We lived still in the shadows of the threatening and frightening scene of the vacant ghetto, of an entire town bereft of life. And we still lived with the trauma caused by the loss of our loved ones.

The meeting with Father strengthened our desire to live, as well as helping us to be prepared to fight for our lives. However, I was afraid. How was one to live without Father or Mother, or without a home and family? What would I eat and drink; what would I wear? Where would I sleep and lay down my head? Today, tomorrow, and the day after – what would they bring? Was the suffering and loneliness that I was undergoing a form of punishment, a Job-like infliction? Why had I fled and left the family behind?

No! This was the answer to Mother's prayers that at least a remnant of the family should survive. Perhaps it was due to her that we would be protected. I had survived and was honor-bound to fulfil her bequest: 'that a remnant of the family must survive'. It could not get worse, but heaven forbid that we should be caught alive! We must flee and even get shot in the back, rather than be caught.

Those were the early summer days of the end of May 1942, and the weather was already summery, making it easy to acclimatize to the life of the forest. Above our heads, there were the long and densely foliated branches of the fir tree bowing down to the ground, protecting us from the rain, the wind, and the sun. Our mattresses were the pine needles that had fallen to the ground and the soft branches of the fir tree were our blankets.

With nightfall, when all the farmers of the neighborhood were getting ready to go to bed, we would go out to look for prey. Instead of saying our prayers before going to bed and bidding Mother and Father good night, we said the prayer for the road before going out to visit the farmers to ask for a crust of bread for the following day. And if we returned safely to our hideaway before dawn, Mother was not awaiting us with a 'good morning' and we were absolved of the need to say: 'I give thanks to thee, O living and eternal king, who has restored my soul to me in mercy: great is thy faithfulness.' Many of the prayers and precepts we had been taught and observed from childhood on were now discarded, for they were part of another world.

It took a great deal of self-inducement to accept the injunction to begin 'a new life' within the forest without Father's protective wing and in the shadow and warmth of my big brother Pinchas. There were two and a half years between us, but it seemed to me much more than that. We decided on the times and places where we would meet up with Father, and he would give us news of what was happening in the area and advise us as to where we could get food and which farmers were friendly and which dangerous. He trained us to live as creatures of the forest. He taught us how to approach the farmers: how to talk to them and ask for food. He forced us to behave independently, without relying on him.

My brother was charged with every difficult or dangerous mission, for he was quick to grasp things as well as nimble on his feet. He had an uncanny knowledge of the region and knew every road and lane. I was very attached to him, adoring and admiring his personality. I had long forgotten those days when he was given to hitting me and tried to get rid of me by means of his whip, and I would not return his blows, despite the fact that I was strong and healthy while he was weak and pampered. (He had been pampered because he was sickly, and also perhaps because he was the first child to survive after two other children had died before I was born.) I forgave him for the blows of the past and I would often say to him: 'If, heaven forbid, one of us must die, I prefer that it should be me, for I could not live without you in any case, and you have a chance to survive. Otherwise we are both doomed.'

Having no choice, I resigned myself to the way we lived, every day producing a different mode of existence, which also changed our view of ourselves. Our customs and habits altered, and we became different creatures in the arms of nature and these surroundings; creatures walking on two legs resembling humans.

In the course of time, the forest became our source of maintenance, and we, in turn, became part of the landscape. We found places to hide and ways of escaping. We discovered clearings and dense growths. Little by little, we became accustomed to life in the forest, discerning the various voices of the wood and noting the trails left by the animals of the forest. We not only changed our habits but also our ways of thinking. But we did not succeed in changing our skins, nor did we grow horns or were our teeth sharpened, and winter pelts remained the domain of the animals. In this respect, we were inferior to them.

We learned from the local farmers that some Jews from Dowgalishok who had succeeded in fleeing from the ghetto were wandering around in the forest. We tried very hard to pinpoint their whereabouts and after some weeks, we managed to meet up with some of them. They told us that in fact the majority of Jews from Dowgalishok had succeeded in escaping with their families.

We would get together in the forest, generally on Friday or Saturday nights. For reasons of security, we did not meet regularly, nor were we aware of one another's hideouts. At these meetings, we would exchange news and advice. Some hid in the houses of farmers, and from time to time, they would leave their hiding-places in order find out what was happening outside or to transfer goods or valuables from one farmer to another.

Even before we had become accustomed to life in the forest, we heard that the Radun ghetto had been razed to the ground and the remaining Jews were moved to the ghetto of Lida. We began to wonder if we had done the right thing by fleeing to the forest. We thought that perhaps in the Lida ghetto, in a big city with a large Jewish population, we could have lived like the other Jews, as long as this was possible.

The approaching winter aroused all sorts of fears. We were aware of the fact that the war would not end by then, and we did not know how we would fare when the winter set in, or indeed how we were to exist until then, for we could no longer return to the ghetto. Anticipating the winter was very alarming, for the temperature could easily reach 20 to 30 degrees below zero. One could freeze to death while merely sitting or sleeping, and the footprints we would leave in the snow when we went out on forays to get food or to wash ourselves would reveal our existence and location in the neighborhood. We could then be collected like stray dogs.

In moments of despair, we almost decided to return to the ghetto without Father. He too was helpless in this situation, for on the one hand he could not take on the responsibility of maintaining us during the winter, and on the other, he would not advise us to return to the ghetto. As for himself, he stated quite explicitly that he would on no account return to the ghetto. His decision and the freedom we had experienced in the forest, stopped us from returning to the ghetto. Rivka Rudnitzky, the daughter of Reb Kaddish, also fled from the Lida ghetto and returned to the forest, which supported and strengthened our determination to stay there. Rivka and her younger sister Nomka succeeded in escaping to the forest from the slaughter in Radun, but when life in the forest became too much for Rivka she returned to the ghetto in Lida in mid-summer. Towards the end of the summer, however, when life in the Lida ghetto hung by a thread and became unbearable she again fled to the forest. Finally, however, both girls disappeared in the forest, and no one knew what had happened to them. We could only guess at their fate.

In the meantime, we began to seek advice and to make plans for the winter. We prepared for the coming winter by digging ditches in various hidden corners of the forest as well as storing food for the winter months, or at least for some months to come. While we were planning the underground bunkers, Father was going from farmer to farmer to look for hiding-places with friendly farmers in exchange for payment or goods that we had left in keeping with farmers before our expulsion from the Radun ghetto. In any event, we made arrangements to dig a hidden hole in the forest, to be used for any emergency.

After the Jews of Radun were transferred to the Lida ghetto and the ghetto of Sch'uchin, the police and the Germans in Radun were free to look for Jews who had escaped to the forest and the villages. Every day we would hear of instances of murder, searches, and the scouring of different forests. This situation made our daily life troublesome, for even the friendly farmers were afraid of hiding a Jew or offering food. At the same time, there was also more informing as to the whereabouts of Jews in the region as well as informing on farmers who gave the Jews refuge. The shepherds became the most dangerous enemies, because it was almost impossible to hide from them. They were everywhere, and a whisper from a shepherd to the effect that he had seen Jews was enough to prompt the Germans to search the area. We were obliged to look for places where the shepherds did not venture with their herds. Such places were hard to find, for the shepherds wandered from place to place, and as a result, we had to do the same.

The hunting for Jews in hiding intensified, and we were unable to find a safe corner in the forest. We would have to disappear from the area and avoid the sunshine and the open skies of the Almighty. The only solution was 'to bury oneself alive', that is, to hide under the earth. We found a spot between shrubs and low trees in which to dig a hole – a tiny sparse part of the forest where there was no pasture and where the shepherds did not go. It was an open space, and it would not have occurred to the Germans or anyone else that it had been chosen by Jews to hide in.

We spent many a night digging the hole. The displaced earth was distributed far from the site in order not to arouse suspicions. The entrance to the dugout was very narrow and we could only enter it by crawling in on our stomachs. It was no more than half a meter in depth (we could not dig deeper because the ground water was near the surface of the earth). In width, it could take three people lying on their backs, who with difficulty could bend their knees or move their limbs. We closed the entrance and camouflaged it with a young tree, dragging it by its roots to the mouth of the entrance when we were crawling inside. We spent more than two months in this hole. We would stay there throughout the day, and with nightfall, we would come out cautiously, stretching our limbs. Like fieldmice and moles, we lay in the dark and damp hole and envied those creatures for having more spacious and comfortable 'bedrooms', and better means of escape.

We were pleased with our 'home' and prayed that it would not occur to a farmer to enter our domain to look for trees or mushrooms, and so discover our existence. We were always plagued by doubts and fears lest someone should come across us without our being aware of it and we could be finished off and buried alive by someone blocking up the entrance. Our major problem was cleanliness and the performance of our needs. We became used to refraining from bowel movements during the day, and for urinating, we equipped ourselves with bottles. In the course of time, we learned how to control ourselves to quite an extraordinary degree, which for a person living under normal conditions would have been impossible.

Our nights turned into days, and the longer the hours of the night, the happier and more secure we felt. Like that of the animals, our senses of sight and hearing became sharper. The same applied to our sense of smell and touch. During the long summer days, as we lay in the dark and dank graves for the living, our minds were pursued by thoughts of the events we had experienced, and which were undoubtedly still going on, leaving us little peace of mind. So we lay: daydreaming and occasionally dozing off, during the seemingly endless hours.

During that time, I found some encouragement and support in the many dreams that visited me in my sleep. After days of despair and depression, I would often dream about the rabbis who taught me at the small yeshiva, and especially Rabbi Mordecai Baer, head of the small yeshiva, who I admired so much. They would come and converse with me, putting their hands on my shoulder and encouraging me, inspiring me with a feeling of hope and belief in the days to come. After every dream of this kind, I would awaken as fresh as if I had been reborn. For a moment, it was difficult to believe that I was lying in a dark hole in the earth.

These dreams were a source of tremendous spiritual sustenance. I believed in them and wanted to believe in them, for they were dreams of love and affection. It was seldom that Mother appeared in my dreams, though I wanted so much to see her and talk to her, even in a dream. When she did appear, she would not weep and be sad, but seemed to be listening to my conversation with the rabbis, and she was pleased with me. On waking, I was comforted by the encounter. I lived in the belief that that day and those that followed would be peaceful and untroubled. The dreams and their visions stayed with me for many years, accompanying and illuminating my darkened path, at times lasting until the appearance of an another dream.

Once I dreamed that I had had a tooth extracted and I awoke with fear in my heart. I did not tell the dream to my brother, but I began to be afraid and there was some justification for my anguish. Not many days passed when a terrible catastrophe occurred: a number of Jews were caught and killed in the forest. I do not know whether my dream had warned me of what was to occur, for the number of cases of murder and slaughter in those days was greater than the extent of my dreams.

With the setting of the sun, we would revive and go on our way to get some food for the morrow. And if it were feasible, we would approach a friendly farmer to get some news of the area, and to check whether there had been rumors concerning our existence in the neighborhood. We always tried to hide our whereabouts from everyone, and if we thought that anyone was aware of where we were hiding, we would immediately change our location. For the same reason, we were obliged to get our food from great distances, lest our hideout become known. This secrecy concerning our hideouts was kept religiously among the Jews, so that if one of us was caught, that person could not lead the Germans to other hideouts under the pressure of the cruel torture the Germans imposed on them. A number of Jews vanished in this way without anyone knowing how or who was responsible. It was also possible that those very farmers who had originally given them refuge killed them, and when the Jews no longer had any money or property to pay for their being kept in hiding, they murdered them.

Our belief and devotion to the teachings of the Almighty was not affected, and we tried to observe both the simple and difficult precepts. In order to maintain our *kashrut,** we existed during the early months of the summer on bread, water, and potatoes. Later on, we permitted ourselves milk and dairy products. As we ate only the latter, we had a constant argument with Father over the eating of meat, for he claimed that it was perfectly proper to eat anything that would keep us alive, even pork, for it was filling and provided energy, and could be kept in an edible condition in the forest for days on end. This was not the case with dairy products, which went bad and soured quickly, and in order to be able to exist on them, we had to go out to the farmers every evening and thus place ourselves in danger.

For many months, we roved around the forests in the neighborhood of Dowgalishok. Every night, like rats slipping out of their holes, we would emerge into the open country in order to get food. The situation became worse from day to day because the Germans had instilled such fear amongst the gentiles lest they assisted or offered refuge to Jews. Whoever was caught disobeying these orders would have all their property expropriated and they and their families would be shot. On the other hand, whoever caught a Jew and handed the Jew over to the Germans would receive a large reward. Thus farmers who were prepared to help us were frightened to do so. They were afraid for themselves and their families, as well as wary of their treacherous neighbors. Differences and enmities between neighbors were exploited to spread rumors that so-and-so was giving food to the Jews, or that another was hiding a Jew for payment. The atmosphere among the inhabitants was poisonous: they suspected one another, friend and brother alike. These were the circumstances under which we would steal up to the doors and windows of farmers, asking for a crust of bread. We had first to make sure that there were no strangers in the house, carelessness on our part would not only put us in jeopardy but could also result in the death of the farmer. Other farmers would be afraid and hesitate to come into contact with us.

Despite all this, and the general fear that hovered over the region, many farmers who had been friends in the past, managed to overcome their fears and help us out with food and advice. More than once, they endangered themselves in the process.

In the summer months our situation deteriorated even further and it seemed that there was no place for us. With the declining conditions in the Radun ghetto, there were attempts to escape from the ghetto into the forest and a number of Jews reached the forest in which we were hiding. These Jews who had recently escaped from the ghetto had still to learn how to exist among the farmers without being seen or attract attention, and without placing those farmers whom they approached for help in jeopardy. The rumors that there were Jews in our area reached the ears of the Germans, and police units and German soldiers began to visit these villages more frequently – the same villages where we requested food. The danger involved in seeking food increased on all sides, and Father, sensing the danger, made every effort to find hiding-places for us among friendly farmers in exchange for payment.

16 In the Stall and Pig Pen of Kaj'uk

On the highway leading from Dowgalishok to Radun, at a distance of a kilometer and a half from Dowgalishok, was a farm belonging to an elderly couple. Their grown-up children had left the place many years before, and only the youngest son, Kaj'uk, remained with his parents. Kaj'uk, a bachelor in his early twenties, knew Father from early childhood, when he would visit our smithy with his father to shoe the horses or to repair a plough. The friendship grew stronger when the running of the farm fell on Kaj'uk's shoulders and quite often he would need Father's help in fixing agricultural implements. Though he was not always able to pay for these services, Father would not let him go away without doing what was necessary, out of a sense of neighborliness. Being a bachelor, and having an eye for the girls, he was always out of pocket, and the limited payment he would receive for his produce would be spent on drinking spirits on Sundays. Now that he had the opportunity of laying his hands on a dowry of money and goods in exchange for providing a modest corner in the attic of the barn or the pig pen, he could not withstand the temptation and refuse the generous offer. At that moment, the thought of possible dangers did not enter his mind.

Without informing his parents or other members of the household, Kaj'uk agreed to provide cover for three people: my brother and myself, and a young boy of our age, Haim Paikovsky, the son of Meir the carpenter and the grandson of Joshe Luja, the builder from Dowgalishok. Father did not join us, in accordance with his principle that we should not live together.

The place Kaj'uk assigned us was in a building used as a

cow shed, stables, and pig pen. Under this one roof, the cows and horses, the goats and the chickens all lived together in harmony. And now human beings were added who had been created in God's image. The pigs, which smelt rather strong, were fortunately housed in a separate pen. We were situated on the middle storey, in that part of the building which was above the cows, and was used for keeping straw, the horse blankets and saddlery, and for storing hay.

As agreed with Kaj'uk in advance, we sneaked into the middle storey where we hid among the stacks of straw and hay. Kaj'uk was to bring us food when he could manage to pinch some from the kitchen.

Only yesterday we had been lying in the dank earth and now we were 'riding high', but there was a drawback. We would lie for hours on end, for days and nights, listening to every sound and rustle, while the barking of a dog would freeze our blood. Every movement in the courtyard or the nearby road would stimulate our imagination to believe that now they were coming to get us.

Lying enclosed like birds in a cage, we waited for Kaj'uk to bring us food and water. Generally, when there were no mishaps, he would bring us food during the twilight hours or the small hours of the night. The food was dry and insufficient, as it was stolen from the kitchen and brought to us secretly. We had to beware lest the shepherd should see us when he came to take the herd out to pasture or when he returned from the fields. Similarly, we would hold our breath when Kaj'uk's old mother would come to milk the cows. We learned to lie absolutely still without moving a muscle and we learned to restrain our coughing and sneezing; pinching our noses until the tears came lest we sneeze, and holding our breath in order not to cough. We developed all sorts of methods to control our natural needs.

Nor did we trust Kaj'uk entirely, for he was young and liked to drink, and we doubted his sense of responsibility. As he was doing this for money, we suspected that he was capable of handing us over to the Germans for a reward.

There was a certain amount of security, however, in the fact that Father was not staying with us and therefore Kaj'uk would not dare to harm us as he would fear Father's revenge.

My father, Moshe David the blacksmith, was known among the farmers as a proud and honest man, courageous and no coward. In better times, no one would have dared to injure him, knowing that he would repay them in kind. In the summer of 1939, on a Sunday, the gentile Sabbath, a group of young hoodlums in Dowgalishok, bought vodka in one of the Jewish shops, got as drunk as Lot, and started to run wild in the town. They came from a neighboring area and knew the Jews of Dowgalishok well. The first to be assaulted were the yeshiva students of Radun, who were not exactly known for their bravery or heroism, and usually struck dumb with fear of the gentiles.

During some rioting in the village, a few of the hoodlums tried to break some windows. By chance, Father was standing with a group of farmers who had come to discuss business affairs with him, and when one of the ruffians behaved badly and spoke to Father offensively, he grabbed hold of him and punched him in the face, sending him sprawling beyond the fence. The effect of the alcohol wore off quickly and the boy immediately became sober. Whereupon he asked Father's pardon and ran off with the rest of his pals. Had Father had needed the help of his farmer friends at that moment in time, they would have undoubtedly come to his assistance.

One morning, the old lady came in to milk the cows as usual. We were lying with bated breath, without moving, waiting impatiently until she finished her task. Unfortunately, on this occasion her dog accompanied her and he started to sniff around. With his keen sense of smell, he sensed our presence and started to bark incessantly, inclining his head in our direction. The old lady felt that there was something unusual in his barking and started to speak and shout towards the attic. We were frightened that she would mount the stairs to the attic in order to find out what was happening there, or that she

would call for help. We also feared that she might faint from
fear on discovering strangers in her house, and if the matter
were made known to the neighbors, both her son and we
were lost. We decided that we had no choice but to reveal
ourselves to her and quieten her. We called her by her
Christian name, softly, so that she should not be alarmed, and
made ourselves known, telling her that her young son had
hidden us for a day. We calmed her and explained that she
must not tell anyone at all, even her husband, that we were
there, for if the fact became known, a great misfortune would
befall both her and her son. Her great love for her son encouraged her to keep our existence secret, and from that day
onwards our situation was much improved. We no longer
needed to beware of being discovered by her and she herself
would bring us much better food. The 'good' days did not last
long, however, and some days later, Kaj'uk informed us that
we would have to leave. His mother was not sleeping at night.
She was in constant fear that our presence would become
known to the neighbors. In order to emphasize the urgency of
the matter, he added that the neighbors were already hinting
at the fact that he was hiding Jews. We had no alternative but
to leave the place at once. The payment that he had received
from us in the form of money and Sabbath clothes and fabric
for a new suit was not returned of course. And we had to
return to the forest.

17 Preparation for Winter

The summer was coming to an end and the autumn was showing signs of arriving, with darkening skies and clouds shadowing the sunlight. We, too, felt the impending darkness of winter and feared what it might bring. Our most urgent concern was what would happen to us in the winter and how we were to obtain food. It would also be impossible to go about every night and beg for bread, for our trail in the snow would reveal our whereabouts. The hard wintry weather threatened our very existence and our fears of freezing to death were very real.

Once again, we considered the possibility of penetrating the Lida ghetto and passing the winter there, but the news was not good. There was hunger in the ghetto and there were also rumors that the Germans intended to slaughter those Jews who were still alive and do away with the ghetto altogether. In order to survive, we understood that we would have to find the solution in the forest and among the farmers living around it. We found a number of sites that would be suitable for digging underground holes. We intended to prepare at least two such holes in different parts of the forest. We also realized that we would have to store up sufficient quantities of food for the winter, such as potatoes, flour, semolina and dried bread, even before the first snowfall. The purpose of this was to avoid having to leave our hole in order to find food, and to prevent leaving a trail of footprints in the snow. Only during those nights when there were snowstorms would our footsteps be covered by snows and only then would we be able to go out to ask the farmers for additional food.

At the same time we did not despair of the possibility of

finding a refuge at the home of well-disposed farmers in exchange for the small amount of goods that we still possessed which we had left with other farmers. If this did not work out, then we would still have the underground hideouts we had prepared in the forest.

We sought a location high up on a hill which would enable us to dig deeply, and which would not be near ancient trees and dense foliage, for the farmers were likely to look for firewood there and uncover us in the process. At the same time, Father was seeking two places with two farmers, for now, as before, he decided that it was not sensible for us all to stay together. One refuge he found with the Kaschitz family, our former neighbor in Dowgalishok, that same family which had bought Cousin Berl Lipkunsky's land and farm. This land and farm bordered on ours, and Father promised them that when the war was over he would leave them our land and farm if they would take in one of us.

Illogical as it may seem, there was evidently a place for us to hide in the former Jewish Dowgalishok, for it would not occur to anyone that a Jew would dare to enter this village where all our property had been publicly expropriated. Those who had become heirs by force were certainly not interested in the survival of Jews, nor were they interested in anyone who could demand the return of their property after the war was over and the allies had won.

The entire Kaschitz family, the mother and three children, understood the situation. The neighborly relationship between the family and ourselves had always been smooth and amicable, and the greater part of our property and possessions had been left with them to keep for us. They were Polish nationalists, and they believed in the eventual victory of the Allies. They even believed that Poland would be greater and stronger than it had been before. The middle son, Franek, was the same age as my brother Pinchas, and they were great friends. During the summer holidays they would spend many a day together, talking for hours on end. Their friendship had intensified even further during the prewar period of Soviet domination. Franek, who was intended for the priesthood, was forced to leave his studies at the Lida gymnasium (high school) and my brother also had to leave the yeshiva when the Soviets took over, so the two of them spent much time together. The decision to take in one of us was made by the entire family, and it was agreed that my brother Pinchas should stay with them and that Father and I would go to another farmer.

18 The Underground Bunker

In the meantime, the three of us, that is Pinchas, Haim Paikovsky, and I, began jointly to plan and prepare an underground bunker that would suffice for four or five people. We knew that we had to finish the work in one night. If we did not complete it in one night, including camouflaging the place, it would be out of bounds for us because of the danger of someone discovering it.

We did not have working tools, and we could not borrow them from a farmer lest our purpose in borrowing them should be revealed. Obviously, it had to be a complete secret. We decided we would get the tools by dragging them from afar. One night, we walked a number of kilometers from the site we had decided on for a bunker, and stole from a farmer – for the first time in our lives. The loot included a double saw, three axes, and three shovels. This was the first theft we had to carry out in order to survive, but it was not the last.

We planned the work in great detail. We prepared the necessary tools and kept absolutely silent on the subject, even to other Jews. We cut down suitable trees to use as supports for the ceiling of the bunker, clearing them of their branches and cutting them to the proper length, hiding them far from the place we cut them down and also from the proposed site of the bunkers, as we did not want to deplete this area of trees and so arouse suspicion.

In 1942, during the first half of September, by the light of a full moon, we began our work. As the nights were getting longer then, we could finish the job. We dragged the heavy beams from afar, and it was not long before we had them on the spot. We must have had a fantastic energy, for in normal times we would never have been able to move such beams from their place, and now each of us carried a huge beam on his shoulders for quite a distance. Before beginning the digging, we cleared the area of pine needles and deadwood that had gathered there for years, and which afterwards we used to cover up the disturbed earth. For many hours we three worked persistently without pausing, using those hidden reserves of strength that had suddenly emerged. We arrived at a depth of 2.8 meters and a breadth of 4 by 4 meters in this sandy soil, and calculated that there would be at least one meter of soil above us, so that even if someone were standing or walking on it, there would be no indication of the bunker below. The height within the bunker would suffice to enable a man to stand up, and the width would be enough for four people lying on their backs, in case Father wanted to join us.

With the appearance of the morning stars, the ceiling beams were put in place, close up to one another. We covered them with soft branches and pine needles in order to prevent the sandy soil from seeping through the ceiling beams as well as to deflect any shaking that might take place when someone walked above the bunker. We spread earth over the branches, densely and tightly, up to the level of the ground. The earth which remained after digging, we poured into sacks and scattered it over a wide area far from the spot, so that no sign of our activity was visible. On that night we must have moved tons of earth in sacks on our backs.

We replanted the trees which we had uprooted and arranged the site as it had been before. With the rising sun, we respread the pine needles and the fallen leaves and deadwood where they had been on the ground, finishing off the camouflage. For ventilation, we left some fist-sized holes alongside the roots of the replanted trees.

The opening to the bunker was about the width of a man's shoulders and one let oneself down by a ladder. We arranged a box-like frame, which would fit into the entrance like a cork, and in this box frame, we 'planted' a young pine tree similar in size to the surrounding trees, making sure that its roots were well-hidden. On entering the bunker, we would draw the tree by its roots together with the frame and thus seal the entrance. The entrance to the bunker was so adapted to its surroundings that even we had difficulty in finding it at times, and we had to pull at various trees in order to find the right one. Inside, we had arranged sleeping bunks made of wooden slats and in one corner we built a stove made of stones to be used for heating and for cooking, with a well-camouflaged chimney to allow smoke to escape.

Autumn was already with us and the nights were becoming long and cold, and we could no longer sleep out of doors in our thin clothing. We began to spend the nights in our new home. We needed to check whether shepherds came this way and whether the place was adequately camouflaged.

So for almost an entire month, we stayed in the bunker by day, and learned that shepherds did indeed pass the place with their herds from time to time. This sounding out of the situation taught us that our 'enemies' (the shepherds) were difficult to avoid. If they did not succeed in uncovering our hiding-place, their dogs running back and forth around the herd and sniffing about probably would do so. Thus we had to change our location frequently.

During the time we spent in the bunker, shepherds would pass overhead with their herds almost daily. We would register the sound of the tread of the cattle's hooves and hear their mooing and lowing, but we could not see them. It was a terrible experience to be buried beneath the earth, to hear voices, to feel the earth trembling, and not to know whether our secret had been discovered.

After a few days, we learned that as long as the shepherds went on their way whistling and humming, it was evident that they were not aware of anything untoward. Days and weeks went by without them discovering anything; they were unaware that beneath the ground were living and breathing human beings directly under their feet. We began to believe that our bunker and its camouflage was successful, and started to store food and wood for heating and cooking, so that we would not have to leave it when the snow fell. The only thing we did not need was water, as we would have the snow.

Jossele Zelver, a student from the Radun yeshiva, was known for his wonderful singing and intoning when he was poring over the Talmud and submerged in a Talmudic problem. Now he wandered alone in the forests around Dowgalishok, looking for shelter. He remembered the region from the good old days when he would come to Dowgalishok for the summer, together with the other students of the yeshiva of Radun. When we met, we advised him to prepare a place for the winter. During one night we helped him to dig a smaller hideout. He burrowed into the earth underneath the roots of the trees, and made a sideways entrance. He dug for a number of long nights, transferring the displaced earth in the pockets of his clothing, carrying it afar and scattering it among ploughed fields.

While sitting in the bunker one day, a herd of cows and sheep passed overhead and we felt the earth trembling above us. The shepherd and his dog dallied for a while over the bunker, cut off one of the branches of the tree we had planted and started to hew it into shape with his knife. Being within the bunker was like sitting in a drum, for every movement outside would reverberate loudly within. In cutting off the branch, we felt as if he were cutting off one of our limbs. We did not know who was treading above or whether he had discovered anything suspicious or was just biding his time. Naturally, we were anxious lest he suspected something which could lead him to bring the Germans there that very day to arrest us. Perhaps he was looking for the entrance. We were trembling with fear and a sweat broke out all over our bodies. We did not know what to do: to jump out and catch him and do away with him before he betrayed us, or to hope for the best. While we were considering what to do, we heard

159

him whistle to his dog and go on his way after the herd. When all was quiet, we slowly opened the cover and peered outside to see if there were any suspicious movements, if he was alone, and in what direction he had gone. When we saw that he was following his herd, which had by this time gone some distance, we were inclined to believe that he knew nothing. We breathed a sigh of relief.

This drama was repeated again and again, when the same shepherd and his herd of cows would pass over our heads. The tension we felt down below would rise and fall with his coming and going. We began to think, however, that if he had not discovered our hideout by now, then he probably would not do so.

Then one day, when the herd was passing overhead, the bull suddenly began to bellow loudly: he roared as if he felt something, as if he wanted to say something, like Balaam's ass. The shepherd, who was upset by the roaring, suspected that there might be a wolf in the area and began to gather his herd together and abandon the place, and so we were saved again.

We did not know what caused the bull to roar in such a manner; it was indeed a mystery, which we could not solve. The following day, the same thing happened again. This time, however, the shepherd suspected that there was a stranger in the area and he began to look more carefully. He sought and sought but found nothing.

We were forced to endanger ourselves by sitting quietly in the bunker in order to see how things would turn out, for if he discovered the bunker, this would show that it was not adequate for the purpose and dangerous to stay there. If, however, he did not find it, then it would serve us through the winter. We hoped that the shepherds would shortly stop coming to the forest with their herds and we would then be relieved of this burden.

Unfortunately, the same thing happened again on the following day, and when we heard hooves approaching, we began to discuss and decide what was to be done should he discover us. We thought that we should catch him and that if it seemed that our lives were in danger, then we would have to kill him. So a cruel and bitter reality had turned us not only into wild animals of the forest but into predators.

With bated breath, and ready to pounce on him if necessary, we again heard the footfalls of the bull overhead, as if someone or something was drawing him to us. Again he began to sniff the earth and bellow, as if he were possesed. This time his anger swelled and he started to paw and lick the earth. The shepherd realized that there was something strange and suspicious here, and he pulled at the very tree planted over the bunker entrance. In doing so, found to his amazement that there was a huge hole deep in the earth!

He uttered a fearful cry. We blinked at the sudden daylight streaming into the bunker. The shepherd, stunned and frightened by his discovery, abandoned his sheep and fled for his life. When we managed to jump out after him he was already far away.

We left the bunker, closing it carefully, and followed in the wake of the herd in an attempt to find out who the shepherd was, thinking that we may know his parents or the owners of the herd. We could then persuade them not to tell anyone of our existence and could continue to use the bunker we had worked so hard to create and which was so essential in the winter.

Following the herd, we arrived at the house of the same farmer in whose attic we had hidden some weeks earlier. One evening we came quietly to see the owner of the herd and warned him that he should not reveal to anyone the existence of the bunker which was now our only home, and that if he would not keep it secret (thereby endangering our lives), we would not hesitate to set his house on fire one dark night and all his property would go up in flames. We added that we would not be occupying the bunker, but we did not want its existence to be known about. (Privately, we thought that we might be forced to use it at some time during the winter months if we had nowhere else to go.) The farmer trembled on hearing our warning. He swore to God that he would not tell a soul and that he would also see to it that the shepherd kept the matter a secret. We could not wholly trust his promises, for the shepherd was not a local man, and a stranger at that, and had abandoned the farmer a few days earlier for fear that he would be murdered. So were obliged to leave the place and start all over again. This was the month of October 1942 – a very bitter month for us.

The riddle of why the bull was so attracted to the bunker and did not want to leave it gave us no rest. We also wanted to know whether the new shepherd who was replacing the one who had fled knew of the existence of the bunker, so we decided to trail him and his flock. We discovered to our amazement that all the cows licked the trees and even the ground around the bunker. We understood then that we ourselves had brought about our discovery, because we had directed our salty urine towards the branches and the ground nearby. (Our greater needs were performed at some distance lest we arouse suspicion that there were people in the neighborhood.) Little did we imagine, however, that urine on the ground, which quickly evaporates and is not visible, could endanger our lives. The cows were very attracted by the salty smell of the urine and licked it with great excitement. They did not want to leave the spot, and this had led to our being discovered. There were so many things against us – both the obvious and the not so obvious.

Having no choice, we continued searching and attempting to pass the winter in hiding with farmers. Father arranged a place for my brother Pinchas with the Kaschitz family in Dowgalishok. I was to join Father. As long as it was possible to remain in the forest when the cold was still bearable and the snow had not yet fallen and would not reveal one's trail, we did so in order not to endanger the hideouts among the farmers. After our bunker was uncovered, we also parted from Haim Paikovsky.

Rumors began to reach us of the existence of partisans in the forests of Natche, Mezantze, and Kovalka, some 50–60 kilometers from Dowgalishok. In these regions, ancient dense forests spread out over tens of kilometers in length and breadth. We called them the *Puszcza*.* The rumors, which were passed on from person to person until they reached us, left us with a very vague impression. We did not know who the partisans were, how many they were in number, and who supported them. One thing was clear, and that was that there were Jews amongst them. We began to try to find out exactly who they were and how to contact them. This called for great caution, as we had heard of various groups that roamed the forest. There were separate groups of Jews and Russians, and also mixed groups of Jews and Russians.

The Russians in the forest were the remnant of the Soviet army who had been stranded behind the German front and not taken prisoner. Among these groups there were those who were murderers and thieves and they were prepared to rob, rape and kill whoever they encountered, especially Jews, out of blind hatred.

One night in October we heard the rumor that there was a mixed group of Jewish and Russian partisans in our vicinity, and we began to seek them out in order to come into contact with them. The rumor that there were partisans in the area quickly spread around the forest. The rumors went the rounds and in the process the number of partisans said to have been seen or met in the woods increased out of all proportion. It was also said that the Germans feared to enter the area because of its proximity to the forests and woods. At the same time there was a change in the attitude of the farmers towards those of us, the new beggars of the area, who were in the habit of asking for bread. This was now offered with a smile and no longer accompanied by resentment. (Until recently it had been given with a warning: 'take the bread and get lost, before the Germans come', which actually meant 'before I call the Germans because I am fed up with you'.)

At that time, Father was in hiding at the home of a farmer named Andzielevitz from the village of Zapashniki, near Dowgalishok. My brother Pinchas, who was staying with the farmer Kaschitz, came to me in the bunker which in the meantime had been discovered, and mentioned that he had heard about Jewish and Russian partisans who had visited Andzielevitz, adding that if the rumors were true, then certainly Father had met them and knew more about the partisans in *puszcza*. He suggested that we go to Father and get more details and find out whether there was a possibility of joining them.

One night in October 1942 we set out to meet Father. Because it was still early and the sounds of barking dogs could still be heard in the village, we did not take the short cut through Dowgalishok but a roundabout route on the edge of the forest. We stole through the back gate into the barn and met Father, who was standing at the doorway and had heard our footsteps through the cracks of the door. During our conversation, he confirmed that the rumors were indeed true and that the previous evening, the partisans had visited Andzielevitz, that most of them were Jews and the minority Russians, and that they were armed with weapons that included rifles, revolvers and hand grenades.

Farmer Andzielevitz, who feared that they might take a pig or rob him of clothing or other things, brought Father out of hiding in order to show them that he was anti-German as well, so that they should do him no harm. This proved to be the case, for they did not take advantage of him but merely spent the night in the haystack in his barn, and used it as resting quarters throughout the following day.

A group of partisans went to obtain arms from one of the farmers in the neighborhood, after having received information that he had a stash of hidden weapons. When the Soviet army was retreating in panic because the Germans were pursuing them, the Soviets left many of their arms behind. They simply wanted to get rid of them. While changing their army uniforms for simple farmers' clothing, they handed over their rifles or machine guns in exchange for a pair of pants or a shirt, and the farmers collected these weapons and buried them in the ground, in the woods or on the edges of the forests near their homes, so that they could keep an eye on them and use them if necessary. Father talked to the partisans at length and tried to find out if there was a possibility of joining them and spending the winter with them in their forests.

In the course of these conversations Father learned that these partisan groups were not organized or armed, and that the existing groups did not execute or fulfill military roles according to orders received from Moscow. There were indeed smaller groups and some of their members had very old weapons. The rest had none at all. They lived in a similar fashion to our groups in the forests of Dowgalishok. The difference between us was that we received food from the farmers on the basis of our former good relationship from better times. The farmers gave us food and clothing of their own free will and also in exchange for goods that we had left other farmers. They, on the other hand, had to buy their food from farmers living near the *puszcza* and had no choice but to steal and plunder in order to stay alive. They went to farmers far from the ancient forest and seized what they needed by intimidating them. Threatening them with arson was also effective if the farmer was reluctant to supply them with food. Generally they went to farmers who were known to be collaborating with the Germans or those who possessed Jewish property.

From the same source, he also learned that there were instances of attacks on groups of Jews by farmers who were collaborators with the Germans, and the Jews were killed. There were also a number of cases in which informers led the Germans to the hideouts of the Jews. In the neighborhood of the ancient *puszcza*, were also many Jews who had returned to the ghetto of Grodno out of fear of the approaching winter with its cold and snowstorms.

Their advice was, 'It's not worthwhile coming to the ancient forest, to an utterly unfamiliar region. Try to pass the winter here in a neighborhood where the farmers know you and where it is comparatively peaceful.'

Unlike the partisans, we did not carry weapons, nor did we try to obtain them, though we could have had them for a comparatively cheap price. There was a sort of unstated agreement among the Jews of Dowgalishok not to use arms as long as there was no need to, so that the farmers would not be frightened when we came to ask for food and that they would not feel they were being forced to give us it. We did not wish to antagonize a community which accepted our existence and had been tolerant towards us. We did not want to give them an excuse or pretext to drive us away. Farmers who wished to could easily get rid of us themselves or inform the Germans and their helpers that there were Jews wandering around the place.

The forests in this area were small and spare compared with the ancient forest. The farmers knew every path and lane. They could waylay us or watch us go on our way after giving us a piece of bread and see where we were hiding, if they so wished. And as long as we managed to get food without using weapons, and as long as we did not need weapons to defend ourselves from the farmers, we did not try to obtain them. And indeed the use of small arms such as rifles or pistols against the Germans and their helpers was tantamount to suicide.

The bitter truth of what was about to happen proved this to be so, for all the Jews in this area were killed within a few weeks, a short while before the return of the Red Army to the area, after they had succeeded in surviving in this neighborhood for nearly two years. As we found out later on, they were not wiped out by the Germans but by the White Poles, the AK, and this could only have happened with the help of the farmers of the neighborhood, who also supplied much of the AK's manpower.

Despite these considerations, we began to try to get weapons, not for our immediate use but to prepare for the time when we would have to leave the area or for any emergency that might arise. We were disappointed in Father's meeting with the partisans, when we realized that the rumors about them were exaggerated, and that it was not possible to join them. We were, however, greatly encouraged by the fact that it was possible to exist in the old forest in unfamiliar territory, without having to rely on the goodwill of some gentile who was prepared to hand out some bread and thereby save our lives. Under duress, it was evidently possible to get enough food to stay alive by using our weapons, although we did not intend to follow this path. In addition, there were many gentiles who had robbed the Jews of a considerable amount of property, and from the moral aspect, there was nothing to prevent us from taking back by force what they had robbed us of.

During that same meeting with Father, we decided to contact the groups of partisans in the Meizanze forest, but at the same time to look for a suitable place to dig a new bunker in place of the old one. Also, it was decided that my brother should return to his hideout with Kaschitz in Dowgalishok for the winter months, and that I would join Father in the home of the farmer Andzielevitz. This had not yet been agreed with him, but after the visit of the partisans and the protection he had achieved by Father's presence, we thought it likely that he would agree.

Thus we parted from Father in a good spirits, feeling that things were indeed going our way and that somehow we would get through the winter. Afterwards, in the spring and the summer, the forest would be our most secure home, and we already knew and understood it. We left the barn filled with certainty and trust, and playfully made plans to obtain weapons and join the partisans in the dense ancient forest, so that we should not have to go about nightly begging for dry bread at the doors of the farmers, and receiving it with knees knocking only when he was so inclined. In the past, even the recent past, it would not have occurred to us that this bread which we received from the muddy and kind hands of the farmer would be so tasty.

19 The Fatal Ambush

We strolled along by the light of the moon, buoyed up with our hopes. We did not suspect that Satan was guiding our steps onto the shorter path from Pashkevitz via Dowgalishok, straight into the hands of the murderers who were waiting for us. At the late hour of midnight, when the moon was full and the sky was dotted with myriad sparkling stars, and all the world was fast asleep, we also imagined that we could walk safely and securely on our way.

The peace and quiet gave us the feeling that there were no strangers in the area. There was no reason to believe that a dozen or so Germans and a similar number of Polish policemen and White Russians were hiding behind the wall of our house in Dowgalishok. They were waiting in ambush for the partisans who were roaming about the area. Normally there was no Germans or policemen in this neighborhood after sundown.

As we learned later, the gentiles who had inherited the property and homes of the Jews of Dowgalishok were alarmed and frightened by the partisan movement in the neighborhood and suspected that they would be the first target of their revenge: both their property and their lives. Therefore they alerted the Germans to protect them against the partisans who were wandering about in the region. They were guarding the western side behind our house, with its foundations touching on the dirt road which led from Lida to Radun.

When we had gone to meet Father, we had heard the barking of many dogs in Dowgalishok and this was why we had kept away from the village and gone through the woods.

Now on the way back, we did not hear the barking of a single dog. And after we had met with Father, we assumed that the dogs had been barking at the partisans passing through the village. The hope that we might meet up with the partisans in Dowgalishok was what motivated us to go through the village. And thus we walked straight into the hands of the Germans.

An hour earlier we had parted with Father, who was hiding in the house of Andzielevitz, about half an hour's walk from Dowgalishok. We marched along by the light of an almost full moon; its silvery shafts illuminating the world around us and shedding its beams on the dirt road. The moon was shadowed by a white mist from time to time and peeking out at us through the mist with the face of a man. And like the naïve children that we were, we believed that the face of the patriarch Abraham was looking down on us from the moon and escorting and guarding our footsteps, the steps of his children.

The world around us was steeped in silence; there was neither the crowing of a cock or the barking of a dog to be heard – everyone was asleep and at peace. Quietly and confidently, we walked along a familiar route. There to the right was our smithy, standing there neglected and abandoned under the pear tree. We turned away from it, with a stretch of some 150 meters between us and our house in the middle of the village. A strange feeling of disquiet and fear enveloped me and my heart was beating wildly. It was not so long ago that there were sounds of life and joy emanating from the house. Here we had spent some of the best years of our childhood in games and playfulness, and now it seemed to be inhabited by ghosts. Our pace slackened somewhat and we stood still for a moment, straining our ears for any sound, but all was calm and quiet.

Now we were entering the section between the fences bordering the narrow lane, advancing further and looking to the right at the huge stone standing alone and mute alongside the fence. Step by step we moved towards the center of the village. My eyes probed every corner, and I was covered with cold sweat as we approached the houses. We passed the house of Feivke Lipkunsky to the left and took the road paved with cobblestones that continued to the end of the village. Looking to the right and left, we crossed the road. Silence reigned throughout the village and there were no lights in the houses. With bated breath, we passed our own house. Strangers were now living there.

Then, suddenly, as we passed the cowshed, the blackened end of a muzzle appeared under my nose. There was a shout: 'Halt! Who goes there?' A round of shots followed.

Without thinking, I found myself running back in the direction we had come from. My more agile brother was ahead of me and I ran after him like a hare. We ran to the other side of the road and once again took the path between the two fences. The sound of firing from rifles and machine guns cracked through the air. The fear I had felt earlier left me, and masses of tiny red stars, like shining copper or the sparks from a red-hot iron, seemed to be flying in succession past my eyes. Bullets were exploding at our feet as we managed to advance a few meters and then another few meters along the narrow road without being able to turn left or right.

In a few moments we would reach the cover of the smithy. But alas, this was not to be, for the next thing I heard was my dear brother's cry: 'They have killed me!'

I will remember Pinke's last cry until the end of my days. It will go with me to the grave. I saw him fall to the ground, his body sprawling out opposite the huge stone on which as children we used to play on our way to our smithy. And I, in the momentum of my flight, did not stop to embrace him, or hug and caress him. It was as if an unseen hand was pushing me further and still further, until finally I sank exhausted onto the ploughed field behind the smithy, helpless and in a state of shock.

For a while there was silence all around. Suddenly I came to myself and thought I should go back. Back to my brother, embrace him, remain with him, lest I remain alone in my dark world. And yet another thought drove these impulses from my mind: 'Get up quickly and flee. Your father is awaiting you, do not make him unhappy. It will make his life unbearable if he learns that both of you have gone at the same time. Do this for your father's sake, so that at least one living soul remains of this great family.' For I was no longer a private person, living the life of a lone child, but somehow I bore the lives of tens of dear ones who were cut down and annihilated. I felt that they were commanding me to safeguard their continuity.

The murderers pursuing us soon concentrated my mind, and even while struggling with my soul, I found myself crawling on all fours, like a worm. By this time advanced some 100 or 200 meters from the spot where I had left my dead brother lying on the ground. I lay and waited while my pursuers came nearer with torches in their hands. Then I heard a single shot and understood its significance. I could no longer help Pinchas – they had released him from the burdens of life.

The shot roused me, and crawling on my stomach and running on all fours, I managed to drag myself to the open field. Lying down once again for a moment, my thoughts returned to my much-loved brother Pinchas. He had been my protector from the moment we had left home – how could I live and exist without him. How could I leave him alone? Perhaps he was still breathing and alive, perhaps he needed my help, my warmth? Why I left him alone with his murderers all around him?

In a flash the image of Father came into my mind: the grieving father who had now lost two children. Only half an hour earlier we were together; what would be the point of his life now? And I seemed to hear his voice telling me to get up quickly, to run to him, for he had heard the shots and knew what route we were taking. He would be waiting for me. Do not help the murderers – do not make it easier for them!

Running on all fours, and jumping from clod to clod, I made a sharp left turn towards the village of Pitzelunze, in the direction of the meadows and the marshes, in order to get rid of my footprints. And some distance behind me, the lights of the torches following me were flickering and looking around for traces of me.

Before dawn, I arrived at Father's hideout in Andzielevitz's barn via a long and circuitous route. I knew that I had to reach Father before he was told that two sons had been killed. I stole into the courtyard quietly and approached the back gate slowly, without arousing the dogs that were lying in their kennels like lords. The gate opened sufficiently for me to put my head in, I crawled in and fell into the arms of Father who was waiting for me at the doorway. He took me into his arms and without asking questions, said in a weak and choking voice, with the tears streaming down his face and his lips trembling: 'My child, you are a gift from heaven, I had already believed that I would not see you alive. I thought I had lost both of you at one and the same time'. Thus he understood that Pinchas had died, that he was bereft of his oldest son.

This was one of the few occasions on which I saw Father weeping like a child. I did not know whether these tears were for the loss of one of his sons or whether they were tears of joy over my remaining alive. He said that we would never now be parted from one another. I wept bitterly over the loss of my beloved Pinke, who was both friend and brother, and mother and father to me during all our experiences together. Father tried to console me by saying, 'My dear son, I thank God for having left you to me, for what am I now without you, a dry tree, a corpse among the living.'

He did not go on speaking and crying, and pulled a sheaf of grain from a whole stack of sheaves which were being stored for the winter, and put me into the narrow space created by the absence of the sheaf. Moving backwards after me, he drew the sheaf back into place, filling in the empty space. I crawled on my stomach through the narrow winding burrow beneath the sheaves of corn that were piled one on top of the other crosswise to a great height, until I reached an underground hole.

Father felt all the limbs of my body to see whether or not I was hurt or if I needed medical attention or some wound attended to. Surprisingly, there was no injury of any kind. He told me that he had heard many shots being fired from different weapons, and his instinct told him that we had been ambushed by the Germans, as he was aware of the route we were taking and the time it would take to reach Dowgalishok. Judging by the sound of the shots, he no longer believed that he would live to see us alive. This was why he had been standing in the doorway of the barn, peering out from a crack, in case one of us should return to him. He also feared that the Germans might have reached him in our wake. He asked me how I had arrived there and whether I had left a track that would lead the Germans to his hideout. I explained to him that I made every effort to erase any signs of my course and that I had gone in the opposite direction, toward the meadows and the marshes of Pitzeluntze.

Father decided that the fact of my coming to him and being with him must be kept from the farmer, lest he should be afraid and insist that we leave. We did not sleep a wink that night, for we also feared that when the farmer learned of the death of Father's two sons, he might take advantage of the situation and out of greed, hand him over to the Germans. By doing so he would gain the property we had left with him without placing himself in danger.

We also feared that the Germans might somehow discover my trail, and planned how we might defend ourselves. We stuffed up the hollow leading to the hole and opened up another passageway underneath the grain as a means of escape. Father also possessed some matches and lighter fuel. We decided that if the worst came to the worst, we would set fire to the barn, and in the ensuing commotion would try to escape. If we did not succeed, then it would be better to be burned alive than to fall into the hands of the Germans. This was to be our last expedient as long as we were hiding out with the farmer, for we never felt entirely secure. We were always afraid that in certain circumstances, the farmer might turn us over to the Germans and exonerate himself.

In the early hours of the following morning, the farmer entered the barn and said: 'Mr Moshe, I am sorry to have to inform you that the Germans have killed your two sons.' He added that the older boy was shot in the heart and died instantly. The younger son was also killed but his body had not been found as yet. It was thought that he was probably lying dead in some field. The police and the Germans were continuing their search, following in his wake to Pitzeluntze. The Polish police said that they were so close to the boys, that they could have murdered them with their sticks. In the afternoon, the farmer informed us that the body of the second son had still not been found and that the Germans had withdrawn and returned to Radun.

20 The Hideout at Andzielevitz

The farmer Andzielevitz was counted among the Polish nobility of the neighborhood and as such he had connections with the Polish intelligentsia of the region. He was kept informed of what was happening among the Germans as he was connected and involved with the Polish underground, and he also received news from the Polish government-in-exile. His home was used to house the committee of loyal Poles, and they would occasionally publish an internal account of what was happening on both the Allied and the Russian fronts.

For similar reasons, the only Jewish apostate in Radun who had married a Polish member of the intelligentsia found refuge in the farmer's home, where she lived as a member of the household and not in hiding. Despite the fact that she was registered as a Pole, she left Radun where she felt insecure, in order not to come in contact with the Germans. For them, she was still a Jewess in every respect.

Bearing a strong prejudice against converts, whom I thought to be trouble-makers and Jew-haters, I was always afraid of her and I would say to Father again and again that I feared she would cause us trouble; that she would try to get rid of Father so as not to endanger her own situation, for she knew of his presence in the barn though she did not encounter him.

Some days had passed since my brother's death, and the atmosphere seemed relatively peaceful. The farmer Shamashka, of Lithuanian origin, who had inherited our farm and property while we, still among the living, took his body to be buried in a part of the forest that had belonged to us. Andzielevitz told us of the undignified and disrespectful way in which my brother's body was treated, for his corpse had been tied by a rope to the harness of a horse and dragged along on the ground to the burial place.

The mystery of my disappearance was still unsolved, and Andzielevitz said that no one knew how or where my body had gone. Father realized that in the course of time, he would have to reveal my presence and therefore decided that the time was ripe to tell the farmer that I was alive and living there with him in his hideout. On hearing this, Andzielevitz was truly shaken and began to cross himself. He was possessed by fear and trembling could not believe that I was really alive, that I 'had risen from the dead', for in light of the stories told by the Germans and the policemen of how they had ambushed and shot at us, it was impossible that I should still be among the living.

Andzielevitz locked the barn and ordered all the members of his household to stand on guard around the barn and the courtyard, to make certain that there were no strangers in the area. He called his wife, his two big sons, the apostate and her husband, and requested that Father bring me out of my hiding-place, for they wanted to see with their own eyes someone who had been resurrected. And so Father showed me off to the farmer's family. Seeing me standing before them, they all made the sign of the cross. At the same time, I saw that the apostate of Radun had tears in her eyes and was looking at me with great compassion, and I felt particularly close to her at that moment, for I sensed that a Jewish heart was beating under that Christian surface. She came closer and asked me if I was not wounded, and repeated the question a number of times. She consoled me and encouraged me to speak the truth, thinking that I was afraid to reveal that I was wounded, for she merely wanted to dress my wounds. The fact that my body had not suffered any injury also came as a great surprise and they saw in this the hand of God.

When I saw the apostate's behavior towards me, I was sorry that I had doubted her intentions and was no longer afraid of her. I saw her as an unfortunate person connected to me by our common Jewish fate, despite the fact that she had abandoned her parents' faith.

The barn for storing grain where we lay hidden under the earth, concealed from the light of day, was built as a rectangle with the shorter sides facing east and west. It had two doors: one on the southern side facing the courtyard and farmer's house and used daily, while the second gate, set in the eastern wall, was used for the entry and exit of horses and wagons and faced the main dirt road leading to Pashkevitz and Dowgalishok. Within, the grain, the straw and the fodder were stored all along the walls. The middle of the barn had a compressed and smooth plaster floor on which the grain was expertly threshed with sticks. Andzielevitz also had a threshing machine, though it was of a somewhat primitive variety that had to be worked by hand. However, not every farmer possessed even such a machine and only the wealthy and privileged, such as our friend Andzielevitz, managed to be the owner of one.

The grain stored against the western wall was stacked in orderly and straight lines and reached the height of a number of meters. At the floor level some distance from the western wall, stood one sheaf, which appeared no different from the other sheaves, and this was used to seal our burrow like a cork in a bottle. The width of our dugout was the span of a man's shoulders, similar to that of an ordinary sheaf, so that one could not differentiate between the sheaves. Entering the burrow, we would draw in the sheaf after us without anyone being able to notice anything untoward. The burrow stretched along the western wall for about four or five meters, and then turned sharply left toward the southern wall. At the corner there was a hole in the floor, also a shoulder's width, which descended a meter and a half into the earth. Here a hole had been dug which enabled two people to lie on their backs and one could just manage to sit up. Wooden beams had been placed over the hole and covered with earth, which was then covered with grain.

The floor of the hole was bedded with straw and we stuffed some hay into the corners to ward off the dampness and cold and covered ourselves with a thin blanket that had been provided by the farmer. The eiderdowns and pillows, which we had given Andzielevitz were not suited to our present lair. We tossed and turned, but managed somehow or other to sleep pretty well. We would have been happy if we could have slept for an entire year, like Honi Ham'aggel the circle-maker, in his time. An oil-lamp with its wick dipped in oil or kerosene, or as the farmers called it, 'the smoker', supplied us with light and gave off more heat than the rays of the sun. When reclining, our feet would touch the wall facing us, that is, the western wall. Without the farmer's knowledge, we arranged an approach to the southwestern corner of the barn, and through a thin crack in the wall, could observe the road leading to and from Dowgalishok and Radun. We could also see what was happening in the farmer's courtyard, catch sight of who was coming and going, and note anything that seemed suspicious. This observation post of a crack we kept secret, for in this way we could observe the farmer's movements and see who he was meeting.

Beyond the western wall, near our dugout, other holes had been dug to store potatoes for the winter. These had been dug up in order to dissemble the yellowish sand that had been unearthed during the digging of our hole. No one could have imagined that somewhere among the three holes for storing potatoes there was another, which served as a parlor for people who preferred the darkness in the valley of death to the light of day.

We had no books, but we did have a book of prayers, the Bible and *tefillin* (phylacteries). Our daily routine was very simple. In the early hours of the morning we would pray and put on our *tefillin*. After that, one of us would go to peer through the crack to see what was happening in the world outside, impatiently awaiting breakfast. We did not suffer severely from hunger but we were always a bit hungry. Perhaps even more than the food, we were avid to see the farmer and hear the news of the day, to note whether he was depressed or light-hearted, to hear about what was happening in the world and the situation at the front, particularly our own front – the movement of the Germans, the Jews, and the partisans.

In most cases, we would be given the bad news with considerable amplification and in black colors, while the good news would be conveyed with restraint, lest we were inclined to belittle the extent and daring of Andzielevitz's action in providing us with a refuge. After all, this was a humane and daring act which demanded unbelievable courage. For by hiding Jews in his home, Andzielevitz was endangering his own life as well as that of his family and their property. In less than no time, everything could go up in flames and he would be the first victim. More than that, he would have to be enormously persuasive in order to convince his wife not to be afraid, and that she should agree to his action, for it was usually she who brought us food and had daily contact with us.

As well as getting news of the front, we would learn at mealtimes whether the Germans or the Russians were advancing. We reckoned we could gauge the situation at the front from the quantity and the quality of the food. On Sundays in particular our hosts would return from church and bring with them news of what was happening. A newspaper was rarely to be seen, for evidently Andzielevitz had his own reasons for not wanting us to know what was happening from any source but his own mouth.

The food was very monotonous. Every day we were served the same things: a meager plate of potato soup ('boullon' in the farmer's idiom) and a piece of bread. This was prepared only for us as their own food was more varied and of better quality. Andzielevitz was quite rich and not at all stingy, but food was his wife's domain. This was somewhat annoying and surprising, for supplying us with food was the least difficult aspect of their deeply humane behavior, but just in this, they did not come up to scratch. We could have paid them separately for food, but we did not want to appear complaining or dissatisfied.

On the days when they thought we had a future, the food would improve, but when they considered our future hopeless, it seemed a pity to waste food on us. After some time, we would go outside, although the farmer was unaware of this, and visit other acquaintances in order to find out what was going on. We would listen to rumors, and even get some concentrated food to keep for an emergency, should we need it. We knew that we had a hard, long way to go – indeed how long nobody knew. Therefore we had to be healthy in mind and in body.

My brother's death had had a devastating effect on me, and for many weeks afterwards I could find no peace of mind. I could not accept this blow and from time to time I would burst into tears. I was haunted by a dream I had about a week before he had died, that had frightened me at the time. I dreamed about Yom Kippur (the Day of Atonement) as if I was the prayer book of that awesome day and could see the printed words 'Yom Kippur'. For days on end I could not forgive myself for not taking note of the warning implied in those words in my dream.

Father tried to console me and indeed would weep together with me, embracing and comforting me. He tried to keep up my spirits, although he himself was a broken man. I sensed to what extent his heart was broken when I had already recovered somewhat. We knew that Father was not in the habit of indulging us as children, but on holidays and other festivities, when we would accompany him to the synagogue, he would not hide his pride in us – his sons. Or he would show his affection when we were gathered around the table conversing during a festive meal. During the rest of the year, he would leave the pampering to Mother. Now that he was beside me, how changed he had become, how soft and motherly he was. Tears would flood my eyes on seeing my strong and healthy father so broken in spirit.

In the many warm and friendly talks we had while lying in the dark and humid hole, Father would pour out his heart to me, not as one might talk to a child but as to a friend and comrade. He would encourage me by saying: 'My darling son, you are young and with the help of God, you will stay alive. The great and wide world will be open to you; you will build yourself a family and forget about all this. You will be happy and things will go well for you. But I will no longer be able to be happy, as I was when mother was alive and you children were at my side. After the loss of my two children, Pinke and Kushka, and Mother as well, I have nothing in life but you. I am now living only for you, that you should stay alive, and that life should go well for you.' I could not accept his words and would tell him that I, too, could never forget Mother and my beloved brothers, whose death I had witnessed with my own eyes. But if we survived, then together perhaps we would fare well, for to me Father was he dearest person in the entire world.

I could sense the scars left by Mother's absence. 'The good life I had with Mother will never be repeated, and I will never have such so close a friend again.' I tried to overcome my feelings and comfort him, saying: 'You, too, will be able to rebuild your life and it is not your fault that Mother died!' And to that he answered with a sigh: 'My child, my dearest child, you are still unable to understand me.'

21 The Germans Visit Andzielevitz

It was the beginning of the winter of 1942. In happier times, we would already have begun to make preparations for Passover immediately after Hanukkah. The nights were getting frosty, and the sub-zero weather was beginning to get a hold, freezing puddles on the ground's surface. During the last watches of the night, when dawn was beginning to color the sky and we were lying awake listening in our hideout, the stillness was suddenly shattered by the rattle of firing and the bursting of bombs. We quickly ran to our lookout in the corner to try to see from what direction the firing had come, in order to be prepared for whatever might happen. Through the cracks in the haystacks, we could see flames rising to the sky, reddening the skyline. We estimated that the location of the fire was a few kilometers from where we were standing. The combination of flames together with the sound of firing boded no good and we feared that something had happened to the Jews wandering about that area, and with fear in our hearts, we awaited the morning in order to hear from Andzielevitz what had happened.

Together with our morning meal, we were told the news that the Germans and the police had surrounded the home of Dashkevitz, a farmer from the neighboring village of Pitzeluntze. It seems that he was host to a group of Jews who had come from the ancient forest, and when the Germans wanted to enter the house in order to carry out a search, one of the Jews assaulted the German and grabbed his rifle from him, pointing it directly at him. The Germans withdrew and an exchange of fire ensued. According to Andzielevitz one of the Jews had a rifle. The door was forced open and the Jews began to flee under cover of the shooting. Most of them were killed by the German bullets, but two men succeeded in escaping.

Dashkevitz was a poor and good-hearted farmer, whose house consisted of only one small room built in a corner of his barn. The recluse Yossele 'the Zalver' (from the town of Zalev) and the cobbler Zusmanovitz from Ivya, hid in the woods near Dashkevitz's home, in one of the holes for storing potatoes in the winter. During the cold nights, they would come into his house to warm themselves and sleep in the barn.

Reubke Hazkels, 'the wedding', who was one of the group of Jewish partisans who had come from the old forest and who had survived that night, described what had happened. They had come to the region to get food and weapons. They were seven in all: Elka Ariovitz, 'Todres' (on account of his freckles), Aizke Tanovitzky, Yankele from Olkenik, and three others whose names were not mentioned. Early in the morning while they were still asleep, the Germans and the police surrounded the barn and tried to get them to come outside. When they learned that the Jewish partisans were armed, they withdrew from the barn, but set fire to it. The Jews who were caught in the fire, jumped out in the face of the rifles and machine guns fired by the Germans and the Polish police. Zusmanovitz, while running from the barn, fell on a German and took his rifle and ran off, but the Germans and the police ran after him and shot him dead.

Reubke took off his boots and discarded his rifle, running out of the barn barefoot, swiftly cutting his way through the Germans. But the farmer Shamaska of Pitzeluntze caught him and started to strangle him, but they were interrupted in the midst of this struggle by the policeman Nosovitz. The policeman told Shamashka to leave him alone and stand aside so that he could shoot him, and at that very moment, Reubke managed to slip out of their hands. He ran for quite a distance, while they followed in hot pursuit, firing at him at the same time. He succeeded in escaping, despite being wounded in the shoulder. Reubke was certain that the Polish policeman, whom he knew well, had fired in the air and not at him, for otherwise he could not understand why he had not been killed.

Elka, who had also jumped out of the barn, fired his revolver at a German blocking his way and managed to escape without any injuries. The remaining five, among them Yossele Zelver, Aizke Tanovitsky, and Jankele from Olkenik, were all killed.

Five months later, in May 1942, Reubke returned to Pitzeluntze with a group of Jewish partisans, in order to obtain a mortar from one of the farmers, who was said to have one hidden. While going to meet the farmer at a neighbor's barn, Haim Paikovsky, who was with Reubke at the time, recognized Shamashka who had tried to strangle Reubke when he was trying to escape from Dashkevitz's burning barn. Reubke immediately dragged him out of the barn. Shamashka threw some sheepskins at him and tried to flee, but Reubke shot him with an automatic rifle. Thus he settled his account with him. This was also done so that others should be aware that Jewish blood would not be always spilled in vain. Reubke Hazkels continued to struggle for survival and seek his revenge both within the framework of the partisan movement and without. He was the only member of his family who had remained alive and he succeeded in reaching Israel, where he now lives with his family in Ashkelon.

According to Andzielevitz's version of the story, the Germans took the entire Dashkevitz family, including the small children, out into the courtyard and shot them on the spot. They then set fire to the barn, so that not a single token of their existence remained. All this was done in order to instill terror and fear in the hearts of anyone who would come into contact with Jews and give them refuge.

We were greatly disturbed by Andzielevitz's account. We also felt his genuine fear and expected that he would ask us to leave him in peace and unburden him of this trouble called Jews. But surprisingly, he was a courageous man, who never-theless decided to endanger his life together with ours, knowing full well that if we were discovered in his barn, all of us would share the same fate. Andzielevitz told us to remain quiet and not to leave any signs of life on our bedding, for the Germans were still roaming about the area, and they were likely to come there in search of spirits and pork. Andzielevitz was known to be a wealthy farmer, and the Germans considered a visit to him worthwhile.

We examined every nook and cranny and tried to disguise and get rid of any object that could arouse suspicion. Andzielevitz did the same outside the barn, and we awaited the next few hours with anxiety. It appeared that Andzielevitz already knew the Germans' round through his connections with the Polish policemen who escorted them. He told us that the Germans intended to continue on their way from Pitzeluntze to the village of Pashkevitz, and as his farm was situated on the highway, it was likely that they would stop off here as well. (We did not know whether his words were intended to frighten us even more or whether they were to emphasize his fine behavior, knowing the danger involved.)

We disguised all the entrances to our hideout, but did not go down to the hole but rather stood on guard, looking out through the cracks between the beams onto the road that leads to Pashkevitz and any suspicious movement in the courtyard. We had the bottle of benzine and matches in our hands in case we discovered that Andzelievitz was planning to betray us and give us up to the Germans. In that event we would set the barn on fire and try to escape in the ensuing turmoil. Unfortunately the only weapons we had at our disposal were fire and knives.

Like people sentenced to death but whose execution had still to be carried out, we sat in the hole, which might become our grave. Our hearts were beating fast and we were tense with anticipation. Would they enter the barn or would they overlook it? If they appeared with Andzielevitz and his wife and household, would they withstand the test and refuse to hand us over. And how would I behave in such circumstances?

The sun was rising slowly to high noon, and we embraced the hope that these unwelcome guests would not visit

Andzielevitz. This wishful thinking soon gave way to disappointment, as from our lookout we saw a column approaching from the direction of Dowgalishok on the road that led to Pashkevitz. This road passes only a few meters from our courtyard and some 50 meters from the barn. We counted every step taken by the column towards Pashkevitz, in the hope that it would continue and not stop here; in fact it seemed to be passing by the gate. And then Satan's hand was at work, and the column deviated left from the highway and straight into Andzielevitz's courtyard. I watched through the crack and saw the devilish faces that I was already familiar with advancing towards the center of the courtyard. My knees were trembling, my teeth chattering, and my entire body began to shake.

I do not truly know why I was unable to control myself at this point for I had already faced death on a number of occasions. Perhaps it was because I was closed in and unable to do anything, and dependent on the compassion of the farmer into whose hands we had placed our lives. And once again we asked ourselves whether Andzielevitz was to be trusted.

Andzielevitz was a shrewd man. He did not wait for the Germans to come into the house and give him orders. He went out and greeted them at the gate of the courtyard, inviting them into his house as welcome and respected guests. He offered them food to stay their hunger, and drink to warm their bodies. And despite the severe ban on homemade spirits, he did not hesitate to take out the spirits in order to offer it to them, stressing that these spirits were kept solely for such honored guests.

He knew some of the Polish policemen, most of who were members of the Polish underground, which was still passive and in the process of organizing. On realizing that the visitors did not turn into a search party and that they were eating to their hearts' content, we were relieved. Still we were frightened and trembling. As long as these angels of death were in our midst, we feared that some intemperate words or the slip of a tongue on the part of a child could endanger our lives.

The Germans had left a police guard in the courtyard, in order to watch the house and courtyard and keep an eye on what was happening in the area. After they had finished eating they filed out to the courtyard. My heart pounded when I saw them turn towards the barn, instead of going towards the gate through which they had come. They advanced to within a hand's reach of the corner where we were sitting and watching them, actually treading on the holes for potatoes, which were dug as camouflage, and standing immediately above our heads.

Then marching alongside the western wall of the barn, and over the frost-covered fields, they went on their way to Pashkevitz. Once again, we had been saved by a miracle, but I was worn out by the long hours of tension. I could not believe my eyes, and again and again, when I replayed the scene in my mind against the background of the flames, I thought about what had happened and what might have happened.

Andzielevitz avoided us for a few hours and did not bring us our daily meal as usual. Evidently he and his household were also in need of some respite. Only towards evening, when he was certain that the Germans had left the area, did he come down and encourage us with a festive meal, together with some home-made vodka of the same variety that he had offered the Germans. He told us that more than anything else, he had worried about his wife's behavior, for she had been very tense. Thankfully, everything passed off peacefully and she had now recovered her equilibrium, knowing that the Germans could also be hoodwinked.

Our trust in Andzielevitz was greatly strengthened after this severe test of his loyalty, and we were no longer afraid that he wanted to hand us over to the Germans. Also, from time to time, he would give us news of the front, which he would get on his hidden radio from the Voice of Free Poland coming from London. From then on, we were more relaxed and at ease, and prayed in our heart of hearts that he would have the courage to keep us until the snows had melted.

Andzielevitz's connection with the Polish underground and his total conviction as to the eventual victory of the Allies, when he would reap his due as a true hero, made him able to withstand these trials. He was pleased with himself for his patriotic actions and we, on our part, were not restrained in our promises. We explained that unfortunately there were few Jewish survivors, and that those who remained would be a unique breed, who would not lack the means to amply repay him for his humane actions.

Bitter reality, however, meant that our hopes were frustrated. The Russia–German front was unyielding. Despite the hard winter, the Germans had succeeded in holding out deep in the heart of Russia for the second winter, striking new blows and advancing in various places along the front. The Allies were in no great hurry to open up a second front and the war continued without any decisive move in one direction or other.

Serious changes along the front were immediately reflected in our meals. If the Russians were advancing and there was the chance of a German defeat, the fruits of victory would appear in the form of potato soup containing bits of meat, together with pancakes, and even a glass of vodka to warm us up, while Andzielevitz himself would suggest that we leave our hideout and walk about the barn. He would even take the liberty to give us various tasks, when he thought that victory was just around the corner.

But when the Germans were advancing and succeeding on the battlefield, our meals were inadequate and barely enough to keep us alive. We were often punished by the Red Army's lack of success in battle, receiving a minimal amount of food as a result.

One night, when a snowstorm was raging outside and no man or animal would dare set foot out of doors, we decided leave our hole under cover of the storm which would quickly conceal our footprints. We went out to look for Jews in the forest and to see how it was possible to live there. We also wanted to hear about what was happening in the region and in the world at large.

Haim Paikovsky was supposed to be with the another Jew who had joined him to stay in the bunker which we had dug in the autumn. We cautiously approached it now, and when we saw that it was open and unoccupied we returned as we had come without meeting a soul. On a number of occasions, we went to visit friendly farmers, in order to hear what was happening in the 'outside world', rather than rely on the news supplied by Andzielevitz. Week after week, we awaited the end of the winter and the melting snows so that we could return to the forest where we could be our own masters.

The Polish underground movement (known as the AK) was supposedly fighting the Germans, however the AK also saw it as their patriotic mission to help the Germans rid Poland of the Jews. They hoped to rid the country of its very last Jew, and therefore what the Germans had not succeeded in accomplishing, they did. The patriotic Poles would not forgo the privilege and pleasure of killing a Jew. Jews caught by the AK were not as a rule handed over to the Germans but rather murdered by AK members.

We knew that Andzielevitz was a member of the AK and heavily involved, as indeed were his older sons, who occupied covert roles in the movement. This worried Andzielevitz and also caused us considerable anxiety. And now we feared them more than the Germans because they lived in the villages and knew everything that was going on there. The local farmers collaborated with them, as they were also part and parcel of the movement. We were afraid that Andzielevitz could do away with us without anyone being the wiser, and without endangering himself. We also feared that unintentionally, when under the influence of spirits, he could reveal to his friends in the underground, just what 'treasure' he harbored in his barn.

Andzielevitz warned us on more than one occasion that his people had no love for us (i.e. the Jews), and suggested that we had nothing to do with them. He explained how difficult was for him at that time to hide us, to watch over us and protect us from them. He made no secret of the fact that he was in contact with the AK and he was more cautious in relation to them than he was with the Germans, for they visited him at any time of the day or night.

On rare occasions, he would bring us a journal of the Polish underground movement. Once we received a newspaper published by Germans in Polish, which contained an article on Palestine. I do not know whether he gave us this publication intentionally or whether he just happened to come by it. Strangely enough, I read it avidly, a number of times, and have not forgotten it to this very day, for I was very comforted by what I read there. Also, I learned something about Zionism, perhaps my first lesson in actual Zionism. As a small child, I had learned about the land of our fathers, the Prophets, and the Kings, from the Bible. I had belonged to various Zionist youth movements: Betar, and Pirchei Agudat Israel, according to whatever was popular at the time and who my friends were. I knew about collecting coins for the Keren Kayemeth and for Keren Tel Hai, but of what Zionism was and what it actually entailed, I was ignorant. And this is what the article in a Nazi publication in the Polish language revealed to me.

The article was a defamatory one against British imperialism, which it claimed was exploiting the Arab countries, and enslaving them in order to serve the Zionist cause, which completely dominated England and the United States through the influence of vast Jewish capital. It was intended to rouse Arab countries to defy the Allies, as well as to prevent any contact with the Allies on the part of the anti-Semitic Poles, and to make the United States repugnant to the Poles via their hatred of the Jews.

The article explained that the British were planning to place the 1.5 million Arabs in Palestine into the custody of the Jewish minority of 600,000. Between the lines, however, I learned that there was an organized and united Jewish community in Palestine, which ran its own administration, and was supported by Britain. Despite the exaggerated claims of British support, I wanted to believe that this was indeed the case, and I had no desire to think otherwise. It was encouraging and at that moment the far-fetched idea managed to invade my subconscious that if we survived, there was an independent Jewish corner of the world and if we were lucky, we could still be happy. If fate continued to play its cruel tricks on us, however, it was good to know that not all the Jewish people were to vanish. We seemed to stand up straighter, and in our meetings with Andzielevitz, we showed him the article written by the Germans and about the common fate of our two peoples, the Poles and the Jews, who were fighting for the revival of their nation. We also pointed out the advantages he would derive from his patriotic and humane actions and the compensation due him when victory came.

Such moments of exaltation were few and far between. The days and weeks of that cold and dark winter seemed endless. From day to day, we felt that the atmosphere was becoming more and more tense and that danger at the hands of the AK was increasing.

Every untoward movement in the courtyard or a stranger approaching the barn aroused my suspicions. I was like a coiled spring and prepared to leave the farmer and go out to the forest at any moment, despite the fact that the winter was still at its height and the snow still blanketed the world outside. The urge to be 'free' among the trees of the forest was strong, as was the desire not to be hidden in the dark and damp hole. But more than anything else, I wanted to be free of having to depend on the goodwill of the farmer who could have done away with us in one swift moment.

In every conversation with Father, I would stress the need for us to leave the little woods surrounding Dowgalishok, and go to the ancient forest to join one of the armed Jewish or Russian partisan groups fighting the Germans. During ten months of suffering and struggling to survive, I had evidently matured, and with the loss of my beloved mother and brothers, feelings of rebellion towards everything around me were generating within me. The desire and need for independence and live at the mercy of those good souls who would offer me a crust of bread and just as willingly, would also be capable of putting an end to my life.

Father had known Andzielevitz from his childhood and youth and trusted him. It did not occur to him that Andzielevitz could betray us and hand us over to the AK. He also believed that due to his excellent relations with the farmers in the neighborhood, most of whom he had also known since childhood, that it would be easier for him to manage in this area than in the *puszcza* among strange farmers and unfamiliar places. He added that he could hide here for a year, taking turns with a different farmer every day.

As I did not know these people, my trust in them was somewhat less than his, and the inclination to leave the region and join a partisan group grew from day to day, and every additional day of staying with the good and compassionate farmer was an ordeal.

The days became longer and the sun's warm rays began to melt the blanket of glittering snow on the ground. Stretches of land were revealed between the banks of snow and the puddles of water. Here and there, one could see clods of earth beginning to stand out. Nights were still cold and covered the puddles with a thin coating of ice, but this soon melted when the sun appeared.

The sun's rays also managed to squeeze between the cracks of our walls, giving us the feeling of spring, and making us long to escape the gloom underground. In the forest we would be free with our fate in our own hands. My fear of the AK intensified. My aim was to get to the old forest, to obtain arms, and join one of the partisan groups, for in the last few weeks, rumors had reached us of their increasing numbers and strength.

The yearning for the ancient forest derived from the desire for revenge. I think it also went back to my childish aspiration to bear arms and be a 'soldier' – a common enough aspiration among children. The reasons I gave Father for going off to the ancient forest were that here we would be wiped out one by one, for the wood was small and every whisper on the part of any gentile who wished to earn some money from the Germans would lead to our end. And if we had to die, at least it should happen in the course of a struggle and rebellion.

During the weeks between Purim and Passover, we would leave the barn in the evenings, to breathe some fresh air and to hear the nearby farmers' opinions on what was happening in the world, as well as locally, and thus we returned to the pattern of roaming about in the night. We relieved our friend Andzielevitz of the burden of harboring us and returned to the forest, to live among the trees and the shrubs. We left him even before the arrangement between us had come to an end and he was indeed pleased to be rid of this responsibility.

When we were taking our farewells, one could tell that he did not believe that we had a chance to survive, for he knew that if the Germans did not get us, we would not manage to evade the AK. He would undoubtedly find it more satisfactory, should anything happen to us, that it should not happen under his roof. He warned us again that his fellow Polish nationalists did not have any love for us, and so we parted on friendly terms.

I did not reveal to him that I was thinking of joining the partisans. I was aware that such a gesture would be abhorrent to him, for his hatred for the Russians was no less than his hatred of the Germans, and naturally he could not abide anyone who came into contact with them. It should be noted that although Andzielevitz received a goodly sum from us, he kept his promises to the letter, and was one of the few who dared to take a stand which could have brought about his end and that of his family and property, and all this entirely on the basis of his own goodwill. He remained faithful to his conscience and stood up against the Germans and his brother Poles, offering a refuge to two poor Jews, who were sentenced to death despite their innocence, endangering his own life in the process. Thus he is entitled to the designation: 'one of the righteous of the nations', of whom there were few among the Polish people.

Subsequently, when another winter and summer had gone

by, and the wheels of fortune had taken another unexpected turn, the Red Army returned in the summer of 1944 and freed the region from the Nazi hordes and began to hunt for the White Poles. Andzielevitz was arrested owing to his connections with them and considered an enemy of the regime. When I learned of his arrest, I did whatever I could to repay him for his past actions and offered him all the assistance that was in my power.

His name and his deeds are engraved in my memory, for he and others of his kind are the few bright spots which illuminate the dark image typifying the Polish people. Not only did they stand by idly while Jewish blood was being spilled, but they volunteered to finish what the German murderers had not succeeded in finishing. Against this ugly and bloody background, his noble spirit shines brightly.

22 Our Journey to Puszcza

The first Passover was spent with a group of Jews we had met up with two weeks earlier in the woods of Petrishonza, some four kilometers from Dowgalishok. In order not to eat leavened bread, we cooked potatoes and permitted ourselves to eat beans and peas when they were available. Instead of bread, we ate flat bread made of unleavened dough on a frying pan. The scene resembled the flight from Egypt in miniature. The only element lacking was a Moses to lead us forth. Instead of leaving Egypt for the Promised Land, we left a dark hole for the thickets of the forest, and we were headed for the entrance to the ancient forest, which was not promising at all.

At that time we met up with Abraham Paikovsky and his only son, Nahum. Abraham was the son of Reb Joseph Jaacov of Dowgalishok, the reader in the synagogue during the holidays and the Days of Awe. During the First World War, he served in the Tsar's army together with my father. He was a wagoner by trade and knew the roads in the area from his frequent journeys. He also knew the way to the ancient forest, which was some 50 kilometers from Dowgalishok.

In the autumn of 1942 he had reached the forest more than once, but he had had to return, as no group would accept him as a member. On the first occasion, he arrived at the forest together with Gershon Haya-Gitls and his family. They roamed around the forest for a month and when they had not succeeded in joining any group, they were obliged to return to their former hideout in the marshes near the village of Talkonza. They hid there among the dense reeds that grew on the banks of the River Dzitva. At that time, there were some groups in the ancient forest made up of some 10–15 people or less, but no group was prepared to have them because of their needs during the coming winter. Obtaining food during the winter was difficult and dangerous because the footprints left in the snow could lead to their underground bunker (*zemlanka*).

The groups in the forest were generally called after the dominant personality within that group. For instance, there was Elka 'Todres' Ariovitz's group. This was the largest, made up of some 15–20 men. Then there were the other groups: Joske Lubatsky of Zabelotz's; the Asners, named after the four Asner brothers from the village of Natche: Jankel, Avremke, and Aharke; and another group led by Haim Itchke (the Gypsy) and his cousin Aharke Berkovitz, and Niomke Rogovsky; and also the group called Shashke, a Russian group of prisoners of war who had remained in the rear.

The groups were closed to people outside the immediate families and their closest friends. Life in the forest was hard, and obtaining food was quite dangerous, not only because of the Germans but because of the farmers living around the forest, many of who were rabid anti-Semites. Surrounding the forest were villages whose inhabitants originally hailed from Lithuania, and most of them collaborated with the Germans. The Polish farmers were not much better in this respect.

The autumn showers, which came down in torrents and marked the approach of winter, were a source of considerable anxiety. Many Radun Jews left the ancient forest and returned to the ghetto of Martzikantz in order to pass the dreaded winter months there. Sometimes they arrived in the ghetto during an 'action', in the course of which Jews were rounded upand sent to 'labor' camps, or murdered within the ghetto. The new arrivals would then be forced to escape amid a hail of bullets and return to the forest.

Abraham Paikovsky and his son Nahum arrived back in the Dowgalishok area after being unable to settle in the forest at their first attempt. They returned again during that same autumn, as they could not find a refuge for the winter anywhere in the Dowgalishok area. Nahum, who was not very old, said to his father sadly: 'Let us return to the forest, they will have to accept us if we insist and do not leave the place – they won't have any alternative.' And so they arrived in the forest with the snow falling, and reached one of the well-organized groups with adequate supplies for the winter and settled nearby.

One bright morning they discovered that everyone had vanished and they were the only ones to have remained in the snow-covered ancient forest. Luckily, the snow had not yet covered the tracks of a sleigh, and with Abraham's keen sense of direction they followed the sleigh track and reached the new location of the group. There they found a large underground bunker well prepared for the winter, and containing ample food supplies. When the occupants of the bunker realized that the newcomers had reached the place via evidence of the sleigh's tracks, they threatened to shoot them for following them as their own tracks in the snow could reveal the location of the bunker. They demanded that Abraham and his son leave the place and when they refused, they kicked them. Abraham begged them to let them stay, claiming that 'what you people discard and waste, would be more than enough for the two of us', but nothing availed and Abraham and his son were forced to leave, returning once again to the vicinity of Dowgalishok, where the snow and frost had taken a hold on the land.

In the springtime, we agreed to go to the ancient forest together. We could rely on Abraham Paikovsky's experience in the matter, as he had been there twice and knew the way. But Abraham was disinclined to try his luck again owing to his bitter experience the previous autumn. However, we convinced him that if no group would take us in, we would form one of our own. We were seven in all: Abraham and his son Nahum, Haim Paikovsky, and myself. Haim and Nahum left for the village of Telkonza in order to bring back Anchke and Zimka Michls, who were staying with farmers, to join us.

197

Father did not want to come with us, perhaps because he had become weak from lying in the hole during the winter, or for reasons of his own which he did not share with me. However, he did not prevent me from going, nor did he urge me to stay with him. I also did not want to press him to come with us as I had no notion of what was awaiting us and the road was unfamiliar and dangerous. Near the ancient forest were Lithuanian and Polish villages whose inhabitants were lurking to attack the partisans. The danger was greatest in the neighborhood of Saltanishok and Kovalka, on the banks of the river near the entrance to the ancient forest. To enter the forest, one had to cross the river, and while doing so could easily be ambushed by the Germans and Poles, not to mention hostile local farmers. People, who were not aware of these dangers could easily fall into their hands. So that when Father seemed unwilling to come with me, I did not try to persuade him. There seemed no reason why the two of us should endanger ourselves and so I parted from him again, for the first time since the death of my brother Pinchas.

Abraham Paikovsky's father, Reb Joshe Jankel, a Jew well into his old age, still lived in the woods with his younger son, Simke the tailor. We agreed that if we would find it possible to exist and join the partisans in the ancient forest, we would return and bring back the rest of the Jews of Dowgalishok. We still had no rifles and our only weapons were sticks resembling guns.

On Sunday, 21 April 1943, we set out on our way. We made our way along bypaths and crooked lanes between shrubs, and left behind the woods of Petrishonza, passing between the villages of Shmilgin and Slabodka. Here we suddenly discovered that Nahum Paikovsky, Abraham's son, had vanished. He usually ran forward in front of the group, and so had evidently gone down a lane between the shrubs and had thus lost contact with us. We stopped to look for him for some time, but when we saw that there was no likelihood of finding him, we continued on our way with heavy hearts. We convinced ourselves and his father that he would turn up, for he knew the way and would return to the vicinity of Dowgalishok and join the Jews who had remained there.

Thus we continued on our way near the village of Poleshok, crossed the highroad that led to Grodno from Radun and reached the neighborhood of Saltanishok. It was dawn when we finally crossed the river, having accomplished the most dangerous part of the journey. With daylight, the gigantic trees almost touching the skies of the ancient forest stood before us. We were relieved and the tension slid away from us as we entered the dense forest in daylight. The first problem facing us was how to find someone in this huge labyrinth. We feared that we might encounter one of the Russian groups, whose only purpose was to plunder and to kill without any discrimination, although if it happened to be Jews, our lives were of no consequence in any case. Fortunately, we managed to reach Torvitz, the farmer, who actually lived within the forest, together with his brother and served as the contact between the various partisan groups as well as bringing them news of what was happening outside the forest.

23 The Meeting with Elka Todres

At first he was unwilling to tell us where we would find the partisans, but after we convinced him that no harm would come to him as a result, he told us to wait and he ran to tell the Jewish partisans that another group of Jews had arrived in the forest. Shortly afterward, we noticed a number of armed riders between the trees approaching us on horseback. When they stood before us dressed as Cossacks, with their rifles tucked into their very impressive belts crossing their breasts and guns decorating their hips, my self-confidence failed me and I did not know whether they were robbers or partisans. They were followed by a horse and wagon, also moving towards us. I immediately recognized Elka (Eliahu) 'Todres' Ariovitz at the head of the riders, coming to greet us. They had brought the wagon to take us to the partisans' camp in the forest.

Suddenly I felt secure, for this was another world and a different rule, unlike the reality and daily experience we had become used to. Here one speaks loudly and fears no one. One can even shout, riding on horses or travelling on wagons, making bonfires, over which the food being prepared sends out savory smells in every direction.

Elka appeared to me as a savior. The freckles which spread over his face added to his charm and good looks. His courageous bearing inspired confidence all around him. I recalled how we had studied together in our first years at school. He was older than I was, but was not one for learning and his heart was not in his studies. We were good friends and on more than one occasion, I helped him avoid trouble with his teachers. The song we learned then still resounds in my memory: 'We have a little goat / And the goat has a beard / He also has four legs / And a little tail.' Now I saw him not as my schoolmate but as a leader, as a great commander and savior. Since our time together at school we had gone different ways: he to study smithing and I to continue my studies at school and at the small yeshiva. Now I was proud to have been his school-mate, and I am still proud of it to this very day. Life in the forest with Elka's group was organized along military lines. It consisted of 70 souls when we arrived to join them and its people included women and children, as well as elderly people who were not able to fulfil any roles that demanded physical effort. Most were single individuals or remnants of families: an older brother with a younger brother or sister, a son with an elderly parent, uncle or aunt, in other words, those who had managed to survive. This was also the reason for it being called 'the family group' as well as 'Elka's group' after its commander and leader.

There were also some younger people, whose task was to guard the camp, and also to supply foodstuffs and clothing. As they did not go in for combative activities their weapons, assuming they had any, were of poor quality. The good weapons were reserved for the fighters who made up a special unit. The kitchen was for general use and supplied food for the entire group in an orderly manner. There was a cook and a storekeeper. Everyone had a role or task that was given him by the leader of the camp. In general, it was the women who did the cooking, the washing, and repairing the clothes for the men and for the fighting unit. The sector sent out on military action would frequently spend a few days with the family group in order to rest and relax.

Every group of people or family would have a sleeping shelter – a sort of hut made of wood and branches. No camouflage was necessary, for within the forest one felt at home and secure. There were guards near the camp, and patrol guards on duty some distance from the camp in every direction keeping an eye on any movement or strangers within the forest. Camouflaged security patrols were placed on all the

roads leading to the forest, and they would pass on information concerning anything suspicious or unusual. Local
farmers from the surrounding countryside were also used to
convey information to the camp's headquarters.

For the first time in many months I did not feel hungry. There
was an ample quantity of fresh meat, since herds of cows or
pigs were brought to the camp and kept at some distance.
There was a shepherd for this purpose, who would also milk
the cows and see to their feeding. The cows and pigs would
be slaughtered according to need, supplying the camp with
cooked food and hot dishes. The only thing that was rationed
was bread, which could not be kept for long. Flour and all
types of grain and pulses were available in quantity, however.
   At that time, there were still non-organized groups in the
forest which did not come under the aegis of the general
partisan headquarters, and were only now beginning to get
organized. Owing to the lack of coordination between the
various groups, there were conflicts which sometimes had
tragic results. There was suspicion and animosity particularly
between the Jewish groups and the non-organized Russian
groups. The source of much of this animosity was the girls in
the Jewish groups. The Russians, who were given to drinking
too much, would fall upon the Jewish girls, and there were
even cases of rape, which naturally led to armed struggles
between the Jews and the Russians.
   The Jewish groups were larger and less mobile, for they
included women and children, as well as the elderly. On the
other hand, the Russians were made up of small groups of
two or three men, who were immensely mobile, and mainly
consisted of former prisoners of war and convicts who had
fled from prison at the outbreak of hostilities, or young people
who had no obligations toward a family. Their groups were
known by such names as Kolka, Sashka, and Vanka. They
were well armed, and terrorized the farmers in the region.
   One day, the Germans paid a visit to Bochka, a farmer
living at the edge of the forest. They tied his hands with a

chain and asked him to lead them to the partisans, saying that if he refused he would be killed on the spot. Bochka, who was used as an informer by the partisans and knew all the groups, deliberately took them to the strongest of the Russian groups in order to teach the Germans a lesson for daring to enter the forest. The Russians, sensing that the Germans were somewhere in the neighborhood, fled. However, Yoshke Lubetsky's group, who were aware of the presence of the Germans, lay in wait for them and assaulted them. In the course of this struggle, Shlaymke Berkovitz of Sabakanitza, Haim Itchke's cousin, lost his life. He had attempted to strangle a German in order to take him prisoner, but was himself killed. The Germans who survived ran for their lives.

24 The Establishment of the Otriad

The organization of the groups into a united partisan movement under the authority of a high command began in the months of February and March 1943, when a small group of men from the east arrived in the ancient forest. They were part of a group of guerrilla fighters and paratroopers who had been dropped behind the enemy lines and whose aim was to organize the various partisan groups hiding in the forest under one central authority with a military discipline, which was to act on instructions from Moscow. These would be conveyed telegraphically, or by runners and contacts between the partisan units in the east, in the region of Minsk and the forests of Naliboki.

At the same time, the Leninsky Comsomol unit was being organized in the forest as a branch of the partisan brigade, active some 100–150 kilometers to the east, under the command of General Mayor Kapusta. This unit was organized along the usual military lines into divisions and platoons, consisting of some hundred men at the time. Most of the men and the divisional commanders were Jews, while the Russians made up some 30 per cent of the unit. Arms also reached the unit via Jews who had bought them or who had obtained them from farmers by force.

The commander at the head of the unit was Lieutenant Stankevitz, who had reached the forest as a guerrilla fighter. The unit set up its headquarters, and among its members were two Jews: Jacob Konichovsky, from Ivya, and Moshe Fefferman, from the town of Lida. Both men evidently enjoyed a certain status within the Communist Party and were loyal to the Soviet regime even prior to the war.

All the young men from the family group who were capable of bearing arms and executing combat missions, moved over to the *Otriad*. All the weapons belonging to the family group were also taken to the unit, and only rather old and useless weapons were left behind, together with the men who were no longer capable of performing military duties.

Elka 'Todres' was made commander and he was responsible for the family group consisting of some 100 souls. They had to get their own food, with the aid of the limited arms at their disposal. Older brothers and sons of those who had joined the unit would sometimes bring them food and clothing. On going out on a food-foraging mission, or *'Bombioshka'* as it was called, members of the unit would sometimes share their loot with the family group, because many of the fighters had little brothers and sisters, and parents or relatives there. In general, however, it was Elka's responsibility to see to the existence and needs of the family group with very limited means. The fighting unit and its command did not concern themselves with the family group's existence; on the contrary, they regarded it as something of a nuisance. Indeed, had it not been for the fact that most of the Jewish fighters came from the family group and had members of their families with the group, it is doubtful whether this group of dependants would have survived at all.

Added to this, there was sometimes an order to round up all the available arms still with the family group, leaving only the most ineffective weapons. Elka, who was courageous and did not lack initiative, would soon acquire substitutes. He had learned to hide weapons from the Russians and use them only when needed on a mission.

Elka obtained arms from the farmers who had collected the weapons discarded by the Red Army during their panic-stricken retreat in 1941. It needed intelligence work to find out who had hidden arms, but by threats and intimidation, indeed sometimes with blows, we would unearth the weapons, which were sometimes hidden in the bed of a river.

There were another two family groups in the forest: the

Lida group and the Grodno group, each consisting of 70 people. Elka's group, however, was noted for its organization and effectiveness, and his reputation stood very high. All the farmers in the neighborhood knew and feared him. They called him 'The Cossack'. Even the Russian commanders of the unit respected him, and some of them were envious of his successes. His handsome and picturesque clothing annoyed them, for they did not know how to dress, and his effectiveness in acquiring arms and military missions were also a source of jealousy.

The chief commander, Lieutenant Stankevitz, also admired Elka, indeed he loved and respected him, but many of his inferior officers saw him in a different light. They could not stand the competition, and viewed him with a blind hatred combined with the inherent anti-Semitism they had absorbed from their childhood, and at the time from the Germans and Polish farmers. To the Jews, however, Elka was an admirable and beloved figure, and they carried out his orders and commands willingly, seeing him as a father: the savior and provider of the family group.

I spent some days with Elka's family group, and before I could become used to the place and its ways, an order was received from unit headquarters to recruit all the young men capable of military duties, in order to transfer them to the unit. I feared that I would be passed over because of my age and height, and I did everything in my power to appear taller. I also asked acquaintances to vouch for me as capable of being a fighter. And so I entered the ranks of the fighters and moved from the family group to the fighting company of the unit.

That 'it is hard to be a Jew' seems to be appropriate anywhere and at any time. Until I arrived in the ancient forest, I had not eaten meat in order to avoid eating non-kosher food, and the taste of pork was foreign to me. More recently, when I was staying in the hideout in Andzielevitz's barn, I permitted myself to eat the meat soup prepared by Andzielevitz's wife, but I did not partake of the pieces of meat swimming about in the soup. I also made a point of praying and laying on my phylacteries every day – the same phylacteries that I had received from Mother (may her memory be blessed). On coming to the forest, I had to face a new reality. I was no longer on my own, but together with a group of people, Jews and Russians, who slept and ate together, went out on missions together, worked together, and even spent their leisure time relaxing in conversation with one another.

When I was with my father or brother, I could avoid eating meat or lard and do with some bread and potatoes, together with dairy products. Or I would go hungry at times. Now the situation was different as we had a common kitchen and everyone received the same meal which was determined by the cook or the storekeeper, and there was no possibility of getting different food. I knew, too, that I had to be healthy and strong in order to be able to fulfil any task I was given, and that I should not lag behind the other fighters despite the fact that I was a lad compared with them. This situation depressed me and I did not know what to do, or how to bear it, and there was no rabbinical authority I could consult on the matter. After some days of preoccupation and self-reproach, I decided that under such conditions it was permissible to eat every kind of food, for any physical weakness on my part could result in endangering life. As soon as I reached this decision and the religious prohibition was written off, I overcame my revulsion about eating pork that was so rooted in my upbringing. At first, it was really an effort which I evidently withstood quite easily, but from then on it was no longer an issue.

Prayers and the laying of phylacteries were a greater problem, however, for I felt that I would be ridiculed if someone saw me praying or laying phylacteries, and that instead of glorifying the Almighty, I would be committing sacrilege in the eyes of both the Russians and the Jews. This did not seem to be sufficient reason not to lay phylacteries, however, for I had sufficient time at my disposal, and I could easily hide behind the shrubs and the trees. It was still a problem, for it was forbidden to distance oneself from the camp area without the knowledge of those who were responsible for guarding the camp. The guards could assume that a stranger was roaming about and shoot him. Having no choice, I would walk a few steps away from the camp and appear as if I was taking a stroll for my own enjoyment, and pray quietly without laying on my phylacteries. Happily, I knew the prayers by heart. Sometimes I would say the prayers to myself without moving my lips, lest someone think I was talking to myself, while the precept regarding laying the phylacteries I fulfilled in a very hasty manner. Of course, it would happen that just that moment, someone would approach me, and I would squat down so that I should not be seen.

This situation did not go on for long and when I moved to the unit, I placed the phylacteries in the pocket of my clothing, which I did not remove, even when asleep. I have never been without these phylacteries, given to me by my mother, and I guarded them close to my body, at all times and across borders and seas, until I reached Israel.

Life in the ancient forest was quite different from life in the woods around Dowgalishok. Here there was no problem of obtaining food, which was plentiful, nor did we lack clothing. When on a mission, we would take off our ragged and dirty clothes and exchange them for others at the homes of farmers. At night we could sleep peacefully without being frightened by every falling leaf. We were relieved of having to care for our personal existence because this was a communal responsibility, and it was the leaders' duty to solve these problems. Conversations generally dealt with military situations, reprisals, and similar matters. During our leisure, we were occupied in polishing our weapons or counting our ammunition. Loneliness was a thing of the past and the dejection caused by having nervously to ask for bread was gone. I was only concerned with carrying out the orders to the best of my ability and returning safely to the warm and peaceful base .

One's personal equipment consisted of a knife, a fork, and a spoon, which were tucked into the fold of our boots, ready for use. During the serving of a hot meal, the entire platoon would sit in a circle and an enormous pot would be placed in the center. The meal generally consisted of meat soup with potatoes, or with semolina, beans or peas. Each of us would dip his spoon into the pot and dole out the soup, and whoever was lucky enough to have a large spoon or a long arm would naturally succeed in getting a larger and meatier portion.

Life, although full of bereavement and loss from the past, and charged with danger from moment to moment, had a kind of gaiety. There was a joy in living that derived from our very existence, despite all that had happened and indeed all that might happen. Life continued along new lines, and every reprisal, no matter how small, against the German murderers, was reason for rejoicing. The very fact of having survived and being able to determine one's own fate to a certain degree, and to fight for the continuation of life, was a source of happiness. When tragedy occurred and a friend fell in battle, we were full of sorrow, but it did not affect the course of our lives – we were immune to catastrophe. As long as life went on, we had to eat and drink and what happened to one person today might happen to another tomorrow. This attitude to life became our natural outlook.

In the jungle of partisan life in the forest there were quarrels and intrigues, as well as ambition to achieve status. Despite all the upheaval and instability young men and women still managed to have relationships, though these were few in number. On a calm and peaceful day, a boy would lie on the grass and win the heart of a girl, until his happiness was shattered by having to move to a more dangerous area. The few girls were attracted to those boys who had the reputation of being good fighters and were known to bring them pretty clothes when they returned from a mission. Naturally, success was generally the lot of the commanders, and if the reputation of one officer declined, he was abandoned without a word and it was the turn of the next 'star'.

The women generally saw to domestic matters or secretarial

work, but this was not always the reason for being accepted into the unit. There were exceptions. I remember one instance of a Jewish girl from Lida, who was taken into the unit because she was a courageous fighter. She was sent out on all the difficult and dangerous missions and was capable of carrying out any task imposed on her no less successfully than the men, who all respected and admired her, and did not dare to impose on her or trouble her in any way because she was a woman.

The unit's activities were varied, and included destroying railway lines, blowing up trains that brought supplies and reinforcements to the front, destroying granaries which had been taken from the farmers by the Germans as well as places where they kept their stores and roadways when they were on the move. There were also planned attacks on police bases, especially those close to the forest. Bridges, which were essential for the movement of military forces and the transfer of supplies, were blown up. We also had to get supplies of food and clothing for the unit.

Food was generally taken from wealthy farmers and estate-owners, rather than the poor. First and foremost among the victims of forays were those who collaborated with the Germans. Their possessions were appropriated and destroyed. The partisans also took food from the farmers. They would tell the farmers that by order of Moscow he had to pay the partisans a tax, as they were representatives of the regime there. The farmer would then receive a document in return, declaring that the partisans had received a certain amount of grain and a certain number of cattle and pigs from him. This document would serve as proof to the Germans that he had nothing left to offer them, for the partisans had taken everything. Such documents were also given to farmers even when nothing had been taken, in order to fool the Germans.

A few weeks after I reached the forest, a group of partisans went out on a mission to obtain food for the unit in the neighborhood of Dowgalishok. I joined this action, together with

Abraham Paikovsky, as we knew the roads and farmers of this area. We also wanted to meet the Jews of Dowgalishok, tell them about the forest and try to convince them to return with us. We managed to locate them and stayed with them for a whole day. I met Father and urged him to return with me to the forest. Abraham Paikovsky also tried to convince his brother Simke and his father Joshe Jankel to join him. I told all the Jews we met about life in the forest, warning them that one day they could all be wiped out here, because they were dependent only on the mercy of the gentiles, and when they decided – heaven forbid – to get rid of them, there would be nothing to stop them from destroying one and all. Unfortunately Father did not react to my explanations, nor did the rest of the Jews. He did not refuse point-blank to go with me, but merely repeated his former arguments: 'Here I know everyone since I was a child and everyone knows me. I have worked for them and served them for many years, and they are my friends and would not do me any harm. Proof of this is that they have helped me until now and treated me with affection, as a friend. And what is more, now the area is ruled by the partisans, and the rumors of large Jewish partisan groups, they woul not harm the Jews out of fear of reprisals.'

To this day, I do not really know the reasons for his refusal to join me in the forest; whether they were to do with his roots in the place where he grew up, the landscape and the people among whom he was raised, and from whom he derived his vitality, or whether there were other factors. Undoubtedly, it was difficult for him to part from this place and the Jews of Dowgalishok, among whom he felt at home. Whatever he was feeling at the time, my own conscience is still troubled that I could not convince him to join me. We never saw each other again, and that too was the last time I saw the good, kind Jews of Dowgalishok.

A short while after I had parted from Father, another group of partisans set off for the Dowgalishok neighborhood, and I asked them to take him with them back to the forest. On their return, they gave me the terrible news that they had not met him and that the White Poles (the AK) had attacked all the Jews of Dowgalishok on the eve of Shavuoth and killed most of them, my father among them. He was 45 years old. Some time later, I heard that among those who lost their lives in that pogrom were Reb Joseph Jaacov, at the age of 85, a decent and honest man who worked the land and revered his God; Leah Rudnitzky and her son Leibke, and her little granddaughter; and Frieda Babroinik, who leased Uncle Jacob-Leib's lands when he did not return from Argentina.

They were all Dowgalishok Jews. Those Jews who survived were killed a short time later, and no one knew how or where. One thing was certain: that they were all killed by the AK, whose aim was to rid Poland of its Jews, for their slogan was: 'A Poland without Jews'.

Father's death was a terrible shock and I was utterly depressed. Now I was all alone in the world, without a relative or benefactor. My loss sent my thoughts back to the death pit in Radun, to Mother and my little brother Kushka, and my brother Pinchas. Now I had no one to care for or to make happy and no one to look after me. I was freed of all obligations, for no one awaited me any longer and I no longer cared about anything. For many days and nights, I withdrew into myself and could not come to terms with the fact that I had left him. Although no one had told me with absolute certainty that father had been killed, I assumed he had perished along with the rest of the Jews of Dowgalishok. In my heart I knew that he was lost, and I could not forgive myself for not having managed to take him back to the forest with me. This was the first time I doubted the Almighty and my trust in his personal care and infinite justice was open to question.

25 The Trial of Elka Ariovitz

One fine day we were shocked to learn that Elka Ariovitz had been summoned before the headquarters of the Kotovsky unit and sentenced to death. The gist of the charge was that before the establishment of the unit, back in the past, he had robbed farmers and taken food and clothing from them 'illegally', and that this accounted for their unwillingness to cooperate with the partisans. A number of other charges were also invented to justify the sentence.

It was obvious to the Jews amongst us that behind the mask of so called 'justice', lurked blatant anti-Semitism and personal envy. His reputation for competence and organizational ability went before him, and his missions were successful. What was particularly painful about the matter was that those who were accusing him of supposed robbery had themselves participated in these actions together with him, but Elka had taken food and clothing in order to support his group, whereas they had robbed and plundered in order to get drunk and behave wantonly. The past actions of Sashka, the former lieutenant in the Red Army, were well-known: he and his fellow soldiers had remained in the rear, and afterward fled to the forest and there joined Vanka, a recognized murderer.

Their hatred and envy of Elka stemmed from his success in obtaining weapons. His elegant clothing also annoyed them and his reputation as a courageous fighter and leader of his group made them see red. They hated him even before the establishment of the unit, when he prevented them from harming the Jews and raping the Jewish girls. They were also anxious that he knew of their unruly behavior. Therefore, they took the obvious way of getting rid of him – that of using him as a scapegoat for their own crimes.

It was true that Elka would punish gentiles who collaborated with the Germans or who attacked Jews in the ghetto and during the slaughter in Radun. And he would also appropriate the possessions of Jews who stayed with gentiles. Elka would take action and go out on forays against gentiles, when the Jewish account generally called for it, and he was under the impression that the partisans approved of avenging Jewish blood. He felt that anyone who collaborated with the Germans against the Jews was an enemy of the partisans. But the anti-Semites among the partisans, who had learned from the Germans that one could gain possessions and 'friends' for Jewish blood, did not like Elka. His punishment suited the general policy of acquiring supporters of the partisans. One of the reasons for his conviction was the reprisals he took against the murderers of Jews.

In the winter of 1942–43, before the existence of the family unit, Elka on his own initiative, took action against Rakoczsky, who had initiated the murder of Berl Lipkunsky in the Lida jail, and the destruction of his family in the ghetto of Radun, by informing the Germans that he was a communist. Elka avenged Berl's death and that of his family by killing Rakoczsky and destroying his property by fire.

On another occasion, Elka set out to get food, and encountered a Polish wedding on the way. Among the guests at the wedding, he recognized a Polish policeman with his young wife. That same policeman had taken part in the slaughter of Jews in Radun. Elka did not hesitate. He took the young man to the forest and reported to the unit that he had taken a Polish policeman prisoner, and requested that he be tried by the unit court. The unit command's natural response was, 'you caught him, so do with him whatever you think proper in the circumstances'.

In the meantime, the affair became known to Marusek, a former Polish communist, who was a member of the unit's command. He tried to free the policeman by all sorts of means. Elka suspected that he might be freed and quickly issued a sentence. He had him executed before Marusek could do anything about it. When the Polish Marusek, the 'devout communist', ran shouting to Elka not to fire, the shots avenging the death of Jews were already ringing out. Marusek, who had supporters at headquarters, was furious, and from then onwards sought opportunity for revenge.

These actions served as a pretext to weave a criminal plot against one of the leading partisans who had paved the way for the resistance movement in the ancient forest.

The opportune moment to get rid of Elka came when the commander of the Leninsky Comsomol unit (afterwards commander of the Leninsky Comsol Brigade), Lieutenant Stankevitz, went on a mission to the east with a group of partisans, taking with him the finest of the Jewish partisans who were Elka's comrades. The trial against Elka was staged during Stankevitz's absence. In order to provide evidence that this it was not motivated by anti-Semitism, two Jews were co-opted who were in the headquarters of the unit: Jacob, from the village of Varonova, and Moshe, from the village of Ivya. According to some rumors, they were members of the Communist Party, and they were also signatories to Elka's death warrant. In their fervor to prove their loyalty to the party, they did not hesitate to lend their signatures, together with the other 'guardians of justice and lovers of Israel' to the death warrant, for they wanted to show their Russian and Polish friends that on no account could they be suspected of loving the Jews.

While the trial was being conducted in secrecy, and without him being present, Elka was arrested and put under guard. He was deprived of his weapons and partisan uniform, which were given to one of the Russians as booty. The Jew who was assigned to him as his guard was Jossele Hamarsky of Eishishok, and as I was told by Lipa Skolsky, Jossele turned to Elka and said: 'Elka, perhaps we should run off together, for the matter appears to be dangerous', and Elka replied: 'I'm not afraid of them.'

At that time, I was still with the family group. I remember the commander who organized us and explained the regulations and orders of the unit headquarters. The people staging the trial considered carrying out the sentence within the forest and in front of the unit, officially and openly. Behind this, there was also the notion of breaking down the unity of the Jewish groups which existed before the establishment of the unit. Before the Jewish groups joined the unit there was a certain amount of tension between the Jews and the unit. The Jews suspected that after their groups were dissolved, they would also be deprived of their weapons, and then they would be at the mercy of the unit. They had been taught by experience, however, and remembered earlier attempts to deprive them of their arms, on the pretext that the family groups did not execute fighting missions, and had no need of effective weapons. Evidently these suspicions were still justified. And indeed, while the partisans were hurrying to carry out their plot and execute Elka in full view of the unit, a riot broke out among the rows of Jews. They grabbed their weapons and threatened to use them if the perpetrators of the plot persisted in carrying out the sentence. The Jews demanded that the death sentence be commuted to something milder. They also demanded that the trial be postponed until the brigade commander, Stankevitz, returned. On seeing that an armed struggle could emerge within the unit, the people who staged the trial were forced to change their tactics and the death sentence was commuted. Elka was instead given three extremely dangerous missions. There was no objection to this on the part of the Jews, as we were certain that Elka would carry out the most dangerous missions successfully. With the trial ending as it did, the partisans were obliged to return Elka's personal weapons and uniform, but it was decided to transfer him from his role as commander of the family group to the fighting unit. We were convinced that the matter would end there and that Elka would rise to his proper status in the unit.

A few days later, some people from the unit's command

invited Elka to go out on an important action with them. Among them were the two Jews who had been signatories to Elka's death sentence. Niomke Rogovski recalled that Elka consulted him, and asking his advice as to whether he should go with them or refuse. Niomke told him to join them and that he had nothing to fear. However, when the command force returned from their action two days later, Elka was not among them. A muster parade of the entire unit was held, and everyone was warned that serious punishment would await anyone who disobeyed the commanders' orders or attempted to undermine the military discipline of the unit. We were then told of the execution of Elka at the village of Lipkonza.

As we learned later on that the show trial was staged before the entire village. It was explained to the astonished villagers that the sentence was being carried out against Elka Ariovitz for acts of robbery and murder against innocent inhabitants. The village of Lipkonza was one of the villages which supported the partisans and which admired and respected Elka in particular. The villagers wept as the sentence was carried out. One old lady of 70 shouted at the executioners: 'What are you doing? he is like our god.' The farmers of the village told how, in the forest, the organizers of the trial had already bound him and shot him in the legs lest he should try to escape. Only afterwards did they shoot him in the head from behind when he requested that they kill him and not torture him. Even today, no one knows who shot Elka – whether it was the entire group or whether it was one of the criminals. There was a rumor that it was one of the Jews, but there was no one who could provide evidence of this apart from the criminals themselves.

This ugly affair cast a dark shadow on the courageous struggle for survival and salvation during the difficult clouded days of our people. It was a sad end to the life of one of the best of the Jewish partisans, who had saved many Jewish lives. His death caused the Jewish partisans much sorrow and embarrassment, partly because of the deceit and villainy that could not be rectified. As a result of these events the *otriad* grew into a brigade, which was called the Leninsky Komsomol, while the Jewish partisans became the 'Kotovsky unit'.

In the meantime, Stankevitz returned from his mission in the east and was very disturbed by what had happened. He recalled how Elka would perform the most dangerous deeds for him, and greatly regretted the loss of such a courageous and capable fighter. As the general commander, he could not dismiss his entire staff and ruin the unit, and he was therefore obliged to accept a situation, which he could not alter. However, we knew that Stankevitz hated the perpetrators for their criminal act and waited for an opportunity to repay them for what they had done, perhaps after liberation.

Unfortunately, Stankevitz did not live to see that day. Shortly afterwards, he fell in a battle with the White Poles, alongside his faithful aide, Leibke Kaganovitz, while the latter was trying to save his beloved commander's life.

Elka's death was not only a personal loss but also a heavy blow for the entire camp's families who now numbered some hundred souls. Elka had seen to their feeding and clothing and had given them feeling of security and hope. Now they were left without a leader to care for them and abandoned to the many dangers facing them. Two other commanders were appointed in his place: Berl from Oran, and Elka Shmilginer, who had been Elka Ariovitz's right-hand man, but neither had the stature and ability of the talented and courageous Elka.

Soon we were to face hard times, as the Germans decided to clear the forest of partisans. They recruited a large number of policemen from among the collaborators – White Russians, Lithuanians, Ukrainians, and all sorts of traitors – and together with help from the regular army and the air force, tanks, and cannons, they laid siege to and raided the forest.

The military unit succeeded in getting out of the area in

time, but without Elka's leadership the family unit was abandoned to its fate. There were many victims. May Elka's memory be blessed and remain with us forever as a brave Jewish fighter and guardian of Jewish honor during the dark days of weakness and helplessness.

26 The Blockade of the Forest

In the general confusion that prevailed in the family unit's camp after Elka's death, the order was given to collect all the available firearms in the camp. All the effective arms, rifles, and machine guns, and personal weapons in the family camp were transferred to the unit, leaving only a few useless rifles. Thus, without weapons and without a leader, the family camp was abandoned in the face of the approaching German blockade.

There were rumors concerning the increasing German presence in the vicinity of the forest, but in the absence of Elka, no one would give the order to move the camp away from danger.

At the time I was returning together with five other men from a military unit mission. We had brought back with us a herd of cattle. On orders from the unit command, we stopped at the family camp in order to leave them some cattle. It was then that the Germans attacked the area in which the camp was located. We had thought that they would not dare to enter the forest, for it was thick with trees and shrubs, and the dense foliage covered large regions of waterlogged marshland.

On Wednesday, 16 June 1943, in the early hours of the morning, airplanes could be seen overhead, and shortly afterwards, the heavy bombing began. Their main target appeared to be the family camp of the people of Lida and Grodno, and there were many casualties among them. This was my first experience of direct aerial bombing, with bombs falling only a short distance from me. It was alarming. The sound of bombs echoing in the void of the forest was terrible, and we feared the possibility of a direct hit. The tall dense trees gave a resounding thud as they fell to the ground. And even before the sound of the exploding bombs resonated throughout the forest, again and again we would hear the sound of the trees falling. The odor of fire and smoke wafted on the air, increasing the sense of approaching doom, we were afraid of spreading conflagration.

The bombing continued in spurts for a few hours, with groups of bombers circling overhead, releasing incendiary bombs from their bays, and sending their long-range missiles in clusters one after the other. When the bombing had subsided, machine gun fire was heard from the direction of the camps of Lida and Grodno, which were some kilometers from us. Without a leader to determine what was to be done and where to move, the Radun family camp was in a state of turmoil. However, they managed to contact the military unit and received some instructions, the gist of which was to camouflage the camp and move some hundred meters further in the direction of the marshes (on the assumption that the Germans would not go into the waterlogged swamps).

Six of us from the unit were first in the Lida and Grodno camps. We managed to get to the Radun camps on Wednesday before sunset, but did not succeed in reaching the unit, which was a distance of a few kilometers from us, and waited for daylight before trying to reach it. The general feeling was that we should get out of there as quickly as possible and flee to the 'Reich' (German-occupied Poland), in the direction of Grodno. But no one gave the order to do so, for Elke, the leader and commander, was absent. Everyone knew that something must be done at once to leave the place, but the right person to say exactly what had to be done, to say 'follow me', was not there. Everyone was saying 'If only Elke were alive, we would have left here some time ago.'

Early on Thursday morning, we received news that the unit had succeeded during the night in safely crossing the river of Dobitz and getting far into the 'Reich'.

This then was the manner in which the family group unit was forsaken by the military unit. First they murdered its leader; after that they expropriated the few weapons it possessed; then they deserted it without orders or guidelines in the face of the heaviest German attack ever to have been made on the forest, while the military unit itself managed to break through the German blockade of the forest and escape.

Standing knee-deep among the dense shrubs and the tall grass, in cold and slimy mud, we waited to see what would happen. We began to hear the sound of dry branches being broken by marching feet, alternating with the sound of boots sinking squelching through the mire. We still could not see anything, for the mist and fog was thick in the air and it was impossible to make out anything, much further than a meter away. But we felt the impending danger, and at that point also realized that the Germans were not hesitating to venture into the mud and water up to their knees. We started to retreat.

It is possible that the Germans would not have dared to enter the waterlogged marshes on their own, but they were supported by a horde of Lithuanians, Byelorussians, and Ukrainians, who were used to wallowing in this mire all their lives, and who were driven on by their desire to kill Jews.

The retreat turned into flight, as we did not have enough firearms to defend ourselves. All around us we could hear echoes of shots from all types of weapons. We soon discovered that we were surrounded on all sides and that there was no means of escape. Pathways divided the forest and the field of view between each section was some meters wide. The Germans placed heavy machine guns and light cannon, at every intersection of the forest, and at every prospect, in order to make it impossible to cross from one section to another. In this way they took over the entire forest. It was clear that the local farmers had guided them, or they would not have known how to find all the paths and close off the forest so effectively. Also, they went straight to the family camp as if they knew its whereabouts beforehand.

The Germans who were combing the forest marched

forward in close ranks, almost touching one another. Before advancing a step, they would fire at the shrubs facing them in order to clear them and force anyone hiding there to come out into their range of vision, opposite those posts where machine guns had been placed, ready for action. We ran wildly from place to place, as if enclosed in a box, and were met by a barrage of bullets in whatever direction we chose to run. At noon it started to rain, and continued to do so throughout the day. We hoped the hunt would cease because of the weather, but this was merely wishful thinking. It soon became clear that we would not succeed in escaping from the circle of death, and that we had no choice but to try to hide amidst the shrubbery and vegetation. Behind every shrub we encountered dead bodies, which were strewn all over the forest.

The six of us had managed to stay together throughout the ordeal. We decided that when we were cornered, we would take a defensive stand and at least try to kill as many of our pursuers as possible before they finished us off. Until then we saved our ammunition as we had little of it and it was a pity to waste even a single shot unnecessarily.

At a certain point later in the afternoon, when we were forced to come out into a clearing with only a few trees standing amidst the small and sparse shrubbery, we were met by hellish fire and it was a miracle that none of us was hurt. Bullets were lying all about us on the ground and embedded in the trunks of the trees behind which we were hiding. Crawling and running on all fours, we managed to evade them and cross over into another sector of the forest and hide among the low shrubs and tall vegetation.

Here, in this part of the forest, we met and joined up with a group of people from the family group of Radun. The rain continued to fall and the shadows of the tall trees anticipated the approaching twilight. Lying on the ground, we awaited nightfall with relief, in the hope that the darkness would offer us cover. We spread out in a single line facing what we imagined would be the direction from which the Germans would approach.

The sector we were now in had already been scoured by the Germans and we hoped that we could remain there until nightfall. I lay to the left of the group, which numbered some 20 men and Kushke, the watchmaker, lay to the right of me. We had only five rifles in all, and I had a Russian-made hand grenade with a handle, that could be enveloped in shrapnel if need be. Suddenly we saw a line of Germans coming towards us from the right, their machine guns poised for action.

Using sign language, we warned each other to keep down until the last moment, for we were under the impression that the Germans had not spotted us. If we tried to escape it was likely that many of us would be casualties, for we had only limited and ineffective weapons. The ring of soldiers advanced at an angle and reached the point where they faced our left wing, with me at its end. I quietly prepared the grenade, taking out the pin in order to be ready to throw it directly they discovered us. The others would deploy their weapons at the same time and we would try to escape during the exchange of fire.

I shall never forget Kushke's appearance at that moment. On seeing the Germans advancing in our direction, he was unable to control himself and lay stretched out on the ground, trembling in every part of his body, as if he had been struck down by malaria. His teeth were chattering and his body was bouncing as if he were lying on springs. I observed every movement made by the Germans, while at the same time glaring at Kushke, lest he give us away.

The group of soldiers advanced almost to our front line, some 20 meters to the left of us, while we watched them with bated breath. Suddenly there was a loud swishing sound of wings echoing through the tall trees above the Germans. A miracle had occurred! The soldiers who had been marching confidently towards their assembly point, were startled by the sound and aimed their rifles in the direction of the trees, thinking that there were partisans hiding up there. Without being aware of it, they passed us by without noticing us. But they were not partisans; they were wild pigeons, whom the

Germans had also alarmed. I just caught the words: 'What lovely pigeons', while all the Germans watched the birds fly off and passed us by without seeing that their target lay at their feet.

While they were marching away from us, we lay on the ground unable to utter a word until they were out of sight. When evening came, we breathed easily at last. With nightfall, we began to seek a way of getting out of the forest. We aimed to cross the river and join the military unit in the 'Reich'. As luck would have it though, throughout the night we followed winding paths without reaching our objective, and when the dawn arrived, we noticed that we were back at the spot we had started from. In fact this was to our advantage for the roads and lanes through the forest were still closed off and we would have encountered endless danger.

On our way out of the forest, we passed by what had formerly been the family camp and found it razed to the ground, with the embers of the fire still alight. We did not go too near, for fear of danger or an unexploded mine. At noon, we met up with scouts from the military unit and learned that the unit had managed to evade the blockade without suffering casualties, except for the protective wing of the rearguard, who had a short exchange of fire with the German vanguard. A strange thought occurred to me at that moment: had the family camp perhaps been intentionally sacrificed to the Germans in order to serve as a cover for the military unit? Had the partisans misled the Germans by making them believe that they had encountered and liquidated the main partisan force, thus enabling the military unit to gain time and withdraw to a safe position?

The scouts also informed us that the unit command's orders were that all the fighters were to disperse in small groups and that only after the blockade was ended and the Germans had withdrawn from the forest, should they return to the chosen meeting-point. We understood that we had to abandon the forest for some time until the blockade came to an end. We organized into groups of four to five men, and together with

Maimke Dolinsky, Haim Paikovsky, and Benjamin Frankel, we set out for the woods of Mezanze. We walked throughout the night, without being seen by anyone. When daylight came, we entered a field of oats, and lay among the furrows for the rest of the day. It was a sunny, summery day with intermittent showers, and we took off our clothes, trying to dry our wet and dirty clothing which reeked of sweat and decay. In the evening we reached the group of Jews who lived in these woods and found them in a terrified state. The siege had passed them by, but they had heard of the attacks and the massive bloodshed in the forest. We also found others who had succeeded in fleeing from the forest during the blockade. Everyone had his own escape story; everyone had experienced a miracle which had enabled him to survive.

Haimke Gitels, for instance, then a lad of 11, had been separated from his mother Gittel and his elder sister Leah during the flight. When he saw that he was alone and that the Germans were shooting in every direction, he climbed up a tall tree and sat in its branches through the long day, waiting for a German to finish him off. After the Germans left, he began to look for his mother and sister in the battlefield, and while he was walking among the corpses, he noticed a skirt hanging on a tree and recognized it as belonging to his older sister. She, too, had been saved by climbing a tree, but when she tried to escape from the forest, she was killed by the Germans or the AK.

Haim Berke's story was somewhat different. When he saw that there was no way out, he lay down among the corpses, smearing himself with their blood as if he were one of them. Only after the Germans had checked that they were all dead, did he continue his flight. Though shot at, he was miraculously saved by a spoon which he had in his pockets.

The blockade lasted 15 days, after which the Germans withdrew from the forest.

For two weeks, we wandered about the woods in the neighborhood of the villages of Yewonza, Mezanze, and Karkodi, near the groups of Jews who had been there since they had fled from Radun. From time to time, other Jews looking for a refuge would appear on the scene, after having to leave the place they had lived in until then. The Jewish haven in this area was used as a sort of hostel for wayfarers and also as a source of information as to what was going on in the area. Armed Jewish partisans would appear here from time to time in passing. The more permanent residents were not armed and lived on food purchased from the local farmers, if they had the wherewithal to pay for it. If not, they would rely on handouts from the farmers, who would give them some bread, or a potato, or flour, and sometimes dairy products.

Cultural life was a continuation of life in Radun. Everything was kosher and people kept the Sabbath and resumed their daily prayers. After the blockade and manhunt in the forest, scores of people who had escaped came here and the whole place was like a beehive. The few good farmers in the area were too few to feed the 'inhabitants' of the woods, and in addition, the increasing number of people begging put too much pressure on those farmers who gave of their own accord. The most recent arrivals were not acquainted with the situation and did not know whom to approach or whom to avoid.

Despite my knowledge of Dowgalishok and life in of the forest. I could not relax here. I felt that the Germans could attack us without warning and that then we would have nowhere to go. I considered these woods only as a way-station until the storm passed and the Germans lifted the siege and left the forest. Then would I return to the forest and join the military unit.

27 Burying the Victims

When we learned that the Germans had left the forest region, we organized a group of ten men and started out for the forest. We, who had survived the German pursuit, felt morally obliged to collect and bury the victims before we rejoined the unit. To whatever extent it was possible, we would not leave them to be prey to wild animals and ravens, and on the 18th day after the manhunt in the forest, we arrived at the former location of the family camp which had been razed to the ground.

It was the season of the ripening corn, the first days of July, and at this time, there are occasional summer rains to relieve the heat of the day. We supplied ourselves with shovels and some blankets that we found strewn about the ground, and went out to the marshes to look for the victims' corpses. We were confronted with a scene of sheer horror, which in normal times we would not have been able to face. From quite a distance, we were aware of the strong odor and knew that the bodies were somewhere in the vicinity. When I was a child, I had heard stories of the body-snatching angels who tampered with dead bodies, particularly with those who had sinned when they were alive. Now, the horrible spectacle of open graves all over the ground lay revealed before us under the sun and the skies. The bodies, which had lain disclosed to the rain and the mud under the warm rays of the sun had lost all resemblance to human beings created in the image of God. Those same friends, with whom only three weeks previously we had fought for our lives, were now unrecognizable. It was only possible to identify them by their clothing or shoes. The bodies themselves had turned into a heap of some other form of life, a worm-eaten, decaying form of life on which myriad angels of destruction had wrought this nightmarish spectacle. The scene that I witnessed for the first time in the short span of my life was beyond the imagination of man or the work of the Creator. It is a vision which will not leave me as long as my memory retains the events of those days.

One of the corpses was that of Shimon Radiks of Brisk, a scholar from the Radun yeshiva, who had married my cousin Sarah Lipkunsky, the daughter of Berl, the tailor of Dowgalishok. The fine head full of learning and wisdom, had become a worm-eaten mass of creeping things. I found some consolation in contemplating the fact that this was the end awaiting all of us.

In addition to the horrifying spectacle, it was also difficult to go near the putrifying bodies because of the terrible smell. It was so strong that even at a distance of ten meters in the open air, it was impossible to go nearer. We had no means of disinfection and a lighted cigarette in one's mouth was the only way to cope. It took an enormous amount of will-power to overcome all weakness and hold one's breath in order to get nearer to the corpses.

Abraham Paikovsky, who had been a soldier in the First World War, and had seen a great many dead bodies on the battlefield, said that he could not go near the corpses. He asked us to pardon him, for this was the most horrific scene that he had ever witnessed.

Although ten of us set out, only a few were able to bury the corpses. The thought that I, too, could be stretched out somewhere out in the open under the sun, at the mercy of wild animals and ravens, forced me to overcome my weakness. Also one's moral obligations to render the last honors to the dead gave me the strength and ability to perform this holy mission. We all drew our strength from the same source and these motives enabled us to withstand this difficult trial.

It was impossible to touch the bodies and we had to use the branches of trees in order to roll them into blankets and carry them through the marshes to graves, which we had dug earlier on. We could not assemble all the corpses into one communal grave because the bodies were too dispersed over too large an area of the forest and marshes. Also, we did not have the strength to do so. For such a mission one would have needed additional men and the means to exist for some time. However, to some extent, we carried out our obligations towards those in the immediate vicinity and dug the graves deeply enough so that the wild foxes could not get at them. After we had filled in the graves, we said Kaddish for the holy, and engraved the date on a sturdy tree: 16.6.1943.

As I recall, those that participated in this mission of rendering the last honors to the dead were Abraham Paikovsky and his son Nahum, Haim Paikovsky, Benjamin Fraenkel, Maimke Dulinsky, Jacov Stolnitsky, and me, Avraham Lipkunsky.

The sun was setting and we hurried away from this place in a state of sadness and utter dejection. We met up with no one in the forest and did not succeed in contacting the unit, which had subsequently been divided into a number of smaller sectors. The major part of the unit, together with the command headquarters, had moved over to the 'Reich' in the neighborhood of Grodno and Novodwor. We split into two groups: one returned to the region of Mezanze, and I, together with Abraham Paikovsky and his son Nahum, Haim Paikovski, and Jakov Stolnitzky, went to the marshes of Lipkonza.

The family group established by Elka had ceased to exist after the manhunt, for there was no one to consolidate the survivors. Many Jewish fighters did not return to the military unit for a while because they could not abandon their families, but a few did manage to rescue their young brothers or parents, and they took them to the unit with them, where they helped with the various services.

The Asner brothers, who were known as courageous fighters, were fined and deprived of their weapons because they did not return to the unit immediately after the manhunt. And so they unearthed other weapons from where they were hidden and formed a separate unit of their own. However, the third brother, Abraham, managed to return to the unit together with his beloved Liebele. After some time, he, too, was forced to leave the unit because they expelled Liebele after she had been with them for over a year. The partisans' objective was to free the unit of all non-fighting personnel in order to be more mobile.

Our group of five men settled in the marshes of Lipkonza for some months. It was that in the village we learned the details of Elka's trial and execution from the local farmers. They had not forgotten him, for he had been much loved.

We sat amidst the dense shrubbery of the marshland without anyone learning of our existence for some time, until the shepherds discovered us. They kept the matter secret, however, and did not reveal it to a soul. Moreover, they would bring us news of the Germans' movements in the area, and later on, those of the White Poles. The village consisted mainly of Lithuanian farmers and Byelorussians, who had no fondness for the White Poles, and therefore no sympathy with the Polish underground movement.

As there was no bare dry ground in the marshland, we would hang hammocks made of branches between the trees and lie in them like monkeys. We stored away a supply of potatoes, and would go out from time to time to obtain chickens or dairy products. And then we would prepare potato soup, living quietly and unadventurously for a time.

One night we became aware that someone was trying to light a fire in the marsh area. We knew that only people in hiding like ourselves needed a fire in the marshes at night. In the morning we cautiously approached the place to see who this had been. To our surprise, we found a primitive still for producing vodka, and we understood that our guests in the night must have been the local farmers making the home-made vodka known as *samogon*. The discovery of the illicit production of vodka brought with it the death sentence, since the Germans needed the grains of wheat for bread and not vodka for the farmers. The farmers would come to the marshes where no one would see them. The distilling process involved cooking the pressed grain extract and letting it steam for many hours. The most suitable time for this was obviously at night. We found in them a certain kinship, for we were all in hiding. Throughout many nights, we would stand by assisting them, talking to them and getting news of what was happening in the area and in general. This was a period in which we felt a little more secure as the local farmers were well informed as to what was going on in the region and our fate was linked with theirs.

Under these circumstances, we became accustomed to being night-birds. During the day, we would lie in our hideout and sleep. One day, as we lay sleeping, hidden among the shrubs, a young shepherdess who knew us from former encounters when she was tending her herd in the marshes, burst in on us alarmed, asking us if we had not heard the shots. She told us that the White Poles were looking for us and that we must leave at once for they intended to kill us. Trying to pinpoint their whereabouts, we saw from afar a group of White Poles, bearing their national flag of red and white, leaving the marshes. Evidently it was something of a miracle that we had not heard their firing, which was intended to draw us out of our hiding-places in the marshes in order to murder us. It was only due to the fact that we had been asleep and not heard the shots that they wandered about in the marshes in an attempt to find us, and when they did not succeed, returned to whence they came. It was obvious that someone had informed them of our existence in the marshes, for they had reached the very spot where we had stayed a few days previously. Fortunately, with our safety in mind, we had changed our location the previous day and thus saved our lives.

This and other similar incidents warned us that the White Poles were following our movements and that it would be wiser to leave the marsh area to which we had become accustomed and acclimatized, and were even beginning to enjoy. These were the Days of Awe, a few days before Yom Kippur, and we were eager to spend the Day of Atonement with other Jews in order to fast and pray together. We decided, therefore, to go to the Mezanze woods to be among the Jews there. *En route* to Mezanze, we passed through one of the nearby villages and stole a few chickens for the ritual sacrifice on the eve of Yom Kippur (*kapparot*). Later on, we were ashamed to learn that we had taken the chickens from a friendly farmer. He complained to the Jews who came to see him that chickens had been stolen from him. We were truly sorry about this and sought ways of making up to him for our errant behavior. Throughout the holy days we stayed in the woods with the Jews.

28 The Jews in the Woods of Mezanze

In the woods of Mezanze, I had had a number of opportunities to enjoy being a guest on short visits, staying near Jewish families whom I did not know personally. This time I lived among them for many weeks and I had the opportunity to get to know them better, to get acquainted with their way of life and opinions, as well as to form friendships. Generally, few groups would welcome the arrival of additional Jews intending to settle amongst them, for the simple reason that every additional Jew affected the amount of food available from the local farmers. Too many Jews in one place strained the goodwill of the farmers of the region. They also attracted informers, which led to pursuit by the Germans, the White Poles, and anti-Semitic marauders of all kinds – all of which could result in loss of life. Actually, there was a sort of nominal distribution of roles among the Jews: who should go to this farmer and who to another, in order to avoid being too great a burden on the farmers. And yet they tried to welcome the arrival of fellow Jews in a friendly manner, following the ideal of hospitality laid down by Abraham, the patriarch.

The families of Reb Moshe Davidovitz were permanently settled in the woods between the villages of Karkodi, Mezanze, and Ivonza, as was Libe Shlosberg, the only daughter of Reb Shmaya Mendel and his wife Frieda, relatives of the Davidovitz family. We even called this part of the woods after them, as if it were their territory. From time to time, other families as well as single individuals also settled nearby, but the Davidovitz family had been here from the very first day after fleeing from the ghetto of Radun.

I had known these families and their households, their

homes and their occupations, merely superficially, for prior to the war I had been a little boy and we had not been in touch with one another. I remembered Moshe Davidovitz from childhood, when I had crossed his courtyard without his permission. His house had stood at the corner of the marketplace and faced the main road leading to Grodno, almost touching it. On the opposite side of the road stood the only gas station in Radun. Reb Moshe and his wife Dvorele, fled to the forest with their three daughters Haike, Liebele and Estherke. The fourth daughter, Zlatke (may she rest in peace) was killed while they were escaping from the ghetto, on 9 May 1942.

Reb Moshe was a keen scholar, well-versed in Bible and Talmudic lore and an observant Jew, as he interpreted this. Although he was related to the prevailing rabbi's court, he was not accepted by them. He did not toe the rabbinical line and had no axe to grind, distinguishing between the teachings of the Bible and making a living. He would dare to question the eminent and based his creed on rational thinking rather than on blind faith. For some reason, he had always displayed an interest in secular literature and found that in the blend of religion and science, the one did not deny the other. His religious creed was based on Maimonides' *Guide to the Perplexed.* The rabbi's court disapproved of the Enlightenment and its leaders.

Reb Moshe's livelihood derived from his restaurant and the alcoholic beverages he was authorized to serve there. Naturally, he maintained good relations with the local farmers, who would visit his restaurant for a drink when they came to the market on Wednesdays, after they had sold all their produce and had plenty of money in their pockets. They accepted him as a decent and honest Jew and they respected him.

Reb Moshe and his family, lived in the woods for 26 months, without stealing or taking anything that did not belong to them. He would obtain food by paying for it with money or goods, or receive it as a gift from the farmer offering it. Throughout the entire period he spent in the woods, he preserved his Jewish identity in every particular, as if he were still in his own home in Radun. He would not eat non-kosher meat but did not look down on anyone who did, saying: 'You youngsters have to be strong and healthy in order to fight and preserve your lives.' He would pray every day and did not light a fire on the Sabbath, but every Jew, even those who had desecrated the Sabbath in the past, he now viewed as pure and innocent. He was proud of every fighting and coura- geous fellow. Reb Moshe was delighted when he had a chance to exchange biblical arguments and Talmudic casuistry with someone, and during my stay in his company, I would use the opportunity to listen to him hold forth on biblical and Talmudic interpretations which he knew by heart. He would posit a question and then reply with originality and deeply felt answers. The result of these exchanges was that I was rewarded with his friendship, as well as that of his daughters, who had the greatest respect and affection for him. They saw in me one of their own kind, attached to and loving Judaism, although at that time I was no longer conscientious about observing the Sabbath or *kashrut*.

Reb Moshe's wife Dvorele was a typical Jewish woman, devoted to her husband with all her soul, and following in his footsteps. She never left him and accompanied him even when he went to obtain food from the farmers. She consid- ered his every utterance sacred, as did the rest of the house- hold. His daughters had already reached a marriageable age and two of them had found husbands in the forest. And despite the differences that would at times arise between the old and the young, the father and his daughters, and although they were independent and not reliant on their father, he was still on a higher level as far as they were concerned. He was blessed with a strong body and good health, and felt like a young man despite his 50 years. He was always trying to understand the idiosyncrasies of the young, even when these went counter to what he considered right. His neighbors in the forest recalled that once, on returning from an expedition to get food, he succeeded in obtaining a whole sack of bread and standing over it, he kept examining the contents, shouting: 'The messiah has come! The messiah has come! A whole sack of bread! '

Life in the forest still included such fundamental elements as love and jealousy. Although the conditions of life were primitive, the fear of death hovered over us permanently and there was not a shred of hope or salvation to be seen on the horizon, yet the people remained much as they had been, with the usual weaknesses and desires and lust for life. And so declarations of undying love were made by many a young man and woman. Because of the difficult nature of life in the forest, particularly for women, few women came to the forest, and it happened quite frequently that a number of young men courted the same girl, and she would favor one and then another in turn. Even in the midst of these harsh conditions, pretty clothes and delicate fineries still attracted the girls, and any young man who understood this and succeeded in offering her such gifts would win her smiles and perhaps even her affection. Betrayals also took place alongside the endless loyalties, and there were women who risked their lives in order to bring food to a wounded or sick lover. Quarrels and angry exchanges between lovers were also part of the scene, and these sometimes lasted for months on end.

Without knowing what the morrow would bring, accounts were still made for the distant future. The lust for life was great, perhaps greater than in normal times. It was very hard to support a whole family, but the mere fact of having a family was considered something to envy by those who had remained alone. Most of us were as lonely as a tamarisk in the desert, but the fate of those who had not made friends was even more sad and bitter.

One of the best of the young men from the yeshiva of Radun had an eye on one of the daughters of Reb Moshe even before they had fled to the forest. As fate would have it, the Germans took him to the Lida ghetto and the young pair went their separate ways. A year later, the young man managed to escape from the ghetto shortly before it was wiped out. The remaining Jews were sent to extermination camps, but he reached the forest and met his beloved once again. Unfortunately, he arrived there sickly and weak from his stay in the ghetto and everyone thought him a failure and that he would not be able to withstand the conditions in the forest for long. His sudden and unexpected appearance in the forest, and the knowledge that someone else was courting his beloved, may have turned the subsequent events into one of the tragic romances of the forest. Time was on his side, however, and the young man from the yeshiva was restored to health, not a little due to the help of his girlfriend who was once again at his side. And he soon became one of the most effective food-foragers. The love of these two continues to this very day in Israel, where they established a family and now have the pleasure of grandchildren.

Life in the forest was harsh and full of danger for a man, but it was many times more difficult and cruel for a woman with small children. This being so, very few succeeded in reaching the forest with their children. One of the few who did manage to flee to the forest, with her tiny, 3-year-old son, was Gutke. The little boy was intelligent and surprised everyone by his cleverness, acting as though he were a born partisan. His awareness and knowledge of the part of the forest they lived in was amazing. He understood why he was living in the forest and who was pursuing them, as well as the dangers. Little Yossele felt that he was a burden to his mother and imagined that she would abandon him and that he would lose her. He would say to her, sadly: 'Gutke, I know that you would like to leave me here in the forest.' And when he was asked how he would ask a farmer for bread, he would answer in Russian: 'Master, give me some bread and something to go with it.' Or he would show us how to hold a rifle as a partisan and force the farmer to give him bread. As a little partisan he would say: 'The world stands on three things: on spirits, a good meal, and something else.'

Gutke was the sister of Hazkel, a wagoner and glazier by trade, who was also known by the nickname 'the wedding' – a nickname also inherited by his two sons, Reubke and Velevke. This nickname was given him during the course of a journey to Vilnius with his old wagon. Vilnius was 80 kilometers away and when one of the wheels or axels broke, he would say, 'Oh, is this a wedding!' and the nickname has remained in the family ever since.

Luckily for Gutke, her nephew Velevke came to her rescue. He was then a young man in his early twenties and very warmhearted. He took upon himself the task of supporting Gutke and her son. (One should remember that every departure from the forest in order to obtain food was fraught with danger.) His kindness not only extended towards his aunt but towards anyone in need. Velevke, who had been an apprentice tailor with Berl Lipkunsky, was a ray of sunshine during those dark days.

Liebe Shlosberg was another heroic personality of the forest. She was the only daughter of Reb Shmaya Mendel and his wife Friedel. There was a family relationship between this family and that of the families of the rabbinical court, and it was obvious that their only daughter would marry one of the elite among the yeshiva students. One summer's day, there was a great to-do when it became known in public that Libele, Shmaya Mendel's daughter was to marry Hirschel the Nimmenzinner, a great and wise scholar, who was also a modest and sensitive man. I remember him from the time when I was a boy at the small yeshiva and we little ones would turn the place upside-down and disturb the studies of the older students. Hirschel would treat us gently and would not scold us, for he was unable to raise his voice on any occasion. The eve of the wedding was the scene of great preparations and all the yeshiva students and family relations of the rabbinical court who were staying in Dowgalishok for the summer, rode on wagons to Radun to take part in the wedding celebrations. Hundreds of yeshiva students were there and half the inhabitants of the village, whether they were invited or not, came to join in the festivities, listen to the music, and watch the dancing.

The young couple were not to enjoy their happiness for long. Hirschel was taken to dig the pits for the Jews of the village on Sunday, 10 May, when all the Jews were slaughtered. He did not return. Miraculously, Liebe survived and managed to reach the forest. Her story, as she described it, is as follows:

On the day Hirschel was taken away, seven of us went down to the cellar to hide but there was no one to disguise the entrance to the cellar, and then Reb Zev Engelzin of Nimmenzin, Liebe's father-in-law, said: 'Save yourselves, children, and I will hide you and stand in your stead.' They descended to the cellar and Reb Zev covered the entrance with all sorts of planks and wood. They remained in the cellar throughout the day, surrounded by Germans and policemen looking for Jews in every nook and crany, in attics and in cellars.

In the early evening, they suddenly heard someone shouting: 'Father, mother, are you alive? Come out! We have just come from the cemetery.' We recognized the voice of Anschel, the barber's son. He cleared away the planks and the wood placed over the entrance by Reb Zev and we came outside. Everyone ran to see whether any member of his or her family was still alive. Mother and I immediately discovered Father and when we met, he burst into tears. He told us that in the place where he had hidden, there were still many Jews, including a crying baby, and that in trying to quieten the child so as not to bring about everyone's end, someone had covered the child with some clothing and the child was silenced forever.

The Germans sent some of the Jews who had dug the death pit back to the village. They carried out a registration of these Jews as people with a craft or profession,

240

and alongside them a number of Jews who emerged from the cellars. In trying to get the Jews to come out of their hiding-places, the Germans announced that they were organizing another registration, and even sent Noah Dolinsky, head of the Judenrat, to call out to the Jews who were hiding, to come and be registered.

Despite all our mistrust of the Germans and their promises, we could not do otherwise. There was no way out and without knowing what was awaiting us, I joined my parents to be registered and we found that 70 people had already done so. The Germans read out a decree whose contents we could not understand, but some inner voice told me to prevent my elderly parents from registering. I entreated them to leave the place while it was still possible. And indeed, they took aside 17 people who were old or who did not have identification documents, and while still in the process of reading out the decree that those Jews who were still in hiding would be shot, we heard the sound of the guns which were shooting them down in one of the parks.

The Germans examined whether one's hands were callused, as proof that there were some among them that had dug the pit to bury their brethren of the village. They were few and we could have risen up against them, but we had no weapons. And even if we had managed to overcome them, we still would not have had anywhere to go or anyone to turn to. Fortunately, a Polish clerk appeared on the scene, who insisted that she had not managed to write down all the names on the previous day, and the Germans, believing her, told her to do so at once. Thus our lives hung in the balance – solely on the words of a clerk.

At the same time, a loathsome policeman appeared and pointed to a Jew from Eishishok who had come to work late. The Germans did not hesitate to order him to be shot. The members of the *Judenrat* who were present swore by all that was holy that this was a mistake, and that the man had appeared at work on time, and so the Germans decided that he might live. The policeman, who did not want to forgo his quarry, said that the man was a communist, so that all the entreaties and explanations were of no avail and he was brought out a few steps in front of the row of people and shot on the spot.

While we were standing there not knowing what to do, Binke Hefetz was brought forward and the Germans informed that he was outside the ghetto. He was immediately divested of his coat and taken some distance and then we heard the 'saving' shot, for from the pallor of his face it was evident that he was already dead when the shot was fired.

Finally, another decree was read out, ordering us to work diligently and conscientiously, that we should not dare to harbor Jews who were not registered, and whoever disobeyed the decree would be executed together with them. And furthermore, that we should take the few items of clothing we had and settle in the crowded ghetto.

Indeed, quite a number of Jews were killed because no one dared to hide them – a situation that lasted for a week. After some negotiations with the *Judenrat*, the Germans agreed to re-register all those who were still alive, evidently intending to get them out of their hiding-places. This continued for another seven weeks, until everyone was sent to the Schuchin ghetto. Many Jews escaped to the forest again and again for fear of being killed but returned to the ghetto because there was no other place to hide.

Liebe added that it was really miraculous how people had survived and emerged from the blood-bath even with bullet holes in their clothing. Neither strength nor wisdom, neither riches nor understanding, made any difference – it was simply the will of God.

Jacob Engelzin, a 10-year-old boy who was Hirschel's

nephew, was not among those who were registered and wanted to hide among the Jews, but they hesitated to harbor him lest they all get killed as a result. The confused boy wandered around not knowing what to do and Liebe said to the Jews: 'What do you want from the boy. Let him be. In any case they will murder us all.' Finally, Jacob Engelzin fled with his Uncle Berka and hid in the forest for 26 months He managed to stay alive, and reached the shores of Israel 12 years later. There he raised a family and lived happily, though he could not forget his past or Liebe's words.

Liebe was one of the 'happy' few who appeared in the list of those who were to survive, but she had to leave the ghetto as soon as possible for her parents were old and not registered, and this too, she describes as a miracle from heaven. Liebe and her parents escaped to the forest and reached the neighborhood of the villages of Mezanze and Ivonza, and they turned to the farmers Winzia, Ambraziuk, and Marishka, and these were their contacts.

These farmers were in the region of Radun and knew where the Jews were hiding. They did them no harm, not even revealing what they knew to others. Moreover, in this sea of hatred and animosity, and the rejoicing of the Polish community at possible calamity befalling the few Jews who managed to survive, these farmers displayed great strength of character. They displayed a praiseworthy humanity that few righteous gentiles were blessed with. On more than one occasion, they endangered their lives in order to render assistance, or when hiding Jews from their pursuers and warning them of impending danger.

Reb Shmaya Mendel was by that time an old man, with a dignified mien and a snow-white beard. Despite his great age, he was a strong man and could have lived for many years to come. When winter came, they did not dig themselves a bunker in the earth to protect themselves from the cold, but sat in a hut and were well clothed with sheepskins. On one of the winter nights, when Liebe and her father went to get food, they took the wrong path and wandered around for almost the entire night. They, asked the farmer Bankevitz for help. When they were riding in the sleigh and their legs were no longer being used, Reb Shmaya Mendel's legs froze, and afterwards swelled and were covered with blisters. Liebe, who loved her parents profoundly and treated them with great respect, did everything she could to save her father, who was also their sole supporter. Liebe ran to a farmer acquaintance, who killed a goose for her in order to rub her father's feet with goose fat. This was the only remedy she could lay her hands on, but sadly all her efforts were in vain, and Reb Shmaya deteriorated from day to day.

Liebe held her dying father in her arms and hesitated to move him lest this would hasten his death. Before he died Reb Shmaya said to Liebe: 'You will outlive this and survive.' He seemed to sense when he would die and foretold that his end would come on the Christian holiday 'Gromnitze' (a Polish Catholic feast of candle-lighting), and indeed so it proved.

While he was ill, they were not far from where the Jewish groups had settled, and yet they felt lonely and isolated. Liebe and her mother had received no help at the most difficult moments when they were most in need of it, and they felt keenly the absence of an awareness of their need and of human sympathy. The struggle for existence was hard, and everyone was preoccupied with worrying about himself and his immediate family. The strong and the capable looked after themselves first of all, and did not always concern themselves with helping the weak, sometimes ignoring them completely. On the other hand, there were touching human revelations that in the way some people did lend a hand to their fellow beings.

Liebe went to Mikhashka, the farmer, and bought some wooden planks which were brought to the forest, in order to prepare her father's grave with her own hands. The ground was frozen and the digging was almost beyond her, and then she remembered the pit she dug before the winter had set in and used it as a grave for her father. These were only some of the trials this fragile and modest woman had to endure during the 26 months of living in the forest. She was one of the few women who remained and fought for her existence in the forest, but each of them had similarly harrowing experiences. Her warm heart, her profound belief, and her boundless devotion, made it possible for her to overcome her trials.

Liebe's strong beliefs would not permit her to overlook any holiday or deviate from those precepts which set a woman's duty. After burying her father, she and her mother sat in mourning for the entire seven days, as it is prescribed. On one of these nights of *shiva*, they awoke and spied a figure lying at their feet. Alarmed, and even imagining that their father had been resurrected and returned, it finally appeared that it was Liuba Bilitzsky of Biliza. Her sister-in-law had lost her way and had remained at the home of a gentile. She had managed to follow some tracks in the snow and, completely frozen, had entered their bunker. (Liebe did not have her own bunker, but when her father took ill, she took over the bunker left by some Jews who feared that they would be assaulted and fled, and remained there until these Jews returned.)

Liebe became an independent and sole provider for herself and her mother, which was not a simple matter in those conditions, particularly for a woman. But this was not all. During the manhunt in the ancient forest, many Jews were killed, among them the mother of 6-year-old Borochel. He was the son of Abraham Bloch (Avremke, the painter), of Radun. One of the Jews brought him to the woods, but no one wanted to take on the responsibility and burden of caring for a small child. Everyone had more than enough to worry about.

One night, Liebe set out with Haim Elka Movshovitz to get some food, and when they entered the courtyard of Vinzia, they encountered two Polish policemen. Naturally, they started to run, with the policemen running after them. Haim Elka threw his coat to the ground and fled. Liebe saw no way of escaping and hid in the garden. The policemen knew that someone had fled through the garden and started to search there. Miraculously, they did not see her, almost as if they had been blinded.

While lying in the garden, with the policemen looking for her, Liebe made a vow that if God would save her this time, she would be a mother to little Borochel. And as she was indeed saved on this occasion, and returned to her old mother safe and sound, she kept her vow and took little Borochel to live with them. She treated him as her own child for more than a year, until the White Poles carried out an attack on them some four months before the liberation, killing some 20 people, among them Liebe's mother Friedel, and her adopted son Borochel.

It is difficult today to appreciate the magnitude of Liebe's act of heroism. In those days, only rare individuals could perform such a deed, for ordinary people would have seen it as foolhardy and nothing more.

29 The Winter of 1943–44

Autumn arrived in full force and with it, the Days of Awe. The days were growing shorter and colder and we felt the heavy autumn rains in our very bones. Anxiety concerning what was awaiting us grew. Now we were entering a New Year – would it bring something better for us? The New Year (Rosh ha-Shana) had passed; the ten days of penitence were drawing on, and the Day of Atonement and expiation was nigh. The few Jews of Radun who gathered together in the woods of Mezanze made their preparations for the Day of Atonement. Those who were fasting, as well as those who had no intention of fasting, carried out the ritual of expiation of symbolically sacrificing fowls despite the fact that these had been obtained by stealth. Together, or on our own, we each did our moral stock-taking.

Everyone reckoned the number of dead victims in his family and the overall number of families who had remained without a living survivor. Who would remember and mourn them? I looked back and recalled the troubled path I had covered during these times. Seventeen months had now passed since the slaughter in the forest. Who could have imagined that this murderous and evil regime would have ruled this world for so long? Had I known that I would have to hide in the woods and forests, that I would be hunted and would lose my beloved parents and brothers, that I would witness so much loss and bereavement, would I have had the courage to carry on? Would I have dared to take my chances and escape to the forest? And yet I was still alive after all this time. Perhaps there was cause for hope.

We were praying together without a cantor the eve of the

Day of Atonement, each with his own prayers, his broken heart, and his pleas, turning his bitter complaints directly to heaven. The form of my prayers had not changed, but their significance and intention were quite different. In former times, when I had said the prayer 'and thou shalt remove the dominion of wickedness from the earth', I had intended it to mean the Soviet regime, because it had challenged the teachings of the Bible and put paid to the yeshiva of the Hafetz Haim. Now, I regretted my former childish prayers, and prayed instead that the Soviet regime be strengthened sufficiently to overcome the truly evil and satanic Nazis. My former concepts were denied when I felt that I was unable to say: 'We have trespassed, we have dealt treacherously, or we have trespassed more than other nations', for I had risen up against the Almighty and against the terrible fate that had been meted out to us.

No one imagined that the war would continue for another winter. We also found it difficult to believe that we could exist for so long, surrounded as we were by the constant threat of annihilation. I still felt a lust for life and was determined to survive in order that some remnant of our family should remain. Thus my thoughts were directed towards life, not death, I wanted to live to tell the story of what the Jews of Radun and I had experienced. I encountered death every day, but my thoughts dwelt on to how to escape it, and I tried to avoid thinking about it. The encouraging dreams which had supported me in the past had disappeared, and now in these days of comparative calm I let my mind run on the good times to come.

The holiday season passed and signs of winter appeared on the horizon. I began to worry about what to do about the winter. With the experience of last year's winter, we were aware that we had to prepare a bunker and food for the entire period of the winter, or at least for a certain time. The Asner brothers, who had not returned to the unit immediately after the German siege of the forest in accordance with the unit's orders, and had been punished by having their weapons confiscated, could not return there because the unit would not now accept the family members of Jewish fighters. Those fighters who had families were permitted by the unit to find somewhere for their families outside the unit. And as the unit had moved west to the area of the 'Reich', that is, to Vilz'a-Nora, in the direction of Grodno, the fighters were asked to serve as their intelligence arm and transfer information to the unit about what was happening in the ancient forest. They had to obtain their own weapons, and as the Asner brothers were old hands at this, they dug out the reserves they had stored away in the earth and organized an independent Jewish fighting group.

After the deaths of Elka Ariovitz and Stankevitz relations between the veteran Jewish fighters and the unit's command had deteriorated. Mutual trust was undermined, and there was some doubt as to the command's intentions. There were still a considerable number of Jews in the unit, some 30 to 50 per cent, but the Jewish fighters were among the unit's founders and had certain privileges, though they were remote from administrative matters because of the suspicion that existed between them and the unit command after they had been duped on a number of occasions and after Elka's execution. They preferred to remain with the unit, but to perform difficult missions elsewhere and not to stay within the confines of the unit. For its part, the unit command found it convenient not to have them participating in the management of the unit, particularly as no solution had been found as yet for the families of those who were not fighters.

In the Jewish group, there were three of the Asner brothers: Yankel the elder, Haim the second, and Aharke the youngest, and their little cousins Rochke and Itzele. Benjamin Rogovsky (Niomke), and his sister Haike, and Haim Itzke Berkovitz and his brother Aharke joined them. Avremke Asner, the third brother, remained with the unit together with his beloved Liebe, who performed various services for the unit.

As many of the Jewish fighters were away from the unit, I did not have anyone to return to, so I stayed with various Jewish groups, cut off from the unit. We were organized into a small, separate group of seven: Abraham Paikovsky and his son Nahum, Haim Paikovsky, and me, Avraham Lipkunsky. We were joined by Moshe Gures and his wife, Haya Sorka, and her niece Etke Moshe. Gures was the son of Jankel, a builder of ovens and chimneys, from Eishishok. In October 1943 we moved some 15 kilometers from the village of Saltanishok, to the region of marshes. We found a spot on a sand-hill within a wood of young pine trees, some meters from the marshes. The hill appeared to be a sort of enclave within the marshes. On surveying the surroundings, one only saw marshes, and though the village of Saltanishok was quite near, it was beyond the marshes.

The Asner brothers came to help us set up the bunker. They brought sawn planks ready to serve as beams, so that we did not need to use the trees surrounding us, and so create noise and leave wood-chippings. They thought of remaining with us, but after some consideration decided that the place was too small and too near the villages. Hence, they decided to find somewhere in the depths of the ancient forest, or to take refuge with a friendly farmer. They helped us set up the bunker with the idea of having an emergency hideout in a crisis.

We dug the bunker deep into the earth, with steps leading down. We almost did not need to camouflage the entrance, for it was clear that if someone reached us and discovered our existence, we would either have to kill him or leave the place and move somewhere else. We built a stove out of stones and bricks that would enable us to cook and bake, and arranged benches of wood along the walls, spreading straw over them instead of mattresses. Conditions were not so bad – if we could only stay there until the end. We stocked up on food for a few months: dried peas, flour, farina, smoked meat, sausage, salt, and other items which would keep during the winter, such as potatoes and carrots.

A guard was on duty all the time. He would also make

quiet reconnaissance tours during the small hours, until the first snows fell. Anyone moving through the marshes could be heard from afar by the breaking of the dry reeds underfoot. In the course of these tours, we would find the trails of different wild animals that moved about the area during the night. We also learned to tell the difference between the footprints of a dog and a wolf. The footprints of the animals were also a useful cover-up for our own.

The village of Saltanishok had a mixed population of Poles, Byelorussians, and mainly Lithuanians. It was also known as a village of murderers from way back. Their attitude to partisans, and particularly to Jews, was not exactly kindly. Until the unit had reached a certain stature, they would waylay anyone going into the forest, and shoot and murder whoever happened to come their way. Only after the partisans retaliated did they stop these activities. The fact that they were known as opponents of the partisans was exploited by us as camouflage, for it would not occur to anyone that partisans were living nearby. Also, we could use their trails to cover up our own expeditions. The surrounding marshes would serve as an area for retreat in case of danger. And with the fall of the first snow, we sat quietly and safely within our bunker without having to go out for food.

30 The Wounding of Aharke Asner

With the onset of winter, the military unit decided to oust Liebke, Avremke Asner's girl friend, and he was therefore obliged to leave their ranks and join his brothers. Through messengers, they arranged to meet at the farm of an acquaintance in the village of Poizil, and as they were about to enter the courtyard of the farm, they were met by a barrage of rifle and machine gun fire. Coincidentally, or perhaps not so coincidentally, some White Poles had reached the farm that night, evidently aware that there were Jewish and Russian partisans in the area. Aharke Asner, the youngest of the Asner brothers, was fatally injured in the leg during this attack. The meeting-place in case of some mishap was to be our bunker, and so they all arrived at our place in Zemlenka that same night, together with Niomke Rogovsky and Haim Itzke Berkovitz – all apart from Aharke, who was wounded and had been left where he fell. They waited for him for two days, in the hope that he would arrive, and when he did not turn up, they went off to look for him, to find out what had happened.

The first snow fell on the night of the attack in which Aharke was injured. He managed to crawl away from the action until he could gather his strength and remained lying on the ground, covered entirely by the snow, so that he was not seen. For three days, he lay in this fashion, but on the third day, the farmer heard his moaning and took him into his outhouse. He gave him food and drink and tended to his wounds. He lay thus for another four days until his brothers managed to find him, as the White Poles did not leave the region for over a week.

It was surprising that Avremke and Liebke were not

caught, for they had reached the farmer's house only half an hour before the White Poles arrived. For some reason they had decided to leave the place. As soon as they had left, the White Poles arrived. The Asner brothers, together with Niomke and Haim Itzke, slipped away with the wounded Aharke right under the noses of the Poles. Using one of their contacts, they informed the farmer where to bring Aharke. The winter was coming into its own, and so the farmer harnessed a horse and sleigh and laid Aharke across it., Thus he brought him to the forest, and laid him down at the spot where he had been told to leave him. Then he fled from fear of the White Poles. The Asner brothers then collected Aharke in their sleigh and brought him to us in the bunker.

The Asner brothers were known far and wide. They were four brothers, healthy and hearty in body and soul. They had grown up in a rural area among farmers who worked their own land, and their village was on the outskirts of the ancient forest. The brothers, themselves, were known by the name 'Asneroki', and they had made a name for themselves as partisans and as good and brave-hearted fighters.

After the slaughter in the Radun ghetto, they were registered with the rest of the survivors, and worked at collecting the dead bodies from the ghetto. When they reached the forest, they met other Jews, and also four Russians who had remained in the rear behind the German army and were not taken prisoner They were Ivan Ivanovitch, Oszipienko Romnienko, Pietro Padkovin, and Ilya Greis, who was Jewish. They bought their first weapons with the 3,000 rubles given them by Moshe Slodovnik, Laike and Zamke's father, who told them to return the money only when they were able to.

There were five brothers and one sister in the Asner family. The father Itzhak had died when Avremke was only 8 years old, and Aharke, the youngest, had been orphaned when he was tiny. The oldest brother, who lived in Olkenik, was killed in the Eishishok ghetto together with the rest of the Jews in the village, while the sister lost her life in the Radun ghetto.

The two elder brothers cared for and protected Aharke, the youngest. And now, despite the fact that he was a strong and brave fighter, they still related to him as if he were small and needed pampering. It seemed as if only now, in the forest, he had grown up. He was a handsome youth and loved to dress up. He always appeared well-shaven and well turned-out, for he was as meticulous about his clothes as if he was in a proper army and had to appear on parade. He would turn up in a uniform of the Polish army, adorned with whatever ribbons and medals he saw fit for the occasion, with highly polished buttons and a well-starched visor cap. His trousers were those of the Polish cavalry fitting as if they were tailored for him, and tucked into shining leather boots. Straps with polished buckles crossed his chest and back in the length and the breadth. Altogether, he gave the impression of a dandyish Polish officer of the good old days.

Now Aharke was brought to the bunker pale and white as plaster, unable to do anything but utter endless groans. He was writhing in pain and there was little we could do for him, for we had no medication and nothing to relieve his pain. The only thing we could do was to dress his wounds with bandages made from clean sheets or linen shirts. He was unable to eat or to drink and there was not a soul among us who knew anything about medicine or healing. Some men went to a farmer in the vicinity of Radun to try to get medicines and bandages, returning with a bottle of Rivanol to cleanse his wounds and some painkillers. But this primitive treatment was inadequate for such serious wounds, which had become infected in the meantime. His right leg was shattered and slivers of bones covered with pus were sticking out. None of us were capable of dealing with the shattered leg of this much-loved friend and brother. The stench from the decaying flesh was terrible. The only one who made a special effort to approach and tend him was his older brother Jacob, and I would assist him. We would separate each piece of shattered bone, cleaning the wound and making an opening in the abscess to enable the pus to drain out. Aharke did not speak but merely watched us and I felt how grateful he was and appreciated our efforts at treating him.

On the following day, the second day of his arrival in the bunker, it appeared as if his condition was improving. The wound began to take on a reddish color and looked more alive, while he seemed to regain some strength and began to speak. But it was merely wishful thinking to think that we could help him without medication. His fever began to rise, his face was burning and his color was high as a result of the fever. His pains seemed to abate, or perhaps he felt them less because of his fever. Evidently, his wound had poisoned his blood. On the third day, he began to expire. I sat at his side all the time, he did not let me go and asked me to come nearer, and held my hand and with his other, supported his head slightly. He was conscious all the time. Only when nearing his end did he begin to hallucinate. Etke, the niece of Moshe Gures of Eishishok, was also in the bunker with us. There had been a time when the two had walked out together, and now, in his most difficult moments, Aharke would glance in her direction and sigh from time to time. He was happy in her presence and would hold her hand when she was standing near him. He died in tremendous pain, among his brothers and friends. Even in his last moment, he was glad to see us around him, not abandoned and alone as he had been a few days earlier.

May his memory be blessed among the hallowed Jewish fighters who glorified the name of Israel in these darkest of times! We dug his grave not far from our bunker in the direction of the marshes, and laid him to eternal rest. In those days, it was a great privilege to die and be buried with one's friends and brothers around one. After Aharke's death, the Asner brothers left their friends and us in the group, as our bunker was too small to include all of us. We were very glad to have them with us, if only for the sense of security these brave-hearted fighters gave to those around them. They went to arrange for a refuge with a farmer or a bunker which had been dug near 'Borovay-Griboz'. The seven of us remained in our bunker, while the eighth, Aharke, lay at rest in the earth a short distance away.

For six weeks we lived in the bunker in comparative safety. Then one fine day, we discovered the footprints of two people leading straight to our bunker. They had evidently followed the sleigh which had brought the wounded Aharke. The footprints gave us no peace as they could prove a threat to our lives. We feared that if the Germans or the White Poles knew of our existence in the bunker, then they could swoop down and capture us. And so in the depths of the freezing winter, we had to leave our warm bunker home and roam about without knowing where to go.

The whole day before we left, we had people on guard at all points, at some distance from the bunker. We dug a hole in the frozen earth and hid some of the provisions that had remained, thinking that we may be in need of them at some future date and unwilling to leave them to be taken by some gentile.

Our family group dispersed. Haim Paikovsky took Moshe Gures, his wife Haya Sorke, and his niece Etka, to the house of a farmer acquaintance where he had taken refuge during the first summer after the slaughter. He relied on the fact that Moshe Gures had money and that for a decent sum, the farmer would agree to keep them throughout the winter. But a group of seven individuals was too much for one farmer, and so we separated into two groups.

Haim Paikovsky and Moshe Gures went to a farmer in the village of Vorla, some seven kilometers from Radun. The remaining three – Abraham Paikovsky, his son Nahum, and I – had no destination in mind and so we accompanied the others part of the way to Vorla, until we went our separate ways. Having no choice, we set forth in the direction of the villages of Vorla and Pitzelunze, in the hope that we might find a farmer who would offer us a haven from the cold and furnish us with some of our other needs.

It was a Thursday when we abandoned our warm bunker, tramping about for two days under the gray winter skies amidst the felled and thinned-out trees of the Vorla woods. The heavens raged. The snowstorms whirled around us, and the cold grew more severe as the day wore on. The snowflakes, frozen hard by the extreme cold and swirling in the screeching wind, bit into us like knives. In sheer desperation, at midday, we tried to light a fire to warm ourselves, but our efforts were in vain as the wind was too strong. We feared that if we tried to walk and keep moving in order to keep from freezing we would be discovered, while sitting in one place without moving and without a fire we would freeze to death. So we dug a hole in the snow, and lowered ourselves into it in order to keep out of the wind, slapping one another and ourselves in an attempt to get warm.

We remembered stories from home about people who were worn out by trudging in the cold and snow and sat down to rest awhile, falling asleep from weariness and eventually freezing into a state of eternal rest. We decided that at all times, only one of us would be permitted to snatch a bit of sleep while the other two would stay awake. I wonder what was the source of our willpower at the time, for we did not even consider the possibility of getting rid of our troubles by dropping into a deep sleep.

With nightfall, we tried to stay with a farmer acquaintance for the night. The farmer gave us some food but advised us to get out of the neighborhood with the greatest possible haste, as the White Poles ruled the village. They had organized groups of six to ten men, equipped with weapons, in order to kill any Jew or Russian who arrived in the village. To our dismay, we knew that he was speaking the truth, having experienced this ourselves and having been smitten by their murderous hands on more than one occasion. Many had been killed by the White Poles after having succeeded in surviving the Germans. The population in this area was mainly Polish and partisans did not often come this way.

As we saw that we had jumped out of the frying pan into

the fire and had nowhere to go, the possibility was broached of returning to the ancient forest and trying to find a partisan group which we could join, or indeed of returning to our bunker with all the danger this entailed. And as these two possibilities seemed inadvisable, we decided to trust to chance and leave matters to fate, whatever it might bring. For this purpose, I used my prayer book that had been with me since I left home, and began to devise combinations of letters, and look for a hint in the contents of the sentences. Finally, it turned out that we were to retrace our footsteps and go back to the bunker. Notwithstanding all our reservations and doubts concerning our return to the bunker, we were comforted by the fact that we were returning to a place we knew: a place that was warm, with provisions that were awaiting us.

On 1 January 1944 we started on our way back. When we arrived at the bunker, we found the entrance closed, as we had left it. There were no signs that anyone had visited the place. Taking even greater precautions, we did not stay in the bunker during the day but went out to the frozen marshes and sat among the shrubs. In order not to leave too many footprints from the bunker to the marshes, we would jump from shrub to shrub onto the frozen mounds of mud and lopped-off branches, trying to obscure the sequence of our footprints.

When we returned to the bunker at night, we would cook potatoes, beans and split peas from our store. We baked bread rolls, which were edible, as long as they were fresh, but within a day became as tough as old boots. We were happy with our lot since we were not harassed. We had learned from experience that even winter does not continue forever, and that if we lived to see it out, we would see the end of our greatest natural 'enemy'. And until then, we would go out to the icy marshes with the arrival of daylight and return at night to sleep in our bunker. For nine long weeks we lived in this fashion. At the beginning of Adar, we left the bunker for good, for we felt cut off from the outside world and were unaware of what was happening around us. We decided, therefore, to go to the Mezanze woods to meet the Jews staying there. The winter still persevered, but the days were getting longer and the rays of the sun begining to warm the frozen earth. The snows and great storms ceased and here and there on the hills and meadows, frozen clods of earth began to appear.

We stayed with the Jews of Mezanze for a week, during which some Jews who had been with the Asners in the ancient forest arrived, among them Niomke Rogovsky and Jacob Asner. Fortunately, they took a liking to me, and agreed to take me with them to their bunker. Indeed, I still do not know what prompted them to do so. Perhaps it was because I had matured in the meantime and no longer considered me a mere boy. They already knew me as a talented youngster who could do all sorts of work, but as an independent youth I could fit in among them and perform useful services, and slowly learn to be a fighter. Attempting to coax them into taking me with them, I said: 'I'm strong enough to fulfil any mission demanded of me,' adding 'even if it is only to mend your shoes, it's worth your while to take me with you.' Jacob Asner remembered that I had helped him to look after his wounded brother Aharke. Niomke Rogovsky and Haim Itchke of Radun also knew me, and added their support. So once again I would be living with an organized group, and not in the solitude of the forest, dependant on my own resources.

31 The Bunker in Borovay-Griboz

The group formed by the Asner brothers and their friends who were forced to leave the unit was made up of ten people. They stayed in a bunker near Borovay-Griboz. They dug this on a hillock among tall and dense trees in the ancient forest which overlooked the area. The hillock penetrated deeply into the marshes like an inlet, and from there it was possible to observe and take in what was happening in the immediate surroundings. It was safe, for no one could reach the place unless they were carried there.

The interior of the bunker was large and spacious, almost like a farmer's house. It was about eight meters long and six meters wide. Along the sides of the wall were bunks constructed from thin poles. In the corner, there was a stove built of bricks in which we could cook or bake bread. Our provisions were ample and varied: there were all sorts of meats, flour, cereals, and even homemade vodka, to warm our bodies and souls. There were guards continuously on duty throughout the day and night, and they would patrol an area of some hundred meters from the bunker. Inside, life went on as it had in the good old days with conversation and laughter.

During the day, we would stand on guard or polish our weapons. Some were busy preparing food, while others would occupy themselves with cards or other social games, without any money for the winners, for they were only playing to pass the time away. Talk was generally about recent events, memories of the recent and more distant past. We almost never spoke of the future, either because we hesitated to broach the subject or because we still did not see the light at the end of the tunnel. Or perhaps we were wary of what the future might bring. The important thing was to live for moment and to let the future take care of itself.

The atmosphere was that of a big family, in which the Asner tribe, with its six members was the largest; there were Jankel, Haimke, Avremke and his beloved Liebke, and their two cousins Itchele and Rochke. Niomke Rogovsky was on his own and without his sister Chaike. Zamke Slodovnik was there with his cousin Michele Schwartz, who had come to the Radun ghetto from Lida – the same Michele whom Jankele Kovalsky saved, together with her brother Joseph, when the Germans took all the Jews of Lida who were in Radun to be killed. Haim Itchke Berkovitz was there with his brother Aharke and his cousin Avremke. Leibke Hefetz and his wife Gitke Kagan. Jossele Hamarsky from Eishishok was alone. Jankele Kovalsky was with the unit most of the time, but considered himself as part of our group. Lastly, there were Esther-Chanke Tanovitsky and her sister Bailke, and Vinzkovsky, a Pole from Radun.

There are many stories told about Vinzkovsky and his motives in joining the Jewish boys in the forest after the slaughter in Radun. It is difficult to understand why someone who could live a comparatively normal life would choose to share the lot of the Jews who had fled from the forest in order to save their lives. The few facts that are known about him teach us that Vinzkovsky was of the 'homeless' mold, despite his being a family man. He had a taste for spirits to the point of drunkenness and preferred being idle to working. In normal times, before the war, he would depend on the Jews for his livelihood. In exchange for performing certain light tasks, he would come by a glass of vodka together with some refreshment, for he liked the Jews and enjoyed being with them. He also mixed with the Polish intelligentsia and, when the Germans were in power, did all sorts of illegal operations for them, which also accounted for his fleeing from the Germans and he again found confederates among the Jews in the forest.

Niomke Rogovsky told that immediately after the slaughter

in Radun, Vinzskovsky was the contact between the Jews in the forest and Lugovsky the Polish police commander on behalf of the Germans. Commandant Lugovsky was a friend of the Jews, and would warn them of imminent decrees, which the Germans were about to execute. It was unusual in those days to receive help even in exchange for money, and he was one of the few who offered help. He assisted Haim Elka Movshovitz, the glazier, to escape to the forest, and sent the Jewish sisters from Natsche with him, recommending them to the farmer Januka of Borovay. A few days later, he himself brought them a sack of flour and other edibles. The same Lugovsky got in touch with the Jews who had fled to the forest and, together with them, planned an ambush against the Germans and the police who collaborated with them in Radun. This was the first opposition to the Germans after the slaughter, and it was long before one had heard or even dreamed of a partisan movement. Lugovsky told the Jews which route the Germans were taking and who they would be, and told them whom to shoot and kill. Ten men participated in this ambush and Vinzkovsky was among them, having been sent by Commandant Lugovsky. It took place near the village of Kurka, some three kilometers from Radun, on the highway leading to Grodno and about a kilometer from the cemetery and the graves of the Jewish martyrs of Radun.

They had very poor weapons: three rifles and a hand grenade. Taking part in the ambush were Yudke Bank from Memel in Lithuania, who had served in the Lithuanian army and knew how to use a rifle, Niomke Rogovsky and Haim Itchke Berkovitz of Radun, who had not served in any army as yet, Jankel Asner from Natche, and his brothers Haimke and Avremke, who had all served in the Polish army, Jankel Koniachovsky from Ivya, Shlaimke Sadovsky from Sabaknica, Aharke Berkovitz from Radun, both cousins of Haim Itchke, and Vinzkovsky, who was sent by the Commandant Lugovsky.

When the Germans were passing on the highroad, the

Jews noted that they were approaching and coming nearer, but allowed them come even closer in order to lessen the distance between the opposing sides, and then began to fire at them. A struggle ensued in which a Polish police sergeant was killed and the head of the gendarmerie was wounded. One Jew – Yudke Bank – was killed also. Unfortunately, he had been wearing a white pullover and was therefore an easy target.

This first action against the Germans was not very successful, but it was highly significant. By this act, the Jews had proved to themselves that they could fight the Germans and inflict casualties on them even with poor weapons, while at the same time the Germans began to realize that there was some danger in their pursuit of the Jews. Vinzkovsky, whose involvement in the struggle became known to the Germans, could not return to Radun now and because of the turn of events, willingly remained in the forest.

Some time later, Lugovsky passed on to the Jews the information that on a particular day, he would be visiting a certain village near the forest with a group of policemen, giving us instructions as to which policemen should be killed straight away and which were to be taken captive. He also asked that he should be taken captive as well, so that he could get out of the police force, which was serving the Germans. This action was executed down to its every detail; the policemen who opposed us were killed on the spot and the rest were taken as prisoners and later released, as Lugovsky had instructed.

Vinzkovsky also took part in this action, and spent all his time together with Elka Ariovitz's group. He was loyal to the Jews and trusted by them. And, since the manhunt in the ancient forest, he was also the patron of Esther Chanke Tanovitsky, Elka Ariovitz's beloved, and the younger sister of Bailke. Vinzkovsky treated the two girls as if they were his own daughters; he watched over them and saw to it that they had enough food and clothing. He did not part from them even when they had to move elsewhere, and they would address him like an uncle or even a father at times.

In the autumn of 1943, during the Jewish holidays, Vinzkovsky and the two girls encountered a group of White Poles. Esther Chanke managed to get away without being injured, but her sister Bailke was badly wounded in her face. A bullet had gone right through her jawbone to her teeth, shattering some of them, tearing part of her tongue, and exiting through her cheek on the other side. As it was described at the time, the Poles pulled her up by her hair and shot her in this position, leaving her lying on the ground bleeding, evidently believing that she was already dead. The Pole, Vinzkovsky, they took with them. How he managed to escape from them no one knows, but he returned to the Asners' group and said he had succeeded in fleeing from them. Afterwards we learned that Bailke was alive but badly wounded.

Taking into consideration Esther Chanke's situation after Elka's death and knowing them from Radun, the Asner brothers and their comrades in the bunker decided to take in the sisters and Vinzkovsky, who had looked after them, for the duration of the winter.

Since the establishment and appearance of the White Poles in the neighborhood, Vinzkovsky's loyalty began to be questioned. There was some information to the effect that Vinzkovsky had met with the White Poles earlier on and that it was they who had persuaded him to join their ranks, and he had seemingly refused. No one knew for certain what were his connections with the White Poles. Had he remained loyal to the Jewish comrades with whom he set out for the forest, staying with them for many months, and even joined them in combat missions? Or had he been freed by the White Poles in order to act as a spy for them? The tension that existed between the Jewish partisans and the Poles, and Vinzkovsky's accidental encounters with the White Poles and his successful escape from them, aroused suspicions of his loyalty to the Jewish partisans, which caused them to keep an eye on him and have him shadowed.

Bailke was miraculously saved and reached the forest

badly wounded. We tended her with all the means at our disposal: washed her wounds, cleansed them with hydrogen peroxide and bandaged them. And, according to the instructions given us by the farmer's doctor, we boiled the bark of birch trees, and would wash her wounds and moisten the bandages with the boiled-bark solution.

The damage to her face and mouth was serious, and she had to be fed. We made all sorts of cereals for her and other foods would be mashed and thinned with water, which she would be fed with an infant's spoon. At the same time, the saliva from her mouth would wash the wounds and keep them clean. The treatment lasted for months and from time to time, bone splinters would emerge together with the emission from the abscesses. She withstood the pain admirably and suffered in silence, without a tear or complaint, but all this was reflected in her suffering eyes. When her wounds had scarred over and the bandages were removed from her round face, the scars were revealed, looking like wild red blossoms. In the course of time, her face slowly slimmed down and took on its former shape.

During the winter when we were staying in the bunker, we noted that Vinzkovsky was looking for a way to escape. Once, for no reason at all, we found him at a distance of some hundred meters from the bunker, after noticing that he was absent. At times, he would try to get away from the bunker and leave footprints in the snow, and we managed to get him back without giving him any idea that we were following him. The unappointed leaders of the bunker decided to follow his movements outside, keeping this secret from the other members, for they wanted to make certain whether or not he intended to flee.

After Bailke was wounded, he wept and worried about his 'daughters', but the suspicion regarding his loyalty was also aroused in the girls after they mentally re-enacted the accidental encounter with the White Poles. After trailing him for a time, it appeared from his behavior and his remarks that there was indeed some foundation to the suspicion levelled against him, and that he was looking for an opportunity to run off and join the White Poles. Once, when he was trying to leave the forest, we found that he was trying to cover his tracks in the snow and get as far from the bunker as possible. Lately and uncharacteristically, he had begun to complain and quarrel in a most unreasonable manner: he was undoubtedly seeking an excuse or pretext to leave the bunker. On the last occasion we found him far from the bunker, and asked him what he was doing there, he became somewhat confused and replied that he had come this far in order to perform his bodily needs. After it was clearly beyond any doubt that he was planning to flee from the bunker and join his fellow White Poles, we decided that he must be silenced. It was no longer necessary to think about what would be the fate of all the bunker's occupants and that of other Jews if he succeeded in escaping and joining the White Poles. Vinzkovsky knew the whereabouts of all the Jews in the forest, as well as their contacts with the farmers in the neighborhood. He also knew how we lived in the forest and the way our minds worked, considering the wide experience he gathered during the considerable time he had spent with us since the slaughter in Radun.

One morning, when everyone was still asleep, we heard firing at the entrance of the bunker. There was a bit of a to-do but after a few minutes it was explained that Vinzkovsky had been shot. We were told that there had been an accident and that he had misfired and the bullet had gone astray and killed him. This explanation was needed to pacify and soften the blow for Esther Chanke and Bailke, who were so attached to him. Esther Chanke realized that this was no mishap and burst into tears and shouted that Vinzkovsky had been deliberately killed. For quite some time, no one knew who had fired the shot from among the three who were designated to do so. Two of them are no longer alive and only the third, who was an eyewitness, can state who was responsible for this deed.

The way it happened, as recounted at the time, was as

follows: Vinzkovsky had to go out on patrol with two men accompanying him; when they reached the exit, a third man shot him in the back and he died there and then. One can understand Vinzkovsky's motives in wanting to go over to the White Poles, for he knew that his life would be much better and more comfortable (after living in the forest for over a year and a half). To this very day, we do not know whether he managed to pass on any information concerning the whereabouts of the Jews to his fellow Poles, but shortly afterwards, only a few months before the Red Army arrived, they attacked groups of unarmed Jews and their families and managed to kill scores of Jews. No matter how painful it was to execute him, it is very likely that getting rid of him saved the lives of many Jews. There was no way of avoiding the axiom: 'If anyone comes to kill you, kill him first'.

It was spring 1944. The snow had stopped falling and was beginning to melt, so it was possible to leave the bunker without leaving footprints. We began to send messengers to renew our contact with the unit, which at that time was in the 'Reich', that is, territory that the Germans considered as wholly German. The way there was known to be highly dangerous because of the extensive marshes one had to cross. Four kilometers of the way there were wooden branches and posts making a pathway across the marshes. These marshes were so deep and waterlogged, that anyone who slipped or fell into the marsh would sink up to the hips or even entirely. The unit had changed its policy to a certain extent: it accepted members of the fighters' families and its store of weapons had increased. This was the period in which the Red Army was severely attacking the German invaders and driving them back westwards and southwards, liberating cities and entire regions one after the other.

Our group, which was serving as an intelligence source in this area, was ordered to remain in the area, which was swarming with White Poles. It is possible that this was the reason why the unit left the area and moved westward to a region where there were few White Poles to act against the Russian partisans. Directives from Moscow were that partisan forces should advance westward and derail trains and harass traffic moving westward to the front. And indeed in the spring of 1944 there were innumerable acts of sabotage against the German trains moving westward to the front with military equipment, tanks and soldiers. Radio contact with Moscow as well as between the various partisan units improved. Whenever information was received about trains moving equipment or men, mines would be laid or the railway tracks would be destroyed at different points along the route. Sabotage methods were improved and were no longer as primitive as they had been at first. In 1943, in order to blow up the railway tracks, the partisans would use a cannon shell, with a rifle directed at the cap; from the safe distance of a few meters they would pull at a cord attached to the trigger of the rifle and so explode the shell. This primitive system was both difficult and dangerous.

The following story is told of Jankele Kovalsky and his comrades when mining some railway tracks. Jankele was an expert at minelaying, using a method whereby the mine would explode when a passing train ran over a pin. This needed considerable precision and concentration. Once, when they were laying mines, they were attacked by two German sentries and had no alternative but to kill them. Then Jankele returned to the railway tracks, took out the mines he had placed there and during the same night, laid them elsewhere, some 30 kilometers away.

The task given to us by the unit was to gather intelligence and convey it to the unit. Once every week or two, five of us would leave for the unit to hand over information and receive instructions. Ours was a small group, saddled with women, operating in an area where the White Poles had a strong hold over the population. We were not equipped nor suited to engage in armed conflicts with the Germans or the Poles. Since our number was small and our mobility limited we were obliged to move from place to place every week or two.

In the second half of April 1944 I joined a group of five men and we went to check the situation in the neighborhood of Radun. On the way, we stopped to visit the Jews staying in the woods of Mezanze, the Davidovitch family and others. There we learned of the struggle between Haim Paikovsky and the White Poles.

Haim had received gold coins from the Jews of Mezanze, in order to buy a rifle or some other weapon, and so he went to a farmer he knew and with whom he had taken refuge at one time. At night, he stole into the barn of another farmer, where he had hidden during the former summer for some time, and hid in the attic in order to remain there throughout the day. Unfortunately, some White Poles happened to visit this farmer, knowing that he had once had contact with the Jews. They claimed that he was hiding Jews, accusing him in order to have a pretext to obtain arms or food from him. The farmer, believing that no one was staying with him, told them that they could search the place to their heart's content. One of the Poles went up to the attic and found Haim. On seeing the farmer, Haim grabbed a soldier and trembled, pretending that he had never seen the farmer before. He told them that he had fled from the Germans and wanted to join the Polish fighters. He looked like a Polish youth, with his light blond hair and blue eyes, and spoke Polish like one of them.

First, they took off his shining boots which they obviously coveted and left him barefoot, and afterwards looked through his clothes and found the gold coins, of which they also relieved him. And as they were pleased with the bargain they had come across, they went into the farmer's house to eat and placed a single sentry to stand guard over him. On seeing that he was in trouble, Haim sought a way out and realized that he had a little time at his disposal. He asked the sentry to allow him to go behind the house in order to answer a call of nature – it is quite that fear had actually stomach cramps and he really needed to go behind the house. The Polish sentry suspected nothing and turned his head away. Whereupon, Haim, taking a chance stood up quietly, and started to run barefoot, with all his strength. The sentry fired at him but did not hit him and he thus managed to escape from the soldiers of the Polish underground. On returning to the Jews of the Mezanze woods, he was as white as a ghost and could not utter a word.

We remained with the Jews of Mezanze for some days. One morning, I was ordered to guard the edge of the woods, and observe movements in the vicinity. I lay quietly hidden by a shrub, and watched the field facing me. I watched the farmer behind his plow, turning one furrow after the other, and I envied this simple man, relaxed and unworried, following his plow-horse, whistling and humming to himself out in the open, without a worry or fear in the world.

In such moments, I would ponder the phrase in Isaiah: 'The wolf also shall dwell with the lamb, and the leopard shall lie down with the kid.' Had we not suffered and been tormented enough? And how long were we to await our salvation? I remembered the article I had read in Polish in a German newspaper about Palestine and its Jewish population, and I felt an endless yearning, mixed with faith and trust, that the day would come when I would tread on the earth of Palestine, the land of our fathers, land of the Judges and Prophets, land of the Bible. It was not very rational at the time and merely daydreaming and wishful thinking; a mystical attachment made up of unseen cords linking me to the land of our fathers. And I saw in my mind's eye the picture of 'every man under his vine and under his fig tree.'

The days when we would load a horse and wagon with provisions to be taken to the ancient forest were over. Not because of the possible danger from the Germans but because of the White Poles, who were lying in wait for us behind every house and every bend and curve of the highways and byways. The White Poles did not need a forest in order to promote their underground movement, they merely sat among their own people. When they so wished they were peaceful tillers of the soil; and when they wished, they took their weapons out of the earth and became partisans, not against the German invader but against the Jews who were trying to escape with their lives from the Germans. Now, on returning to the forest, we packed a knapsack bursting at the seams with food supplies, bearing it on our backs together with the weapon each of us held in his hand. In addition to individual knapsacks, there were also heavier kitbags, which we took turns to carry.

It was an hour before midnight and the moon was rising in the sky, shedding light on the dust road we were walking along in Indian file. I was the last and brought up the rear after Niomke Rogovsky. We passed alongside the colonies of the village Lonki on our way to Saltanishok and Kovalka. All was quiet and only our elongated shadows accompanied us on our way. In this lap of our march, it was my turn to carry the heavy sack that contained, among other things, a frying pan and other cooking utensils. Those who were at the head of the line had already passed the houses along the roadway and the last in the line were just about to pass the houses. Suddenly the silence was shattered by rifle fire, directed at us from behind the houses to the left and the rear. While dashing past, I saw a number of shadows moving around behind the houses. We were few and there was no point in starting a gun battle, so all we could do was to get up and run like the wind. I did not know the roads to the forest well and I was forced to keep up the pace and run after Niomke lest we be separated. He was not carrying anything and ran in front of me like an arrow without looking behind. Without letting go of the sack on my shoulders, I chased after him with the last of my strength, fearful that I would lose him. I did not dare discard the sack, lest someone say I did it because I was frightened. And so we ran some six kilometers, Niomke ahead and I following him, trying to catch up with him though all my strength was dwindling. The frying pan and other utensils were knocking against one another and sounded like an orchestra of drums accompanied by cymbals. When we finally entered the dense forest, Niomke halted for a minute, saying to me: 'How can you manage with that big, heavy, sack; for heaven's sake, throw it away together with that idiotic frying pan which makes so much noise.' I thought it a pity to discard the sack just anywhere after having borne it with the last of my strength, but without saying a word, left it alongside a tree trunk with a great sigh of relief. Niomke turned to me and said: 'Avremke, there are only the two of us, who knows what happened to the others or whether anyone was injured. They could have wiped us out completely – are you hurt?' And he continued to say that we must quickly pass over the river near Kovalka or they might block the road; and as it was already daylight, they would finish us off.

There were many such encounters with the White Poles. They awaited us behind every house and in every dark corner. The Polish Amalek did as his forefathers had in earlier times, and cut down the unfortunate and the survivors who remained after the German massacre. This is the way they were and this is how they will be remembered. It was a miracle that in this ambush no one was killed, and when we arrived in the forest, all were alive and unhurt.

The White Poles were infinitely more dangerous than the Germans, for the latter did not dare to penetrate into the forest or even to remain within the vicinity of the forest with only a small force. The White Poles, on the other hand, were supported and assisted by their fellow farmers. In every village, they had contacts who supplied them with information, and they were aware of the routes we would pass and where we were settled. This was the reason why we had to change our quarters so very frequently, for we had to be wary of every farmer who might reveal our whereabouts.

Only two days earlier, we had changed our location, and still had not managed to get to know it and arrange some protection against the cold of the night, the rain and the dew, when in the early hours of the morning, we heard the sound of an axe chopping not far off. We were alarmed as we did not know just what this meant and why a farmer should have come as far as this in the early morning in order to chop wood. This aroused our suspicions, for since the advent of the White Poles, we no longer trusted any Polish farmer. We spread out in an encircling movement and advanced towards the woodchoppers, closing in on them from every side. Having combed the area to see whether there were others with them, we paid them a surprise visit. Their first reaction was to raise their axes against us, but these were quickly lowered when they saw our rifles and guns aimed at them. We were not interested in drawing any attention by the sound of firing and therefore we quietly bound them up, tying their hands lest they try to escape, and started to question them. This place was near the villages of Podemb and Boodes – villages known for their animosity to the Jews and Russian partisans, and for collaborating with the Germans.

During the winter before that, the farmers of these villages had attacked a group of Jews within their winter bunkers, robbed them of their clothes and whatever had remained after they had escaped from Radun, and finally murdered everyone in their hideouts. We had a long and bloody account with these villages, but until then we had had no opportunity to make our way into these villages and take our revenge without enduring any losses. In the course of the investigation, they claimed that they came from the village of Drutchemin, and that they were a father and his son. They could not answer our question as to why they had chosen this remote place in the forest in which to chop wood when there was plenty of wood nearer their homes. To those among us who were in the know and had experience, they were evidently scouts and contacts of the White Poles or the Germans. We were faced with a difficult dilemma – what was to be done with them? If we were to release them, we would endanger all our lives; we would not succeed in keeping them with us for any length of time, for they might escape; considering the circumstances in which we live, it would be impossible drag them around with us. After some discussion, we decided to kill them quietly – not by shooting. This would serve as a warning to the nearby village's not to enter the forest. So they were hanged, and buried under one of the trees, with the grave well disguised. During the questioning, it emerged that these farmers had played an active part in the killing of Jews or in handing them over to the Germans during the winter of 1942–43, so this proved to be an opportunity to take revenge for the Jewish blood spilled by the villagers of this locality.

32 The Sudden Death of Moshe Gures

Obtaining food in those days involved supreme dangers, even more than any act of sabotage, because the White Poles went about the villages watching our every movement and seeking any opportunity to attack us. One night when we were out trying to get food, we invited Moshe Gures (who was not a member of our group) to join us, as we needed a stronger crew for this purpose. We went out in single file; at a certain point on the way we had to cross a bridge, after which there was a sharp turn leftward. As usual, two scouts would precede us by about a hundred meters. When the scouts turned left, it seemed to those of us who were at the end of the line that someone was approaching us from the side. Avremke Asner, running to see who this might be and also in order to warn those ahead of us, fired one shot into the air. On hearing the shot, everyone stood still and some fell to the ground until it became clear what was going on. Hearing the shot in the rear, the scouts thought that the shot was fired in error, for their friends were behind them and there was no need to panic. Moshe Gures also fell to the ground but when it appeared that the firing had been unnecessary and everyone stood up to continues on their way, Moshe Gures remained lying on the ground. Niomke, who had been walking alongside him, shouted: 'Moshe, get up! What's wrong with you?' But Moshe did not move. Niomke tried to pull him up but sensed that he had lost consciousness. I was among those who gathered round, trying to find out what had happened to him. We undressed him completely but could not find any sign of a wound or a drop of blood. His heart had stopped beating and he was no longer breathing.

We tried to bring him back to consciousness, but to no avail. We lit a fire to examine his body more closely for any possible injury and for any sign of life. After all our efforts, however, we had to leave him there, after taking his weapon and some of his clothing, lest the farmers identity him.

Moshe Gures had been born in Eishishok and was a builder of stoves and chimneys – profession he had learned from his father Reb Jankel. He was a strong and hearty man when he died at the age of 35.

His father was an old man who continued to work until the day he died. He was goodhearted and full of the joy of living. When he was up on the roof repairing a chimney, he would sing amusing songs, many of which had specific and not very complimentary references to the gentiles and the priest, and laugh at the world.

It was told that on his deathbed, he rose from his bed and demanded that he be given a dish of potatoes cooked in salt, and served with a 'drink'. He ate the entire dish and then rose from his sickbed, but some days later succumbed to his illness and died. He was one of those good and simple Jews who earned their livelihood by the sweat of their brows and seemed happy and blessed with their lot. I was a child of 10 when he died, but his cheerfulness remains etched in my memory and I remember him as if it were only yesterday that I had seen him. May his memory be blessed.

33 The Assault of the White Poles

It was the month of May 1944. Unbelievably, two whole years had passed since the slaughter in Radun and our flight to the forest. The news coming from the front was encouraging. The Germans were retreating under the pressure of the Red Army, who were crushing them and taking over cities and village at a rapid pace. However, there was such a large area to take back and the front was still very far from us so that we did not try to figure out when our submission to the Germans would end. Just as the news we received from the front was auspicious, our own situation went from bad to worse. Although the Germans could not spare forces to deal with us, the numbers of White Poles increased each day. They organized themselves in every village and their principal aim was to kill every Jew who was still alive.

Every evening, we would observe from a distance of scores of kilometers great lights hanging in mid-air for hours on end. These were flares to indicate bombing positions or beacons to enable entire units of parachute troopers of the Red Army to land. Sometimes we would hear enormous explosions and feel the earth trembling under our feet, and we would put our ears to the ground to hear the quaking and tremors in order to try to gauge how far they were from us.

We changed our location at that time, but chose to remain in the same forest where we had spent the winter in the bunker near the marshes. After setting up our summer camp, five of our men, Jankel Asner, Haim Itchke, Zamke Slodovnik, Avremke Asner and Niomke Rogovsky, went to the unit to receive instructions and obtain information and news of what was going on. They were supposed to return within three days. Those who remained went out one night on a foray to get food and returned very late, almost near dawn. We were tired and weary from the long night's trek and the heavy load we had carried. One of us was assigned to stand on guard and the remainder went off the sleep. The man on watch was Avremke Berkovitz, 'the wolf', the son of Shalom the glazier and Haim Itchke's cousin.

Our camp was situated on the slope of a hillock, as if in a hollow or a crater, and therefore the camp could not be seen even from nearby. Different-sized huts resembling tents were spread over the area some meters from one another. Everyone arranged his hut according to his needs and the size of his family and it was made of branches and blankets according to the individual's talent for improvisation. Most of the huts had roofs sloping on either side because of the heavy rainstorms. Another problem was the mosquitoes and flies, which came from the marshes. As I was on my own, I found a hut-mate, Jossele Hamarsky of Eishishok, who was also alone, and we became good friends. He was older by a few years, small and lean, and we therefore needed a smaller hut with only one blanket. We cut off green and supple branches, which could be bent easily, struck one end in the earth, and bent them in the form of a bow, and struck the other end into the earth as well, covering a distance that would suffice for two such small men. We stretched the blanket across the remaining branches and tied the ends to the earth to prevent the mosquitoes from entering. We closed it off on three sides, leaving just enough space to enter by crawling head-first into the hut. Inside the hut, we could not stand up straight but had to bend our knees and settle down like sardines, but it was warm and cosy for sleeping.

Returning worn-out from the long way, Jossele and I made our way to our little hut to sleep. I loosened the belt that was tightly encircling my hips in order to breathe more easily, and this time, for some reason, I also allowed myself to take off my shoes. Generally, I would leave my shoes on at night as a safeguard. Our hut was on the edge of the camp, near the marshes, and was lower than most of the huts and hidden on one side by a small hillock. We both fell deeply asleep without sensing anything of what was about to happen to us.

I was suddenly awoken by the sound of firing and explosions that burst overhead. Instinctively I put out my hand to rouse Jossele. He continued to sleep, unaware of what was going on around him. Still befuddled with sleep, I still could not make out from which direction the shots were coming, and without thinking, pushed my head forward in order to get out, but the way was barred – for this was a closed side. As the hut was so low, I had to crawl feet-first and ran out on all fours. It was lucky that the hut was closed on that side and prevented me from running in the direction I intended, for I would have run straight into the gunmen who were only a few meters away. They had spread out along the rim of the hollow with machine guns and riddled the huts below with a rain of fire. I started to run, holding my rifle in one hand, but my pants were falling as, when I had gone to sleep, I had loosened my belt to which the hand grenade and gun were attached. Thus I had to grasp the rifle in one hand and my trousers in the other, lest they hinder my legs, and I ran in this manner, crouched over in order to avoid getting shot at. While running, I glanced back for a moment to see what was happening to Jossele, and I saw him running to my right, running and falling between the small pits in the ground. For a moment I thought he was wounded, but after a few seconds, I saw that he was again running as fast as a rabbit as he disappeared from sight.

I managed to put some hundred meters between the firing, and me and then heard the shooting continue until it ceased. After a few minutes, there were isolated shots and then all was quiet. I knew that a terrible catastrophe must have occurred, for they attacked us when we were all asleep and they shot us down with their machine guns from a distance of only a few meters. At that moment, I did not know whether anyone else had survived, but prayed that Jossele Hamarsky might have been saved, as I had seen him running behind me. I tried to get as far as possible from the place for I knew that they would probably be looking for me. I went deep into the thickest part of the forest, between huge trees and among all sorts of wild animals. Alone, and with the taste of death in my soul, the knowledge that I had lost comrades with whom I had undergone such hard times added to my loneliness. Only a few hours had passed and I was reviewing in my mind how it could have happened and what had happened to Avremke who was standing on guard. I wondered why he had not warned us.

I knew that the five who had gone off to the unit should have returned by now and feared that they might have been ambushed by White Poles on their way to the camp and would have no idea of what had happened in their absence. Therefore I decided to keep an eye on those paths leading to the camp they were likely to take. Throughout the day, I lay beneath one of the trees, shaken by the new disaster that had befallen us, and while lying like a worm in the damp earth, sounds of tremendous explosions pierced my ears, as if the whole earth was quaking. At first, I did not understand what was going on, but I soon realized that these sounds were the echoes of explosions coming from the front advancing towards us, some tens of kilometers away. Perhaps these were the *katushas* that were recently put to use on the battlefield, which startled the Germans and swept them from the region, leaving scorched earth behind them.

Some hours earlier, my life had been hanging in the balance and I was given further time to struggle for my existence. Not happiness but merely a continuation of the effort to survive as long as it was possible. I knew what had befallen my comrades and the fate of those who had remained behind in the crater. Sadness, grief and bereavement were once again at the core of my soul. For the past 25 months, since the slaughter in Radun, they had fought reliantly for their survival, and now just as we could hear the sounds of explosions heralding our salvation, just now, they had to die, without being able to defend themselves. How cruelly fate had dealt with them, for they had fallen not at the hands of the Germans but at the hands of the Polish underground, who were supposed to be fighting the German invader.

The echoes of explosions from the front aroused feelings of hope, which merged with the pain and bereavement, accompanied by fear of what the morrow might bring. Now that the front was advancing in our direction, we would have nowhere to hide, for the retreating Germans were occupying every corner of the forest and the White Poles were running amok in the villages.

This was one of the longest days of my life. I wandered about aimlessly in the dense forest, peering in every direction and listening for any unexpected sound. On my way I passed by an old camp where we had been located the previous year. There I sought for some old rags to have something to cover myself with at night, as I had run for my life from the hut with nothing but what I was wearing. Towards evening I decided to go to the camp to see whether anyone had remained alive somehow, or perhaps needed help. I approached the camp very cautiously and looked around to see whether someone was not waiting to attack anyone returning to the spot. From a distance of 50 meters, all that I could see was burning embers all over the camp and smoke rising and shrouding the entire area. I did not have the strength or the courage to see whether anyone was still alive, but I gathered the little strength I had to withdraw and leave this place. I felt as if I was among ghosts and in the habitat of death. Going as far as possible from the place, I continued to roam from place to place, watching the paths that the five would be likely to take on their return from the unit. I did not drink a drop of water or eat anything on that day and did not feel any need of it. Late in the night, when I assumed that the comrades would not be returning that night, I lay down to sleep. I only had the shirt and trousers that I was wearing to protect me from the dampness of the earth, so I put some soft branches on the ground as some protection. Apart from the cold that penetrated to the bone, the mosquitoes attacked pitilessly. At that moment, I remembered Job and scratched myself as he had. I gathered moss from the ground and the bark of trees to cover those parts of my body that were bare as a shield against the cold and the mosquitoes and managed to wrap my head in my shirt, curled up like a hedgehog, and so dozed off.

In the early hours of the following day, I again began to wander about and follow the pathways in order to meet the men who were to return from the unit. I was feeling hungry but did not want to leave the forest in order to get food before I encountered the returning five, for in this way I might endanger them. So I began to pick currants and wild berries that were growing in the forest. Crawling on all fours and gathering berries, I heard a suspicious rustle as if someone were nearby. Perhaps the White Poles had returned to check the area after their success the previous morning, but it was also possible that this noise was being made by the comrades returning from the unit. Little by little, I crawled nearer the sound, which now could be identified as voices. As I got closer, the sound of Yiddish reached my ears. I was afraid to stand up as they might have shot me if they did not recognize me immediately. I called out their names and when I was answered in the affirmative, I went to them and told them what had occurred and about my visit to the burned-out camp on the evening following the catastrophe.

We decided to go to the camp that very day in order to see whether there were any wounded who were still alive. The scene was indescribably horrible. The camp was destroyed and burned-down, with dead bodies strewn all over the area. Among the bodies we found Liebke Hefetz in a firing position – evidently he had resisted until the very last. Haim Asner's skull was shattered by the butts of rifles – who can say what tortures he had to endure before he died? We dug a large grave and buried all the bodies we could find side-by-side together.

So we parted from our beloved comrades. We paid a final

tribute to their memory, while our hearts were burning for revenge. Those who fell were Haim Asner, Itchele Asner, Leibke Hefetz, Sarah Dobke Gures, Etka Gures, her cousin, and Aharke Berkovitz. That same day we learned that other survivors had reached the unit or other Jewish groups, and heard also that Bailke Tanovitsky had been wounded. We looked for her so that she should not remain in this area alone, for according to instructions which the unit had received from the Red Army headquarters we were to return and join the unit at once.

34 Vengeance

We could not return to the unit until we had made our accounts with the perpetrators of the dastardly crime. The five knew that the White Poles would not have been able to find our camp at night without the help of an informer to show them the way. All the indications were that one of our own contacts had betrayed us and decided to go over to the other side. Evidently it was a farmer from the village of Mantat who knew where our camp was located.

There were six of us: Jankele Asner and his brother Avremke, Niomke Rogovsky, Haim Itchke Berkovitz, Zamke Slodovnik and I, Avraham Lipkunsky. We reached the village just before sunset and three men stood on guard at the entrance to the village to let us know if there were any suspicious activities and the remaining three went to the house of the betrayer. Niomke Rogovsky and Jankel Asner entered the house and I stood on guard outside. On seeing Niomke and Jankel, the farmer tried to jump out of the window and escape to the cornfield alongside his house. Niomke jumped out after him and during the pursuit fired at and killed him on the spot. After this, we informed the members of the farmer's household that this was the result of his betrayal of the location of our camp, which led to the White Poles' assault and the death of our comrades. That same night we were on our way to the unit.

It seems that the White Poles followed in our wake after we returned from this action in the late hours of this miserable night. They went straight to the camp, quietly approached and waited until daylight to carry out their plans more effectively. Unluckily, Avremke Sholom Berkovitz did not take part in our mission that night and did not get up to stand on guard, or perhaps fell asleep. And thus the White Poles succeeded in getting close to the camp without being noticed. And out of 13 that were still alive that night, only six survived: Jossele Hamarsky, Avremke Sholems, Rochke Asner, Liebke, Avremke Asner's beloved, Bailke Tanovitsky, and myself.

All this happened only a few days before the routing of the Nazi forces in our area and the guns of the Red Army heralded liberation and freedom; while we bereaved and stricken ones continued living a 'normal' life. We set out for the neighborhood of Marciknetz, to join the unit located there at the time. On our way, we encountered groups of Jews from Marcikanz and Grodno. Here, too, the White Poles had been active, but they did not dare to run riot as they had done in the region of Radun and Natche, for here the partisans had a strong hold and any animosity towards them would call for an immediate reaction.

When we reached the unit, we encountered General Mayor Kapusta, who had been the commander of our sector. On orders from Moscow, he advanced together with the front line westward, to sabotage the railway and disrupt the routes taken by the retreating Germans. We were not too happy about remaining in the vicinity of the Germans and received these orders with mixed feelings. On the one hand we wanted to savor the taste of freedom, but on the other, we also wanted to take part in the destruction of the Nazi beast. But we feared that the front would engulf us and that we would not be able to hold out as a united force.

The high command of the sector, together with General Kapusta, sat around for days on end drinking vodka as if it was water, and were as drunk as Lot, but the partisan activities continued as usual. Radio contact with Moscow continued throughout the day and night and every advance on the front was reported to us immediately. Planning was excellent and the partisan groups would go out on sabotage missions one after the other. We felt that the front was getting nearer and nearer, but had no notion of when it would finally reach us. We were informed that Radun was already liberated, but we were some hundred kilometers to the west. The last order we had received was not to leave the forest in order to prevent the retreating soldiers from finding cover there. In other words, we were to be the guards of the forest.

35 The German Army in Retreat

One morning, our scouts informed us that the vanguard of the Red Army had already arrived. We doubted that this was true and went out to the villages to see for ourselves. Just as we were entering the village, two horsemen of the Red Army's advance guard arrived. We saw them as angels, as messengers of the Messiah. We clasped their hands in a comradely greeting and with great excitement exchanged a few words with them. They told us that it was in this area that they had broken through the German front and utterly destroyed their forces. They were chasing after the Germans but could not catch up with them, because they were only the advance guard, and the greater forces were some tens of kilometers behind them and therefore unable to prevent the Germans from fleeing. We returned to the forest, agitated and exhilarated, to inform our comrades of the happy news of our meeting with the vanguard of the Red Army.

As an auxiliary force, our object now was to block the routes taken by the retreating Germans. I awaited this face-to-face meeting with the retreating German soldiers in a state of great tension. Was it possible that everything was now turned upside down and that this time we would be doing the killing, that we would arrest them, give them orders, and also imprison them? They were experienced soldiers, equipped with the best of weapons, and this called for caution. Now, in these last minutes before salvation, we needed to be careful for they were many and we were few.

While we were patrolling in the dense vegetation of the forest, we heard some suspicious rustling, and found facing us a German unit which was seeking cover. Our shouted orders in German to put their hands up came as a surprise. They did not have time to think and surrendered at once. With no opposition on their part, we led them out of the forest to where prisoners were being collected. We were a handful of partisans and they were scores of men, and yet they looked so forlorn and miserable. We were excited and stunned by this sudden encounter. We did not touch them, but ordered them to march quickly and keep their hands over their heads. The accumulation of feelings of vengeance, of pain and hatred, were tempered, and when the beast had finally fallen into our hands, we realized that we were not of their ilk.

The retreating Germans tried not to fall into the hands of the partisans for they were aware of the fate that awaited them. They preferred to be taken prisoner by the Red Army. They were not mistaken, for the first prisoners to fall into the hands of the partisans had a very ugly and bitter end. The partisans in the forest killed many and hundreds were taken captive as prisoners of war.

The front passed us by and we remained in the forest for another week in order to flush out the Germans who had penetrated the forest. It was then that I had an opportunity to observe the behavior of this superior race. Some of us disarmed the Germans and then led them like sheep from the forest. More than once, I was alone with many of them and feared at moments that they could easily do away with me. but then I thought of my family and my brethren, and how they were led by the Germans *en masse* and that they, too, displayed little opposition, for they had no reason to believe that their opposition would succeed in achieving anything because the surrounding population was as hateful as their captors. These same Germans, masters of the world, when they were defeated and humiliated, showed no opposition and carried out every order that was given them. They were as submissive and subservient as dogs, and were ready to sacrifice their comrades in the SS without the slightest hesitation. On the one hand, their appearance and behavior aroused disgust, and on the other, compassion for these beings who had lost all resemblance to one's concept of a human being. At that moment, I did not know if these same people were capable of slaughtering children only a short while ago, and of behaving brutally to mothers and their babies. Or perhaps they were just poor creatures who did not have the strength to oppose the arrogant and murderous regime, which drove them to perform such crimes against humanity. Many of the captives were youths who were barely 18 years old, or perhaps less, and there were also a great many older people. We looked for members of the SS among them and these were dealt with immediately, for we said to ourselves that afterwards we would not be permitted to do so, nor would we be capable of doing so. The others were brought to the prisoner-of-war camp in the village of Astrin, where we guarded them and looked after them. And we were still submitted to German bombing, which caused a number of deaths and casualties.

We were a small gathering of Jews from Radun, trying desperately to reach the town. I knew that nothing was awaiting me there, that I would find only the ruins of a Jewish town. I knew that every stone and corner would remind me of the blood that had been spilled, the life that had existed there and had been destroyed. I was drawn to the town and yet recoiled from it. I was frightened to be with myself and my loneliness. What would I find in Radun but pain and bereavement. These days of liberation and liberty that I had awaited for the last 26 months were steeped in grief and sorrow.

When our mission as guards in the forest was over, the partisans sent us to the front to join units of the Red Army. They were sent straight to the fighting at the front and most were either killed or wounded. The unit sent only one group to Radun, and I was among them, perhaps because of my comparatively tender age. I was granted a certificate attesting to the fact I had fought as a partisan against fascism, together with commendations for good behavior, and I was transferred to the special combat sector of the unit. Our task was to maintain order in the town and to purge the area of criminals, meaning the White Poles who hated the Red Army and the Soviet regime.

I was released on 7 July 1944, although the war was still on. On returning to Radun, I found, as I expected, all the Jewish houses gone to rack and ruin and uninhabited, for on 10 May 1942 I had accompanied their owners to their mass grave in the cemetery.

I came across a few lone Jews who had survived in the forest and lived together in one neighborhood. It was difficult to accustom oneself to the ghostly aura of the place. The military framework in which I lived and the many activities this involved, eased my feelings and lessened my loneliness to a certain extent. I was attached to the security police, known as the NKVD,* whose principal responsibility was to help the Red Army uncover White Poles and bring them to the security police to be investigated. It was an unpleasant and dangerous task. The neighborhood of Radun contained hundreds of White Poles who hated the Jews and the Soviets, and who had killed many soldiers of the Red Army hundreds of kilometers behind the front. The ordinary soldiers were unaware of the dangers looming in the rear of their liberated motherland. The first victims, however, were the few Jews who had survived in the forest or had been in hiding with friendly farmers. When they came to claim the property they had left with the farmers, they would be killed by the White Poles. It took many months to overcome them.

As I knew the dusty lanes and paths leading to the villages around Dowgalishok, I was attached to a Red Army unit as guide and scout. I was given a uniform of the Red Army and I would go out mounted on a small horse at the head of a company of soldiers, and lead them to the villages where there were nests of White Poles and show them how to surround the villages and cut off any possibility of entering or leaving them. After that, searches were made in the houses of suspects. A good many weapons were confiscated and scores of suspects were taken to be interrogated. Anyone who objected would be shot on the spot.

Despite my revulsion at the task, I was glad that I had been chosen to fulfil such a dangerous mission, for thus I could take my revenge in some way against the murderer of my father and all the innocent Jews of Dowgalishok.

The security police in Radun were stationed in the spacious house that had formerly belonged to Berl Lipkunsky, the tailor of Dowgalishok. The many rooms were turned into interrogation cells and the enormous storeroom became a temporary prison. The prisoners were crowded into a corner of the storeroom, enclosed and fenced in like in a sheepfold and there was barely enough room for everyone to stretch out. Occasionally, I was asked to be present during an investigation and assist in questioning, which generally took place at night. Some of the methods used during these interrogations are still fresh in mind. It was then that I learned that the interrogator always sat unrevealed in the darker shadows of the room, while a strong electric lamp illuminated the face of the suspect. And when the answer to the interrogator's question was not satisfactory, he would make use of an improvised whip made of supple metal wire and lash the suspect all over his body. I also learned the effect of isolation, hunger and thirst on a prisoner.

Once, I met the farmer Andzielevitz among the prisoners, together with one of his sons. I knew that he had had connections with the political wing of the White Poles, but now I had a chance to repay him for his decency towards my father and myself. I did whatever I could to make it easier for him. I saw to it that he had food and drink and tried to cheer him up. I gave evidence that he had provided cover for partisans and that my father and I had hidden in his barn during the winter of 1943. I do not know to what extent all this helped, but at least he and his son knew that I recognized them and did whatever I could to defend them.

The front was hundreds of kilometers west of Radun but the struggle of the White Poles against the Soviet regime on the one hand, and the means adopted against them on the other, were very cruel. One morning, as I was passing the large community center in the heart of the marketplace, I witnessed a sight one could not forget. Scores of bodies were lying one next to the other along the wall of the building, with their heads near the wall and their feet facing outward. The previous day, the White Poles had attacked soldiers of the Red Army and murdered seven in the most ruthless manner. In response to this act, the Red Army soldiers carried out a search in the vicinity of this incident and killed scores of White Poles by slitting their throats, placing them on public display for everyone to witness the bodies which remained there for two whole days.

The war was still at its height. Many partisans were recruited into the army and volunteered to be sent to the front. Out of loneliness, and also because I wanted to contribute to the war effort against the Germans (as well as to take revenge on the murderers of my family and the Jews), I applied to the recruiting office and signed up to go to the front. When I reported to the captain on duty in the NKVD office, and told him that I had signed up for the army, he began to shout at me in great rage, adding some juicy Russian curses for good measure: 'What's wrong with you, have you gone mad? You will not go!' He immediately phoned the commander of the recruiting office and cancelled my enlistment. Whatever his feeling for me stemmed from I do not know, but it is quite likely that he saved my life, because most of the partisans did not return from the front and only those who were wounded survived. As I was completely alone, I was delighted by the invitation from Haim Itchke Berkovitz (the Gypsy), who had also remained alone, and Michka Dubinsky and his little brother Isrulik, to come and live with them. And so I did. We lived together like brothers – eating together and caring for one another – like a little family.

292

36 Distressing Thoughts

We were focused at first on wreaking vengeance on those who had murdered our families and our people. Only after that did we dwell on our daily lives. We still did not think about how we would build our lives in the future, but sometimes I would try to imagine what my life might be like later on if I did not try to change the path I was pursuing at the time. As the war was still being waged, there was no point in making plans for the future. So we sweetened our lives with food and drink – homemade vodka was the best remedy and morale-booster.

There are times when the least important of incidents arouse dormant thoughts and even changes the course of one's life. Such an instance occurred when I was serving as aide to General Mayor, who had been appointed to the Security Police in Radun. There was still no running water in this town and the inhabitants drew their water in buckets from a well which they then carried to their homes. One morning I was asked to pour water over General Mayor's hands and help him to wash. My appearance was no different from that of any of the town's gentile inhabitants, with my pale blond hair and blue eyes. My Russian too was similar to that spoken by the locals, whose native tongue was Polish. The general did not imagine that I was anything but a Byelorussian or a Pole. He was in a congenial mood and we had a short conversation consisting of a number of questions on his part and replies on mine. Finally, he asked me what my name was and I innocently answered that my name was Avraham. The general straightened up, looked me in the eye, then discharged me with a lusty Russian curse, saying: 'So you're a Jew, Damn it!' 'Yes,' I answered, 'I am a Jew!' And with those words the conversation ended.

I could not stop thinking about his surprise and disappointment at my being a Jew. It gave me no peace. If the high priest of the NKVD, the communist Holy of Holies, and a police officer was so disappointed by seeing a living Jew at a time when the war against the German racist regime was still being fought, what could one expect from these miserable anti-Semites? The new regime did not live up to my expectations, and from that very moment I knew that I could not build my life here and would have to escape from this place or cut myself off from Judaism. Thus the thought that I must reach a land where there was a good and safe life for Jews began to be uppermost in my mind.

The physical transition from the persistently threatening life in the forest to that of a normal one under a roof was comparatively easy. Little by little, I became accustomed to sleeping in a house although it was some time before I could sleep in a proper bed with a mattress. The hard floor with my curled-up fist for a pillow was my best way of sleeping. But as far as my emotional state was concerned, things were not that easy. The more life followed a regular pattern and the feeling of security stabilized, the more I sensed an emotional disquiet. The wounds caused by bereavement and loss had apparently healed during the struggle for survival, but reappeared in full force from time to time. I was looking back at what had been, what no longer existed, and would never return. And the events of the past 26 months repeatedly whirling through my head like a silent film, together with the uncertain and undetermined future, weighed on my mind like a heavy load which could be discarded.

37 Pinchas Receives a Jewish Burial

My brother Pinchas, who had fallen on that moonlit night in October 1942, began to occupy my thoughts once again and would visit me in my dreams almost nightly. I knew that I would never be at rest unless I sought him out and attended to him, somewhere in the forests of Dowgalishok. I would not be able to leave Radun before I had given him a proper Jewish burial, near our mother and brothers and all the Jews of Radun. The idea that I must bring him to be buried in a Jewish grave lodged in my mind and tormented me day and night. Entering that area, however, was extremely dangerous for the neighborhood harbored many gangs of White Poles. My request to the Security Police to have an armed escort was turned down and I was told that I must postpone my plans until the area was purged of these gangs, and that there was no justification in endangering myself. I accepted this without resentment, for I understood that they were incapable of understanding what I felt. However, the summer was at an end, the days would soon be shorter, and if I did not move him now I might not be able to find the exact spot next summer. In the meantime I could not leave Radun. I did not ask the partisans for help because I did not want to involve them in any danger or be refused. But the thought would not leave me and I felt that this is what I must do, no matter what happened.

Towards the end of August 1944 I took my rifle and my gun early one morning, and went out to the end of Mozaika Street, on the road leading to Dowgalishok. I entered the house of a farmer who was a stranger to me, and ordered him to harness his horse to his wagon and to take two shovels. I explained

that the order came from the Security Police and that he had
to take me to Dowgalishok, some ten kilometers away, in
order to exhume the body of a partisan and bring him to
Radun. After carrying out this order, he would be free to go.
He did not ask any questions, but merely harnessed the horse.

We set out on our way. I did not know where Pinchas was
buried, but from information we received at the time, we
knew that Shamashke, who lived in our house in
Dowgalishok, had buried him in our sector of the forest and
he certainly knew where. We went straight to our house in
Dowgalishok, and I told the wagon-driver to call Shamashke.
When he appeared and saw who was calling, he became
deathly pale and could not utter a word. He was certain that
I had come to settle accounts with him. I quelled his fears and
told him that I did want anything from him, neither our house
nor payment, but that I had come to exhume the body of my
brother whom he had buried. And now I demanded that he
come with me at once and help me find the spot. He had no
choice in the matter and jumped onto the wagon, and we
went on our way with the two farmers in front and I behind
them. I prayed that no other farmers would see us as we were
going by. I was aware of the dangers I was facing, as they were
two and I was alone, and I tried to keep some distance
between us at all times and to be behind them. Shamaske
guided the wagon through the narrow lane between the
fences where Pinchas had fallen, near the stone. We passed
our smithy, now uninhabited, and turned right to one of the
paths leading to the forest. We stopped at the edge of the
forest near a small hill covered with grass without any sign or
marking-stone, merely cowpats scattered here and there,
indicating that graziers and their herds frequented the place.

I ordered the two to start digging, and stood on guard at
some distance – knowing the possible danger in their both
having shovels in their hands. Digging in the sandy soil
was quick and easy, and I hoped that I would be able to find
something to identify as my brother's bones. There was
indeed a skeleton. When I began to lift it out I recognized the

clothing he had worn and had been buried in. When I saw the straps of the phylacteries which were wrapped around his bones. I knew then that these really were the mortal remains of my brother. A wave of satisfaction flowed through me for the moment, for I had found Pinchas. 'My dearest brother, I have not forgotten you and never will, and I will take you to those who were dear to you, so that you will not be alone,' I uttered to myself in the depths of my heart. I took great care that no bones should fall away from the disintegrating skeleton. The former tension in the air had dissipated, and the farmers also were calmer after we had found the skeleton and were at last convinced that I had no evil intentions towards them. They did everything they were told to do uncomplainingly. Gathering the remains in sheets and blankets I had brought with me, I put them in the wagon, and replaced the earth in the empty grave. I asked the farmer to make haste back.

Within the hour, we were once more in Radun. I assembled a *minyan* of Jews to accompany me to the cemetery and, alongside the mass grave of the Jews of Radun, where my mother Sara Mina and my small brother Kushka had found eternal rest together with other members of the family, I buried my brother Pinchas, together with his phylacteries. I was disturbed and distressed by this parting with my brother and went about not quite believing that this had been accomplished. But my heart was no longer heavy and I felt as if I was floating in mid-air. I guessed Pinchas would not visit me in my dreams that night.

The following morning, when I came to the Security Police and told them what I had done, they looked at me as if I was a madman. I was severely reprimanded and, if they had not thought well of me, I would have been punished. But when my excitement had subsided somewhat, there was not a happier man and I felt newly liberated.

Time passed and the war was still dragging on. The front was situated somewhere near Warsaw and no one knew why the end was so prolonged. In Radun the war now had little impact, except for the lack of certain provisions, which had always been one of the characteristics of the Soviet regime. One's daily activities were those of normal times and I continued to work under the command of the military police.

In October 1944 I was informed that I was to attend a course for cadets, which was to take place in Grodno. This suited me well for I had always wanted to study, no matter what the subject. Moreover, I desparately wanted to leave the confines of Radun and visit a city the size of Grodno. The course was very interesting and we learned all sorts of things, starting with the construction of an engine for firefighting. I was the only Jew on the course, but experienced no discrimination. In fact, the rapport between the gentile youths and myself was excellent.

38 Escape from Radun

On one of our free days, I went out to explore the streets of Grodno and happened to meet two Jews. From them I learned that there was a way of reaching Palestine via Romania. I had never abandoned the idea that it was possible to uproot myself from this place and go to a land where one led a Jewish life, and I sought ways of achieving this. Under the pretext that I was ill, I stopped my studies at the course and fled back to Radun. To the military police in Radun, I claimed that I had been granted protracted leave. There I learned that all former Polish citizens could return to Poland, and that the Davidovitz family and Liebe Shmaya Mendel's were actually preparing the necessary papers to do so. As none of them was due to be called up for military service, they could do this openly. I, however, had to act in utter secrecy, for I was still part of the military and this could be interpreted as desertion, which had very clear significance in those days. I sold the few possessions that had been left hidden with friendly farmers, and with the help of Laike Slodovnik, who worked as an official in the NKVD and an added 5,000 rubles, I obtained the necessary papers very quickly. With the money that remained, I bought gold coins and dollars for the journey, and arranged to join the Davidovitz family and travel with them.

I kept the matter secret even from Michka and Haim Itchke. I did not want to reveal my plans to them lest they try to dissuade me, and especially because they could have been in danger were the matter were to reach the ears of the military police.

All my personal preparations for leaving Radun were made but there were still some obligations that troubled my conscience. I had not been able to visit Father's grave and that of the Jews of Dowgalishok who were murdered by the White Poles. I did not know where they were buried and it was doubtful whether this could ever be discovered. The fact that my father's body was not alone was some consolation, for number of Jews were killed on that occasion.

Until then, I had no knowledge of what had happened to my uncle in Dzivienishok, that is, the families of Yekutiel and Nahum Joseph Lipkunsky. Perhaps they were still among the living and I should try to find them before leaving Russia. For I might never have another chance to do so. After making enquiries and questioning a number of people, I learned that one child from the village of Dzivienishok was alive and living in an orphanage in Vilnius. So there was a ray of hope after all, and I decided to go to Vilnius immediately and look for the child from Dzivienishok and find out what happened to my relatives there.

The journey to Vilnius, a distance of some 80 to 90 kilometers from Radun, took more than a day if one travelled by horse and wagon. There was also a great deal of danger involved. Public motorized transport was unknown there in those days and the only way I could reach Vilnius would be to get a lift from a military vehicle going in that direction.

On a gray and rainy day at the end of November, I set out for the highway in order to hail any military transport going to Vilnius. My service uniform and my documents attesting to the fact that I was a partisan, helped me to get lifts from one military car to another, and I reached Vilnius in the afternoon. With my knapsack containing provisions for the journey on my shoulders and soaked to the skin, I marched excitedly through the streets of Vilnius – legendary Vilnius. Pensively and full of anticipation regarding the uncertain meeting, I trudged along looking for the orphanage where the boy from Dzivienishok was supposedly living, with the thought that perhaps he was the son of one of my uncles and my only remaining relative. In order to reach the orphanage, in my haste I enquired of passers-by whether they knew of such a place in the neighborhood. And as luck would have it, I found myself an hour later within the orphanage. Children of all ages were running about in the dark and dingy corridors. I stopped a few of the children and asked if they knew anyone who hailed from Dzivienishok. A few minutes later, I was facing a lean and withdrawn child, seemingly frightened of his surroundings. I peered at him and he stared at the floor, hesitating to return my gaze, as if to say: 'What does this man want of me?' I asked the other children to leave the two of us alone and I then explained to him that I had come to look for relatives from Dzivienishok, and that perhaps he could help me. I asked him his name.

'I am Pinchas,' he said, and suddenly my high hopes seemed to have been justified, for my brother was named after our grandfather. And then I hesitatingly asked what his family name was, and he told me that it was Lipkunsky. I trembled with excitement, for I knew that I had found my cousin and that I was no longer alone in the world. My further questioning was merely to convince him that I was his cousin. I asked whether he was the son of Nahum Joseph or of Yekutiel. He told me that his father was Nahum Joseph. I asked about his parents and other members of the family, and whether he had heard about his cousins in Radun and knew that his father hailed from Dowgalishok.

We talked for some time – that is, I did the talking and he the listening. I explained who I was and the relationship between us, taking out of my knapsack the rolls that I had brought with me for the journey to offer him some. After we had warmed to each other, I told him the purpose of my visit: that I intended to leave Russia for Poland and from there make my way to Palestine. He listened without reacting or questioning and, only after turning to him and telling him that I wished to take him with me, did he burst out with a loud, firm: 'No!'

I had come down on him like a thunderclap and he had had no time in which to take in this sudden and unexpected meeting. He was embarrassed, but sufficiently intelligent not to place his trust in me and, quite rightly, was afraid to leave the other children and the orphanage to accompany a young man he had just met for the first time on a dangerous journey to an unknown land.

I was relieved by his negative reply, for I was also afraid of the responsibility. To take a young boy on a dangerous journey to a place that I myself was uncertain of would be rather foolish. I was pleased by his refusal and parted from him hurriedly in order to leave for Radun before nightfall. But I felt that I had left a part of me in Vilnius.

For a long time afterwards, I thought of Pinchas with yearning, until we met again years later. The seeds of this sudden meeting slowly bore fruit in the boy's heart as well. Thirteen years after our first meeting, he arrived in Israel, thrilled that we had both found one another.

A few days before the appointed day for leaving Radun, I felt that I could not keep the matter secret from Michka any longer. He had taken me into his house and treated me like an older brother and I felt that the affection was mutual, for I respected and admired him. One evening when work was over, I said that I wanted to talk to him and we went out to stroll along the pavement at the corner of Grodno Street, where Itzchak Rogovsky's house stood. We joked and gossiped, and I told him what was troubling me, that I could see no future here. Little by little, I revealed that I intended to leave in a few days. His spontaneous reaction was: It's out of the question, I won't let you do this.' He presented some serious arguments against the idea. First, the fact that the war had not yet ended, and that the journey was dangerous, and that I should at least postpone it until after the war. But after I said that I had made up my mind and did not want to be persuaded to change it, he threatened me by saying that he would hand me over to the NKVD and then I would not be able to leave.

But I stood by my decision and was not prepared to change it, for it had been made after much consideration and thought. If he wished to hand me over to the military police that was his concern, but I would not willingly reverse my decision. When he realized that my mind was made up and that I would not succumb to threats, he embraced me and kissed me and, with the tears rolling down his cheeks, wished me a good journey and bade me farewell.

So it was that I left the place of my birth and set out on a new path for a new life.